Contents

Individual Topic Search

4 Spreadsheets   127

6 Presentation and Graphics 269

Introduction

This book is designed to introduce a wide range of popular computer applications. The book assumes no previous knowledge of computers or use of computer applications. The book is divided into chapters, one for each separate topic or application.

The first chapter deals with some computer theory, which is designed to give students knowledge of what a computer is, its origins and development, what the various parts are and what they do. This chapter also deals with common uses of computers along with safety and privacy issues. This chapter has a few simple questions which may be used to assess knowledge as the student progresses through the chapter. These questions are available on the CD and are referenced at regular intervals throughout the chapter.

The remaining chapters deal with specific application programs. Each chapter starts with an introduction to the particular application and works through that application in a step-by-step manner, starting with basics such as how to load the program and progressing to extensive work in each application.

The book includes individual tasks which require the use of a particular application program to complete the task. Tasks are graded, starting with the simplest functions in each application and gradually moving on to the more complex uses of the program. Each task introduces one or more new concepts, which are simply explained and use real-life examples to reinforce the concepts. The task is immediately followed with any new instructions needed to complete that task, thereby gradually building up the student's skill level.

Each task in the book is supplemented with a large selection of additional tasks, which are referenced at regular intervals in each chapter and are on the CD supplied with the book. These additional tasks reinforce the learning at the particular stage in each application. Solutions to all tasks are available on the Gill & Macmillan website (www.gillmacmillan.ie).

The design process of spreadsheets and databases is covered in a straightforward, practical manner. There is a simple example of the design of both a spreadsheet and a database at the end of both sections. These examples work through the design from conception to final evaluation.

The book is not software specific and is therefore suitable for use with any software. However, Microsoft Office 2003 and 2007 have been used in order to explain the solution to each task in each application. Both Internet Explorer and Mozilla Firefox have been used in explaining the use of the Internet and World Wide Web. Outlook Express has been used to explain the operation of e-mail.

USE OF THE CD

The CD contains over 200 additional tasks. These tasks are saved in files on the CD. Each file is saved as both a Word document and an Adobe (.pdf) file format. Each task is referenced in the text and has a standard filename format, which appears as follows: Task 3A-4.doc or 3A-4.pdf.

Each of these files contains a number of separate tasks which reinforce the learning of material from that particular section of the book.

The CD also contains files that are required for performing tasks in the book. A number of graphics, documents, spreadsheets, databases and presentations are included which allow students to perform tasks at later points in a chapter even if they did not create the files in earlier stages. There are a number of text documents on the CD that may be used by the student (instead of typing the text) for some of the word processing tasks. These are supplied in both document and plain text formats. All these files are referenced in the book with both filenames and the folder locations on the CD.

LECTURERS!
SUPPORT MATERIAL

For your support material visit our website at:

www.gillmacmillan.ie

Support material is available to lecturers only within a secure area of this website.

Support material for this book consists of solutions to assignments or tasks.
To access support material for *Step by Step Computer Applications*:

1 Go to 'www.gillmacmillan.ie'.

2 On the left-hand side you will see the heading 'resources'. Underneath this click on either 'Lecturers' or 'Teachers'. The Logon page will appear where you can enter your username (which is your e-mail address) and your password.

3 After entering your details, click on the 'Logon >>' button.

 (If you do not already have a password you must register. To do this click on 'Register to become a member' and complete the online registration form. Your password will then be sent to you by e-mail.)

4 Click on the link for Support Material, e.g. for Teachers it will be 'Teachers Support Material'.

5 Select the title *Step by Step Computer Applications*.

SYMBOLS USED IN THIS BOOK

The following symbols used in this book have the meaning indicated:

Click the left mouse button.

Click the right mouse button.

Double-click the left mouse button.

Triple-click the left mouse button.

Hold down the left mouse button.

Hold down the right mouse button.

Move the mouse to point to an item without clicking or holding any button.

Release the mouse button.

Point to an item on the screen.

Hold down the Ctrl button.

Hold down the Ctrl button and press the semicolon.

Hold down the Ctrl button and the Alt button and press the Delete key.

Hold down the Shift key.

Hold down the Shift key and press the number eight.

Hold down the Shift key and hold down the left mouse button.

Press the Enter key.

Press the F4 function key.

Press the Backspace key.

Press the tab key.

Press the equals key.

Press the plus key.

Press the minus key.

Press the multiplication key.

Press the division key.

Press the comma key.

1 Computers (Theory)

INTRODUCTION

Computers are so common today that it is surprising to learn that the first computer was not produced until 1944. This computer was produced by a team of IBM engineers and measured 15 m long and 8 m high. The power of this computer was much less than the smallest pocket calculator of today. The first commercial computer was produced for a bakery in 1951, and this computer was 10 m long, 2.5 m high and 1.2 m wide.

The first appearance of the modern personal computer (PC) was not until 1971, due to the development of the modern microprocessor by Intel. This chip, the Intel 4004, had a complete processor on a single chip. The power of this chip was totally inadequate by modern standards, but it did set the pattern for future development.

DEFINITION

The simplest definition of a computer is, 'A computer is a machine for processing data.'

A slightly more accurate definition would be, 'A computer is a general-purpose machine that processes data according to a set of instructions that are stored internally, either temporarily or permanently.'

A computer can process numeric and nonnumeric data, for example:

- It can take a list of names and sort them into alphabetical order.

- It can take information about workers' rates of pay, hours worked, tax and social welfare deductions and produce a weekly or monthly payroll.

- Computers are also used to play music, produce drawings, play games, guide aircraft, keep records, produce invoices and numerous other tasks.

Of course, the computer cannot do these things on its own. People must supply the data, give exact instructions as to how it is to be processed and specify what results are required. Instructions are given to a computer by a program.

TYPES OF COMPUTERS

Computers can be divided into three basic groups:

- Mainframe.

- Mini.

- Micro.

Mainframe

Mainframe computers are used by very large corporations and have large computing power and storage space. Modern mainframe computers tend to be about the size of a large storage cabinet. These computers would be stored in a special room with a large number of terminals (referred to as **dumb terminals** because the processing is done by the mainframe) connected to them. These computers are very powerful and process data extremely quickly. Mainframes are very expensive and are therefore only used by large corporations.

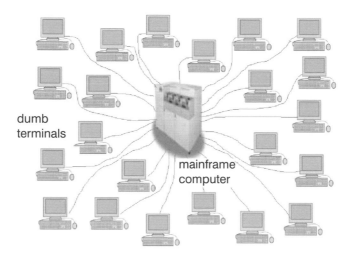

dumb
terminals

mainframe
computer

Figure 1.1

Mini

Mini computers have a similar arrangement to mainframe computers but are smaller – typically the size of a small filing cabinet. These would be used in situations where the large power and storage of a mainframe was not required. This type of computer is not nearly as expensive as a mainframe but still retains a lot of the mainframe features. Mini computers are typically found in sizable companies.

Micro

Micro computers are by far the most common today. They are commonly referred to as a PC (personal computer). The modern micro computer (PC) is as powerful as a mainframe was a number of years ago, they are relatively cheap and have a vast number of programs available for them. They are fast and have large storage (but still small in comparison to mini and mainframe) and are used in a wide variety of businesses. There is a PC in most homes today.

monitor

DVD drive

floppy drive

keyboard

mouse

Figure 1.2

PCs are often networked together. PC networks have taken over from the mini computer in some business situations. In a network situation each computer does its own processing and is therefore referred to as an **intelligent terminal**. Each computer is connected to a server for central storage and printing. Network users can also have access to other facilities connected to the network, such as scanners and the Internet.

The mainframe, mini and networking setups greatly facilitate group working, especially where a number of people are working on a common project. These arrangements allow all members of the group to work on the same files, thus eliminating duplicate files. The arrangement also means that all members are using the same programs, printers, etc.

Laptop

A variation of the PC is a laptop computer. This has all the features of a desktop PC but the components are much smaller and therefore fit into a small case.

Figure 1.3

The monitor is a liquid crystal display (LCD) type and is an integral part of the computer. Laptops may be connected to a standard keyboard, mouse and monitor and in this case operate as a standard desktop PC.

Personal Digital Assistant

Another variation of the modern micro computer is the development of the personal organiser or the personal digital assistant (PDA). These are small computers which fit in a person's hand and receive input by means of a small keyboard or pointer which selects items on the screen. These have become quite powerful and some of the more expensive ones allow the user to edit Word and Excel documents, view PowerPoint files, connect to the Internet, surf the World Wide Web (WWW) and send and receive e-mail.

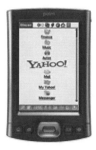

Figure 1.4

Multimedia

A large number of PCs, including laptops, are equipped with the necessary components in order to connect to the Internet, whether individually or as part of a network. Most computers are also equipped with components such as sound cards, cameras, microphones and DVD (digital versatile disc) drives. These features give them the ability to play music, produce graphics, play motion pictures, play games, record sound, etc. These features are commonly referred to as **multimedia**.

Task 1.1

Answer the questions in **Task 1A-1** on the CD.

BASIC PARTS OF A COMPUTER

The computer itself consists of the central processing unit (CPU) together with random access memory (RAM), read only memory (ROM) and the connections to the various other devices such as keyboard, screen, disk drives, printers, etc. These items, which are connected to the basic computer, are collectively referred to as peripheral devices or peripherals.

CPU

The central processing unit (**CPU**), commonly known as the microprocessor or the central processor is, in effect, the brain of the computer. It performs the task of organising the work of all the other components and also carries out arithmetic, sorting and other functions. The CPU contains two units, which are used in all its work. These units are the arithmetic logic unit (**ALU**) and an amount of immediate access memory. The ALU performs all the arithmetic and sorting functions and uses its immediate access memory while performing these functions.

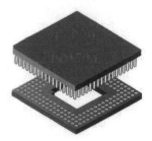

Figure 1.5

The most common CPU in PCs today is the Intel Core 2 or the Intel Core 2 Quattro processor. The six core processor is on the way. This has been developed over the last few years, has continuously increased the operating speed, and is now running at clock speeds up to 3 GHz. This means that the CPU is performing up to 3,000,000,000 instructions per second. The amount of data that can be processed in one instruction has also increased.

Processors are developing at a rapid rate and the next generation where the processor and memory will be completely self contained is already in development.

RAM

The random access memory (**RAM**) is the computer's workspace, where the program instructions and the data being worked on will reside. The CPU can read from, and write to, RAM very quickly (much faster than to a hard disk). In most computers anything stored in RAM will be lost when the computer is switched off or in the event of a power failure – for this reason it is referred to as **volatile memory**.

ROM chips RAM chips

Figure 1.6

ROM

The read only memory (**ROM**) contains certain program instructions that are required by the CPU for its own internal use and these do not change. The CPU can read the instructions stored in ROM, but it cannot write anything into ROM and is therefore referred to as **non-volatile memory**.

Task 1.2

Answer the questions in **Task 1A-2** on the CD.

PERFORMANCE

A computer's performance is dictated by a number of factors, such as clock speed, CPU, RAM, hard disk, bus size, bus speed and the number of applications in use at the same time.

- As mentioned above, the clock speeds are continually increasing and are obviously increasing the performance of the computer.

- The number of operations performed by the CPU during each clock cycle varies – the greater the number of operations, the greater the performance.

- The CPU accesses RAM much faster than the hard disk. Therefore, if a computer has a large amount of RAM it will have very fast access to a large amount of data. If a computer has a small amount of memory then it uses the hard disk as temporary memory, but it takes longer to access this and therefore degrades the performance of the computer.

- The speed at which data can be read from, and written to, a hard disk varies. Again, the faster the read/write operation, the better the performance of the computer. Working from a CD, memory stick or floppy disk will be quite slow, as the read/write operation on these drives is very slow in comparison to the hard disk.

- A **bus** is a channel along which data flows in the computer. This may be compared to a motorway along which traffic passes. The wider the bus, the more data it can accommodate at a time, like a highway having four lanes instead of two. The faster the speed at which the data flows along the bus the better the performance – compare a highway speed of 130 km/hr instead of 70 km/hr.

- Computers are capable of running a number of application programs at the same time. However, each program requires an amount of RAM when it is in use and therefore if a number of application programs are in use at the same time it will slow down the computer's performance.

INPUT DEVICES

In order to give instructions to (or feed data into) a computer we must have some way of communicating with it. The most common method is by using a keyboard. Since the instructions given to a computer must be exact, the accuracy of keying is more important than speed.

Other methods of input include:

- Mouse.

- Joystick.

- Disk drive (hard, floppy and zip).

- Memory stick.

- CD-ROM/DVD.

- Touch pads (laptops).

- Touch-sensitive screen.

- Trackball.

- Scanner.

- Digital camera.

- Microphone.

- Light pen.

- Video.

OUTPUT DEVICES

These allow us to receive output from the computer. The screen (or monitor) is the most common output device. The way in which the output is displayed is controlled by the program instructions that are given to the computer.

When output is required on paper, it is normally produced on a printer. There is currently a large variety of printers available. The most common types are laser and inkjet. The laser printer is suitable for large quantities and good quality but tends to be expensive. The inkjet printers are suitable for low-quantity colour printing. These printers are relatively cheap but the cost of ink is high. The quality of the inkjet printer, in some cases, is now nearly as good as the laser printer.

Other methods of receiving output from a computer include:

- Disk drive.
- Memory stick.
- Speakers.
- Plotter.
- Robots.
- CNC (computer numeric control) machines.

Task 1.3

Answer the questions in **Task 1A-3** on the CD.

HARDWARE

This is the term used to describe all the electronic and mechanical elements of the computer. Hardware is basically something that has size and shape, and can be seen and touched. Examples of hardware are a computer, screen, printer, disk drive, disks (hard or floppy), mouse, cables, etc.

PROGRAMS

The computer cannot do anything on its own. It must be given exact instructions, which it will follow. These instructions are given to the computer by people and they are contained in what is known as a program. The activity of producing a program is called programming.

A program may be only a few lines long or it may contain several thousand lines, depending on what it is required to do. Most programs in common use are written by specialists who are employed by software houses. Most people who use computers today have little or no knowledge of programming – this is not necessary in order to operate a computer.

SOFTWARE

This is the general term used to describe the various programs used on a computer. Software is something that has no size and it cannot be touched, but a computer can do nothing without it. Software is generally supplied on a CD and for this reason the CD, which is a piece of hardware, is often mistaken for the programs that are optically stored on the CD disk. It is in fact the programs stored on the disk which constitute software. Software is continuously being developed and updated versions of software are released regularly. The updated version may have been developed to correct some faults with a previous version or, more frequently, to introduce new features into the software.

Software may be divided into two categories, namely:

- Systems software.

- Applications software.

Systems Software

Systems software is the programs that are produced in order to manage and control the computer's operation. Systems software is normally referred to as the operating system (OS). The operating system transforms the various pieces of hardware into a working computer by allowing all the different components to operate together and perform the function for which they were designed.

The OS accepts instructions from the **application software** and carries them out. It organises the flow of data to and from the various parts of the computer, such as the CPU, memory and hard disk. The OS also controls the various devices attached to the computer, such as the keyboard, mouse, monitor and printer. Without the OS the computer would simply be a collection of parts that would not be able to do anything.

There are a number of operating systems in use today but by far the most common is Windows. Windows is an extensive **systems software** (operating system) program that is designed to be user friendly. There are a number of versions of Windows in common use (Windows 2000, XP and Vista), but they are all so similar that most people would not see a difference when using a computer with any of these versions.

Modern OSs use icons (small pictures or words) and a mouse to perform many tasks. The use of icons and a mouse is referred to as a graphic user interface (GUI). The use of a GUI has become so common that it is difficult to comprehend how the computer was operated before they were invented. The use of a GUI makes operating a computer very simple. The icons used in various application programs are standard and once the user learns how to perform an operation in one program, it is the same in all other programs. Commands are executed by simply pointing to a particular icon and clicking a mouse button. The use of a GUI also allows easy manipulation of text and graphics and the user can immediately see the result of a command.

Even though the icons are part of each program it is the OS that allows the use of the GUI and responds to many of the commands given in the application program.

Applications Software

This term refers to the various programs that are used to perform specific user tasks. Examples of these programs are Word, Excel, Internet Explorer and games. There are literally hundreds of thousands of application programs.

Application programs are designed to perform very specific tasks, such as producing a letter, spreadsheet, payroll or playing a game. The application program works in close association with the OS. Instructions are passed between the two programs as they work hand in hand to perform the various tasks.

Each **application** program used with Windows must be specially matched to the Windows environment. Care should be taken when purchasing software to ensure that it is suitable for the particular version of the OS that is on the particular computer which will be used.

Task 1.4

Answer the questions in **Task 1A-4** on the CD.

DATA REPRESENTATION

When a letter or number is typed on the keyboard it is stored in the computer's RAM. The computer's memory is not capable of storing letters or numbers as we see them. The memory consists of chips with millions of tiny magnetic cells which can either be charged or uncharged. If a cell is charged we refer to it as containing a **1**, and if it is uncharged we refer to it as containing a **0**.

In order to store anything in a computer's memory, each character must be converted into a **binary** code, i.e. a code consisting of a series of 1s and 0s. The most common code used is called the ASCII code (American Standard Code for Information Interchange). Each of these 1s and 0s are referred to as BInary digiTS, which is abbreviated to bits. This ASCII code represents each character as a series of eight bits, which is referred to as a byte.

The following are just a few of the ASCII codes:

Number	Code	Letter	Code
1	10110001	A	11000001
2	10110010	B	11000010
3	10110011	C	11000011
4	10110100	a	11100001
5	10110101	b	11100010
6	10110110	c	11100011

The read/write operation to and from the various storage devices, such as disks and CDs, is normally measured in bits per second (bps), also referred to as **baud**.

MEMORY SIZE

Computer memory and disk space is measured by the number of bytes or characters it is capable of holding. Since these numbers are very large the terms kilobyte (KB), megabyte (MB) and gigabyte (GB) are used:

- 1 KB = approximately 1,000 bytes (1,024 exactly).

- 1 MB = approximately 1,000,000 bytes (1,048,576 exactly).

- 1 GB = approximately 1,000,000,000 bytes (1,073,741,824 exactly).

STORAGE DEVICES

The normal method of storing programs and information for a computer is on a magnetic disk or optical disk. The six most common types of storage devices are:

- Floppy disk.

- Zip disk.

- Hard disk.

- Compact disk.

- Magnetic tape.

- Memory card/stick.

All types of units have certain things in common but there are some distinct differences between them. The following is a brief synopsis of the storage devices.

Floppy Disk

This consists of a disk drive unit into which a floppy disk is placed. The disk has magnetic surfaces and a read/write head is positioned on both sides of the disk. The disks in this case are removable and can therefore be transported. Software for a computer may be supplied on floppy disk. This disk size is standardised at 3.5" and the speed of this device is very slow (less than 1 Mbps).

Figure 1.7

Zip Disk

These are similar to floppy disks but have a much larger storage capacity (usually 100 MB to 750 MB). They are much faster than floppy disks (up to 2.5 Mbps) but not nearly as fast as hard disks. They are most suitable for transporting large files and for backup storage.

Figure 1.8

Hard Disk

This consists of a number of rigid magnetic disks mounted on a common spindle with read/write heads between each disk. The disks rotate at very high speed and the read/write operation is very fast (normally 3 to 30 Gbps). The complete unit is mounted in a sealed container and is therefore not susceptible to dust.

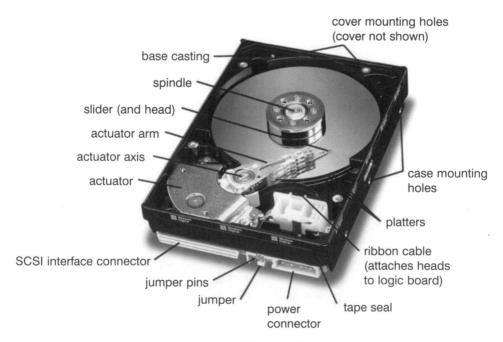

Figure 1.9

Every computer will have at least one hard disk in the machine. Hard disks are also available that are separate from the machine but may be connected to it by means of a cable. Another type of hard disk is capable of being plugged in and out of a socket in the computer, called hot swap disks.

Optical Disk

These are normally referred to as compact disks (CDs) and consist of an optical surface onto which the data is burned using a laser beam. The data is read from the disk using a laser. A variation of the CD is a DVD. This is also a laser disk but is used to store motion pictures. Disks are now available that may be reused and these are referred to as rewritable (RW) disks. CDs normally hold about 650 MB. The read/write speed of these devices is normally less than 10 Mbps.

Figure 1.10

Magnetic Tape

The data in this device is stored on a magnetic tape in the same way as an audio tape, i.e. sequentially. In order to retrieve data from the tape it is necessary to go to the exact point on the tape where that piece of data is stored. The technology associated with tape storage has developed and write speeds up to 15 Mbps are being achieved. However, the read speed is greatly affected by the time taken to find the data required. Therefore, this storage device is usually only used for archival storage. Data cartridges, which fit into the tape unit, are available with storage capacities of 8 GB. Some systems have multiple tape units, which hold up to 640 GB.

tape

tape unit

Figure 1.11

Memory Cards/Sticks

This is a small memory device that is used in a range of digital equipment, such as PDAs, digital cameras, laptops, mobile phones, etc. These devices are simply an amount of RAM which may be plugged into and out of the appliance. These devices are also referred to as flash cards or memory sticks. Read/write speed is usually less than 20 Mbps. The USB memory stick has virtually replaced floppy disks as a means of transporting data.

Many printers are now accepting memory cards to make it possible to print photos from the camera without the use of a computer.

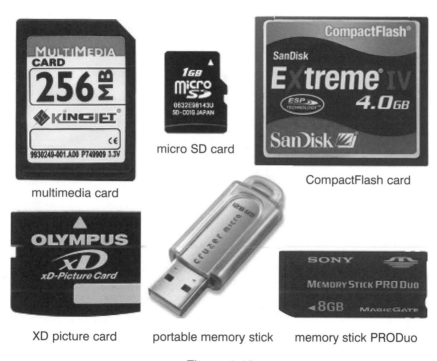

micro SD card

CompactFlash card

multimedia card

XD picture card   portable memory stick   memory stick PRODuo

Figure 1.12

MAGNETIC DISKS

The disk surface in the floppy, zip and hard disk is magnetic – it must be magnetically divided (formatted) into a number of tracks and sectors. Each storage location can then be located by the disk number, disk side, track number and sector number. Data that is stored on the disk is transferred (in a stream of bits) from the computer's memory and stored in one or more of these storage locations. The amount of data that can be stored on a disk depends on the size and density of the disk. Hard disks normally hold from 120 GB to 1,000 GB. Zip disks hold 100 MB to 750 MB. Floppy disks normally hold 1.44 MB.

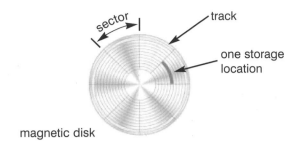

Figure 1.13

Formatting

In order to use a magnetic disk (hard, floppy, zip) it must be formatted. When a disk is produced it is simply a plain magnetic surface that has no method of storing data on it. Formatting the disk is the process of magnetically producing the tracks and sectors on the disk.

Backup

Computers are man-made machines and do break down from time to time. One of the most severe problems which may occur, however unlikely, is the loss of data stored on a disk. In order to recover from such an occurrence it is necessary to keep copies of all data that is stored on the computer's hard disk. The process of copying data to another location or device is often referred to as **systems backup** and would be performed on a regular basis. The frequency of a systems backup may vary from several times per day to once per week, depending on the importance of the data.

Depending on the amount of data to be backed up and the likelihood of having to restore the data, a variety of media may be used, including:

- Memory sticks.
- Zip disks.
- CDs or DVDs.
- Other hard disks.
- Backup tape.

The normal procedure is to have three copies of data that are updated (backed up) at regular intervals. At least one of these copies should be stored outside the building that houses the computer.

In some cases large amounts of data need to be backed up for archival storage. This would require a very large number of zip disks or CDs and the procedure would be relatively slow and labour intensive. In this case the data would normally be stored on magnetic tape, which is capable of holding up to 8 GB on a very small tape.

Task 1.5

Answer the questions in **Task 1A-5** on the CD.

SOFTWARE DEVELOPMENT

Software development may be broadly divided into four stages:

- Analysis.
- Design.
- Programming.
- Implementation.

Analysis

This task involves a careful examination of the business, what it does and how it does it. Usually, a systems analyst examines the operation of the client's business and determines how the business may be improved by the use of computer software. The outcome of this analysis may be to use off-the-shelf software, in which case the software may be purchased, installed and the personnel trained in its usage.

In other cases the result of the analysis may be the recommendation that the business have their own software developed. This solution would be much more expensive, but in the long term it may be more advantageous to the business to have programs tailored exactly to their needs.

Design

The systems analyst will usually progress from the analysis to the design of the new software, where this is considered necessary. This step involves clearly identifying **what** the software should do, but not **how** it should do it. This is similar to an architect designing a building and producing a blueprint, with full specifications for every aspect of the construction. At the end of the design phase the systems analyst produces a very detailed specification of **what** the software is to do.

Programming

This stage involves a computer programmer translating the detailed specification into a computer program – usually a number of programs. Each program contains the instructions needed by the computer in order to perform tasks identified in the design phase. This is similar to a builder who takes the blueprints and specifications and constructs the building. The programming phase will also include testing the programs before installing them for the client.

Implementation

The implementation phase involves installing the new software on computers and ensuring that the software meets the client's needs. This stage may become quite extended, depending on the detail and accuracy of the previous stages. Training personnel to operate the new software is also part of this phase.

COMPUTER-BASED TRAINING (CBT)

CBT takes advantage of the multimedia capability of modern computers and uses interactive programs to train people, namely communicating knowledge and enabling people to perform certain tasks on the computer. The most popular of these programs are ones that teach people **to keyboard**. The more sophisticated of these programs are able to detect the user's ability and adjust the exercises to their standard. Of course, these programs cannot determine if the person is using the correct finger for each key or whether they are looking at the keys as they type, but nevertheless they are very useful and if used properly will enable a student to acquire the skill of keyboarding.

Most CBT programs will use text, sound and video clips, which allow the student to acquire skills without risk to the person or the use of expensive equipment.

The use of CBT allows students to work at their own pace and will usually accelerate the training time and reduce costs. Students may work at home or even over the Internet – therefore there is no need to attend classes and have the presence of a teacher.

There are a number of disadvantages to CBT. The learning tends to be a solitary process and therefore there is little interaction with other students. There may be no teacher involved in the process and therefore no way of obtaining assistance if it is needed. The lack of contact with other students or teachers may lead to a lack of motivation and the student may just give up.

COMPUTER NETWORKS

There are a number of advantages by connecting computers to one another. The configuration of connecting computers together is referred to as a **network**. Networks may be divided into two broad categories:

- LAN (local area network).

- WAN (wide area network).

LAN

This arrangement typically applies to a room or a building where a number of computers are connected together by means of network cables. The arrangement is sometimes referred to as an **intranet** (not to be confused with Internet).

The arrangement usually consists of a computer called a server, which is used to control the network and store shared resources such as files, programs, printers, scanners and Internet connections. Computers that are connected to the server are referred to as terminals. These terminals are actual PCs and therefore perform all processing locally.

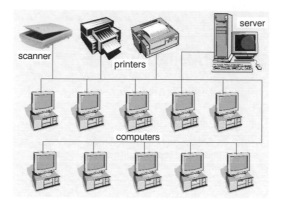

Figure 1.14

This arrangement has some security attached to it, as users have to use a username and password in order to gain access to the network. A major advantage of this arrangement is that different users may work on a single set of files, such as accounts or payroll, while still having other applications that are specific to their computer. This can be advantageous when purchasing licences, as it is only necessary to purchase licences for the number of users of each individual program.

A less popular type of LAN is a **pier-to-pier** arrangement where individual computers are connected together without a server. In this arrangement individual computers may share data directly with other computers.

Intranets may connect to the Internet and thus allow users to access the Internet. The type of connection used would generally be ADSL (broadband). However, there is usually no connection to the network from outside the network. In some cases intranets may be arranged so that authorised people may gain access to the network via the telephone line. This type of network is referred to as an **extranet**. In this arrangement a user may dial up the network and, provided they have proper authorisation, use the network. A firewall is commonly installed on the server in order to control access to the data on the network.

WAN

In this arrangement individual computers and LANs are connected over a large area, e.g. a single country or even worldwide. Typically banks, insurance companies, national governments or lotteries would have their own WAN. Computers in different locations communicate via the use of telephone lines on the **PSTN** (public switched telephone network) or in some cases, satellites.

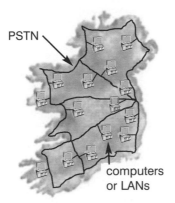

Figure 1.15

The most popular WAN in use today is the Internet. This arrangement allows computers all over the world to communicate either directly or via a LAN.

In order to connect networks on a country or worldwide basis it is necessary to have excellent communication networks. The networks used for computer communications are high-speed digital networks such as **ISDN** (integrated services digital network), **ADSL** (asymmetric digital subscriber line) and satellite communications. These types of networks are commonly referred to as **information superhighways**. The Internet operates on such a network. Individual users normally connect to the Internet via the PSTN using a router.

Task 1.6

Answer the questions in **Task 1A-6** on the CD.

THE INTERNET

The term **Internet** is short for internetworking. The Internet is a collection of worldwide computer networks connected together using the **PSTN**. The information on all these networks may be shared by anyone connected to this worldwide network.

Modern developments have increased the access to the Internet by means of mobile phones and satellite communications.

CONNECTING TO THE INTERNET

In order for an individual computer to connect to the Internet it must be equipped with a network connection. This is a device that is fitted in the computer and allows it to connect to the telephone network via a router. Alternatively, a computer may be part of a LAN that is connected to the Internet. There are a number of different types of connections to the PSTN. The most common is an ADSL (broadband) connection using a standard router.

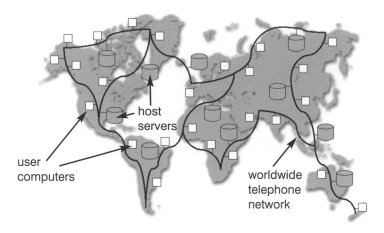

Figure 1.16

ADSL

The most common type of connection to the Internet is the asymmetric digital subscriber line (ADSL) or broadband. This type of connection makes use of existing telephone lines but transmits at much higher frequencies, therefore not interfering with existing telephone traffic. The connection is always on and because of the higher frequencies used, transmission rates of up to 10 Mbps (10,000,000 bps) are available. The term **asymmetric** means that the information flowing into a computer (download) is much faster than the traffic flowing out of it (upload). This is advantageous as the amount of download traffic is much greater than the upload traffic.

An account with an Internet service provider (ISP), such as Eircom, Smart, O$_2$ and BT, is also required in order to gain access to the Internet. Some of these accounts are free.

Modem

In areas where broadband is not available it is possible to connect to the Internet using a modem. The word **modem** comes from two words which describe what a modem does – Modulator and Demodulator. It is a device that accepts serial data (a string of bits) from a computer and converts it into an analogue signal. The analogue signal is suitable for transmission over a PSTN. The analogue signal is receiving by another modem, which translates the analogue signal back into digital data. The reason we need modems for data communication is because the telephone network is designed for analogue communication.

This is a relatively slow arrangement with maximum download speeds of 56,000 bits per second (bps or baud). However, these speeds are rarely achieved and very often the speed will be closer to 28,000 bps.

THE WORLD WIDE WEB (WWW)

The WWW is a global network of computers that uses the Internet to connect and transfer data, pictures, sound and video worldwide. In order to allow this to happen there has to be a standard protocol for connecting computers together and transferring information. The development and adoption of **http** (HyperText Transfer Protocol) facilitated the development of the WWW.

Along with having a connection to the Internet, the computer must also have a program (software) that will allow the computer to interact with the World Wide Web. This program is called a **web browser**, and the most common web browser programs in use are Microsoft Internet Explorer and Mozilla Firefox.

The uses of the WWW are vast and varied. New uses are being found every day and it is impossible to devise any sort of a list of uses. The main uses can be broadly divided into communication, training, research, commerce and marketing.

E-mail

This term stands for electronic mail. Everyone who has an account on the Internet usually has an e-mail address. Even if you do not have an account you may have an e-mail address in your place of work. Alternatively, you may sign on to a number of free e-mail services such as Gmail, Hotmail and Yahoo.

Once you have an e-mail account you may send and receive e-mail from anywhere in the world, provided you have access to a computer. The most popular programs used for e-mail are Microsoft Outlook, Microsoft Outlook Express and Webmail.

The use of e-mail has revolutionised the way in which people communicate. E-mail allows instant delivery of messages at a greatly reduced cost. An e-mail may be sent to a number of people at the same time, and messages may be replied to, or forwarded to, other people very quickly.

E-mail messages may also have files attached to them and in this way any file(s) may be sent from one computer to another almost instantly and at a very low cost. The file may contain data, pictures and programs.

The only drawback is that the messages must be typed, and unless people have good keyboarding skills, this process can be very slow.

Task 1.7

Answer the questions in **Task 1A-7** on the CD.

USES OF COMPUTERS

Use of computers has become so common today that it is difficult to imagine a world without them. Their use has revolutionised every aspect of life, from the home to space travel. Computers are generally used to take the drudgery out of repetitive tasks and increase the efficiency of businesses in general. The vast majority of homes now have a computer, which is used for both work and leisure. However, it should be remembered that computers are not the answer to every problem. There are many tasks that still need human interaction.

The era we are living in now is sometimes referred to as the **Information Society** or **Information Age**, in the same way as we once had an Industrial Age. Many countries rely heavily on the production and use of information technology (IT) to generate wealth. Today, it would be difficult to comprehend how our lives and society in general would change if computers disappeared tomorrow.

In the Home

A home computer would normally be a multimedia machine with sound, DVD, network connection, scanner and printer.

The software on such a machine would normally be off the shelf and typically include a word processor, spreadsheet program, Internet and e-mail programs, graphics programs (for use with a digital camera), DVD player, web browser and numerous games.

The use of the Internet and e-mail have become as common as making a phone call was a number of years ago. Children are using the computer to produce colourful school projects as well as using the Internet to source material.

Using computers to work from home is also becoming more common.

In Education

The use of computers in schools has grown at a similar rate to the increase in general use. Initially computers in schools were single, stand-alone units but now computer networks have become increasingly common. Computers are used for both administration and teaching purposes. In the teaching area they are used to teach the use of applications software, such as word processing and spreadsheets. However, there is a vast range of software available to enhance the teaching of all subjects – this area is becoming increasingly popular as teachers gain confidence in using computers.

The use of computers in other education-related areas include:

- Student registration.
- Timetabling.
- Distance learning (e.g. Open University).
- Project and homework research.
- Computer-based training (CBT).

At Work

Most workplaces now have a computer network (LAN), which is used to carry out a large number of tasks required to run the business. Computers in workplaces generally do not have full multimedia capability and are selected to only perform the business functions.

In general, computers in the workplace will have specialised software that has been written specifically for that particular business or a more general program for that type of business. Computers in the workplace will normally have some off-the-shelf software, such as word processing and spreadsheet programs.

The list of work areas where computers are used is endless but here are some examples:

Banks	New customer applications, account details, transaction records.
Insurance Companies	Applications, claims processing, renewals, quotations.
Manufacturing	Computer-controlled machines, robot assembly, stock ordering.
Government Departments	Tax records and collection, vehicle registration, public records, electronic voting.
Health	Patient records, ambulance control, diagnostic instruments (monitors), specialist surgical equipment.
Supermarkets	Point-of-sale terminals, stock reordering, credit/Laser card payments.
Communications	Automatic telephone systems, mobile phone systems.
Reservations	Cinema, theatre, airlines, hotels, car rental, holidays.
Cars	Electronic management systems, navigation systems.
Aircraft	Autopilot, computer navigation systems, fly by wire.

E-commerce

The term 'e-commerce' stands for electronic commerce. The use of computers combined with high-speed digital networks is allowing more companies to carry out business without face-to-face contact. Video conferencing and electronic document transfer mean that business can be transacted very quickly without the need to travel or wait for the mail.

Shopping online for all sorts of goods and services, from the weekly groceries to a house in the sun, is now possible. The user simply logs on to the Internet and selects the site from which they wish to purchase. The user can then view the items and select what they want as they browse. There are a number of advantages to shopping on the WWW, some of which include:

- Large selection of suppliers.

- Large selection of goods (may cause difficulty in making a choice).

- Shop when it suits you (available twenty-four hours a day).

- Easy to make price comparisons (be sure to check cost of delivery).

Payment for goods purchased over the WWW is normally made by credit card and the items are delivered to your door. When giving details, either personal or financial, care should be taken to ensure that the website is secure (usually indicated by the letter s after the http (https://) at the start of the website address). Some websites display secure certification, indicating the level of security associated with their website. Personal details should be limited to those necessary in order to carry out the transaction. Be wary of websites that collect additional personal information, as this is often used in marketing.

The consumer rights for goods purchased over the Internet are the same as for any other goods purchased. However, returning goods and receiving a refund may be quite difficult. These rights may be summarised as follows.

Under the **Sale of Goods and Supply of Services Act 1980**, anything bought from a retailer must be:

- Of merchantable quality.

- Fit for its normal purpose and reasonably durable.

- As described, whether the description is part of the advertising or wrapping, on a label, or something said by the salesperson.

Teleworking

The increased use of the PSTN and the Internet to communicate has led to a growth in teleworking. This may be divided into two categories, namely:

- Working from home.

- Telecentre.

Working from Home

This has the great advantage of not having to commute to and from work. It also saves the employer having to provide workspace with all the accompanying overheads. There are usually less distractions when working at home, which can result in greater productivity. There is also greater flexibility in work scheduling and work can be scheduled to fit around family commitments.

There are also drawbacks to working from home. Work becomes a solitary occupation with little human contact. This can lead to stress, which is normally alleviated by simply being able to share problems with colleagues. It is also very difficult to engage in teamwork from home.

Telecentres

There has been a large growth in the use of telecentres in Ireland over the past number of years. This has come about due to the advances in the PSTN and the availability of computer-literate personnel. A telecentre typically has operatives using a computer while talking to clients on the telephone. Telecentres are used for such activities as making reservations, offering customer support and telephone banking.

Task 1.8

Answer the questions in **Task 1A-8** on the CD.

USING COMPUTERS

As with the use of any machinery there are good and bad practices associated with their use. Firstly, the computer should be started correctly. This usually involves simply switching on the machine (and possibly the monitor) and then waiting for the operating system to load. During the start-up cycle the keyboard or mouse should not be touched. The computer should also be shut down correctly, which is much more important than starting. All programs should be shut down (exited) correctly and then the operating system shut down.

The room or office where the computer is installed should be well ventilated and have good lighting. Lighting should be such that it does not cause glare on the screen. The computer should be positioned so that natural light does not interfere with viewing the screen.

Health and Safety

The most common problem associated with the constant use of computers is RSI (repetitive strain injury). This is caused by constant use of the same muscles over a prolonged period of time. Poor posture or incorrect positioning of keyboard, mouse or monitor normally cause injuries.

Eye fatigue is another problem that is usually associated with constant use of computers. This is often attributed to poor monitors, poor lighting, incorrect lighting, reflections on the monitor or being too close to the monitor. Frequent breaks are required if a person is using a computer all day.

The person's position while working at the computer is important. People should sit properly in an appropriate chair with the monitor slightly below the eye line. The keyboard and mouse should be at the correct height and comfortably positioned. The user should be able to sit with their arms by their sides while using the keyboard.

The chair is also of great importance. It should be comfortable and the height should be adjustable.

Licensing

All software, including the operating system, is copyrighted and should be licensed. Most computers are sold with the operating system (usually Windows) already installed. However, if the operating system is upgraded then a further licence fee has to be paid.

All application software is licensed separately and a licence must be purchased for the use of each piece of software on **each** machine. When a new program is purchased it automatically comes with a licence. This licence is usually a single licence, which licences the software to be used on one machine only. As in the case of the OS, if the application software is updated then a separate licence fee must be paid.

It is sometimes possible to buy multiple licences for software at a reduced price. Some vendors offer site licences that allow the software to be used on one site (one company, business or school). Site licensing is common in some applications, particularly in the case of accounts, bookkeeping and payroll programs. This is often a better option. Even though the cost is greater than a single licence, the overall cost for a number of machines is much less.

The growth in the use of the Internet has led to many producers offering their software over the WWW. Some of these programs may be freeware, which do not require a licence to use them under the conditions specified. A large number may be shareware, which generally require a licence. Standard commercial programs may also be downloaded directly from the supplier's website. However, it must be remembered that most of these programs require a licence, and while some offer a free trial period, they are only legal when paid for and then usually only on one computer.

Every program will have a product ID number that must match the licence for that product. The product ID may be checked by accessing the Help menu for that program.

Programs may be copied onto storage media such as a memory stick or CD but it is not legal to sell these or even to give copies to other people.

The Environment

Respect for the environment is becoming a very important issue. In this Information Age the proper use of technology may help to reduce its impact on the environment. Printer toner and ink cartridges, and the paper generated by printing should be recycled. The use of electronic documents, without the need for printing, should be used wherever possible. The use of low-power computers, monitors and peripherals should be encouraged together with automatic power management help to reduce overall power consumption.

COMPUTER SECURITY

There are a number of measures which should be taken in order to secure the integrity and privacy of data stored on a computer. The first measure which should be taken is to ensure that the machine itself is not stolen. This can be a particular problem with laptops, mobile phones and PDAs. If the item is stolen then all the data stored on it can be accessed, even if it is protected with IDs and passwords. The loss of a personal mobile phone may mean the loss of contact phone numbers unless they are also recorded somewhere else.

Backing Up

Computers today are generally very reliable, but like any machine they can break down. The most important part of a computer is the data stored on the hard disk. If this data is lost then it may be very expensive or impossible to generate it again. All data stored on a computer should be copied onto backup storage at regular intervals. These intervals may be weekly, daily or even a number of times each day. Some businesses have a system of live updating where the data is backed up as it is written to the hard disk.

Privacy

It is vitally important to ensure that computers are protected from unauthorised use. In the case of computer networks, users are forced to log on to the network. In order to do this they must have a recognised username or ID and at least one password. Computer users usually retain their username or ID (generally their name) but passwords should be changed regularly and old passwords deleted where necessary. Stand-alone computers may also be protected in the same way, but very often this is not enabled on the computer.

Many programs, such as accounts, payroll and employee records, may be separately protected by having their own username and passwords. This means that even though a user may have access to a computer or computer network, they may not have access rights to certain programs or even certain elements within a program. The right to make changes in certain data, such as personal details, may be restricted to a supervisor or manager.

Many companies have information security policies that make personnel aware of their responsibilities with respect to information security. These policies also detail procedures for dealing with sensitive information and for reporting breaches in security.

Physical

It may seem obvious, but computers should be stored on a solid table or on the ground. Monitors should be positioned in front of the user and slightly below the eyeline, and therefore it is not a good idea to have the monitor sitting on the computer.

As already mentioned, computers should be shut down properly. In the case of a power cut this will not happen and the computer may be damaged as a result. Some files may be corrupted, or data lost, if the power is suddenly cut off. In cases where computers hold sensitive information, they should be protected by using a UPS (uninterruptible power supply). This device contains a battery that keeps the computer running for a period of time in the event of a power cut. This gives the operator sufficient time to shut down the computer properly and disconnect it from the mains.

Some of the more powerful UPSs allow the user to continue using the computer for a period of time.

Another problem that sometimes occurs with mains power, particularly after a power cut, is a power surge. This is where the voltage suddenly surges, just for a brief moment, but it can cause damage to data. This may be prevented by using a surge suppressor. Surge suppressors are often an integral part of a UPS.

The computer equipment should be kept clean and free from spills. Cables should be tidy and away from traffic. Computers should be in a well-ventilated area and at normal room temperatures. Overheating can be a problem if the computer is stored in a small space with lots of other equipment.

Viruses

Today the term **virus** is more associated with computers than humans. Computer viruses are programs that are written with the deliberate intention of disrupting the operation of a computer, sometimes preventing the operation of the computer altogether and corrupting or deleting the contents of the hard disk. Where a computer is part of a network the problem is even greater – a virus can spread to the whole network very rapidly.

There are many different types of viruses, the more common ones being the following.

Boot Viruses

These viruses infect boot records and may prevent the computer from working altogether.

Program Viruses

These programs are loaded in memory during the execution of a program, taking the virus with them.

Multipartite Viruses

A hybrid of boot and program viruses.

Stealth Viruses

These viruses use certain techniques to avoid detection. They may either redirect the disk head to read another sector instead of the one in which they reside, or they may alter the reading of the infected file's size shown in the directory listing.

Polymorphic Viruses

This is a virus that can encrypt its code in different ways so that it appears differently in each infection. These viruses are more difficult to detect.

Macro Viruses

A macro virus infects the macros within a document or template. When a macro virus is activated it infects the normal template (Normal.dot).

ActiveX

ActiveX and Java controls have introduced great flexibility and dynamism into Internet activity but may soon be the scourge of computing, as they provide an ideal opening for this type of virus.

Viruses are spread by being carried on files that are moved from one computer to another. This can be done using floppy disks, CDs, on e-mail or even over the Internet.

Most computer users invest in antivirus software in order to prevent infection. In order for the antivirus program to be effective it must be updated regularly (at least every week). Once the program has been purchased it may be updated by downloading the latest update over the Internet.

The following are some simple measures that may help to prevent infection by a virus:

- Check the computer regularly for viruses.

- Clean/disinfect or delete infected files immediately.

- Never use a memory stick that has not been checked for viruses.

- Never open e-mail from unknown sources.

- Only use reputable software (be wary of free software).

- Back up data regularly.

DATA PROTECTION LEGISLATION

There is a vast amount of information collected and stored on computers every day. Many people would be shocked if they knew how many databases contained their personal details and the uses to which this information is put. Database creators include banks, building societies, local government, supermarkets, credit card companies, doctors, hospitals, insurance companies and employers. Effectively, every form filled out is stored in a database. In the past, these databases were often shared or sold to other parties. In order to try and control this situation the government has introduced data protection legislation.

The Data Protection Act 1988 gives certain rights to individuals and imposes certain responsibilities on controllers relating to data stored on computer. The Act gives every individual the right to establish the existence of personal data, to access such data and to have inaccurate data rectified or erased.

The following are some of the main points of the data protection legislation:

- Data shall be kept only for one or more specified and lawful purposes.

- Data shall be adequate, relevant and not excessive.

- Data shall not be kept for longer than necessary for the purpose for which it was collected.

- Data shall not be used or disclosed in any manner incompatible with the purpose for which it was collected.

- Data shall be adequately secured against unauthorised access, alteration, disclosure or disruption.

- Every individual has the right to:
  - view data stored about her/him.
  - have inaccuracies rectified or erased.
  - have personal data taken off a direct mailing list.
  - complain to the Data Protection Commissioner.

Task 1.9

Answer the questions in **Task 1A-9** on the CD.

2 Managing Computers and Files

SYMBOLS USED IN THIS CHAPTER

The symbols used in this chapter, and their meanings, are as follows:

Click the left mouse button.

Click the right mouse button.

Double-click the left mouse button.

Hold down the left mouse button.

Hold down the right mouse button.

Move the mouse to point to an item or to another area without clicking or holding any button.

Release the mouse button.

Point to an item on the screen.

Ctrl — Hold down the Ctrl button.

Ctrl Alt Del — Hold down the Ctrl button and the Alt button and press the Delete key.

Press the Enter key.

Alt F4 — Hold down the Alt key and press the F4 function key.

INTRODUCTION

Modern computers have been designed to be user friendly. This has been accomplished mainly by the use of Windows-based operating systems. These systems provide a range of programs that may be used to manage the computer.

Task 2.1.1

(a) Start up the computer.
(b) Shut down the computer.

STARTING UP THE COMPUTER

Most computers are started by simply plugging them into a power supply and pressing the power button. The monitor may also have to be switched on, but generally it is powered from the same supply as the computer. After a short delay the monitor should show what is happening as the computer starts up (boots up).

As the computer starts up, the operating system the computer is running will load automatically and some information may appear on the screen. Most computers use Microsoft Windows as the operating system and the version of Windows the computer is running will be displayed. After a short period the computer will display a login window or the Windows desktop, depending on the configuration.

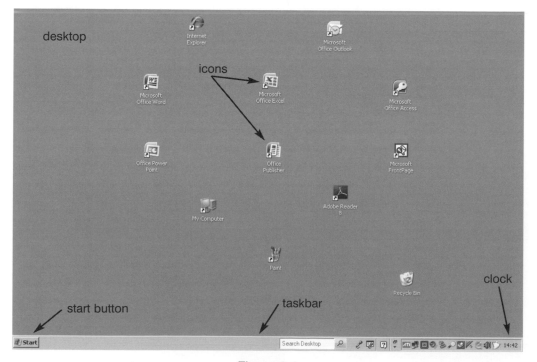

Figure 2.1

When Windows is loaded it displays a screen, called the desktop, with an icon (a graphic picture) for some (or all) of the programs available to the user. The user selects the program required by simply moving the mouse so that the arrow on the screen points to the icon for that program and pressing (clicking) the left mouse button twice in quick succession. If you have not used a computer before this is a skill you will need to develop. The desktop will also have a taskbar (usually at the bottom of the screen), which may also be used to load programs. The taskbar will always display the Start button and may also display other buttons and files that are open.

The arrangement of the icons on the screen will normally be set to automatic, in which case they will line up in columns on the left of the screen – this option may be changed if required.

The layout of the icons can be arranged as follows:

- ▣ Blank area of desktop 🖱. (*A pop-up menu will appear.*)
- ▣ Arrange icons 🖱.
- Select the arrangement required. (*Remove the tick from auto arrange.*)

When the Auto Arrange is switched off and none of the **Arrange By** options are selected, then it is possible to position the icons in any position on the desktop.

Icons are positioned as follows:

- ▣ Icon 🖱.
- Drag the icon to the required position 🖱.

Networks

If the computer is connected to a network then the network login window will automatically appear when it is switched on. The computer requires the input of a username and password in order to gain access to the network. After logging on to the network a desktop will appear.

SHUTTING DOWN THE COMPUTER

When you have finished using a computer it is necessary to shut it down properly. This is necessary in order that Windows deletes any temporary files it has set up and to undo any connections made during the time the computer was working.

The computer is shut down as follows:

- Exit all programs.
- ▶ Start button 🖱.
- ▶ Shut down 🖱.

A window may appear that offers a number of shut down options. Select the one required.

If a computer stops responding to commands (hangs) it may be necessary to perform an emergency shut down. This should only be done when it is not possible to shut down the computer in the normal way.

An emergency shut down is accomplished as follows:

- Hold down the Ctrl key and the Alt key and press the Delete key once or twice in quick succession. (Ctrl Alt Del).

A window may appear from which the shut down option required may be selected.

Some versions of Windows use the following procedure:

- Hold down the Alt key and press the F4 key (Alt).

Task 2.1.2

(a) Load My Computer.
(b) Display the following information:

- The total capacity of the C: drive.
- The used space on the C: drive.
- The free space on the C: drive.

(c) Close My Computer.
(d) Load Windows Explorer.
(e) Display the following information:

- The total capacity of the C: drive.
- The used space on the C: drive.
- The free space on the C: drive.

(f) Close Windows Explorer.

DISPLAYING COMPUTER INFORMATION

The simplest method of seeing what the various components on a computer are, is to use some software programs that are part of the Windows software package.

My Computer

My Computer is one of the programs that is automatically installed with the Windows operating system. There will be an icon on the desktop for this program. The program is loaded by simply pointing to the My Computer icon and double-clicking the left mouse button.

If the icon is not on the desktop then the program may be started as follows:

- ▣ Start.

- ⊕ All Programs.

- My Computer.

The My Computer window will appear on-screen showing the various items on the computer. The diagram below shows that this computer has a 3.5" floppy drive (A:), a single hard disk (C:) and a DVD drive (D:). A DVD drive may sometimes appear as a CD-ROM.

Figure 2.2

The single hard disk in a stand-alone computer may be partitioned, that is, split into two or more parts. This would appear in My Computer as two local disks, namely **Local Disk (C:)** and a **Local Disk (D:)**. The DVD drive would then be labelled (E:).

The hard disks in this case could be two separate hard disks or a single partitioned hard disk. In either case the computer's operating system treats them as if it has two separate hard disks.

> The contents of the various items displayed may be viewed as follows:
>
> - ▣ the item 🖱.

> More information about the various items may be viewed as follows:
>
> - ▣ Item (C:, D:, etc.) 🖱.
> - ⊕ Properties 🖱.

The properties window will appear, showing all the information about the item selected.

The program is closed by simply pointing to the close icon ☒ in the top right-hand corner of the window and clicking the left mouse button.

Windows Explorer

Windows Explorer is simply My Computer with the left-hand pane displaying the resources available on the computer. It is sometimes easier to work with files in this mode. Windows Explorer is displayed by simply loading the program as follows:

Method 1	Method 2
Load My Computer. ▣ Folders (on the menu bar) 🖱.	▣ Start button 🖱. ⊕ Explore 🖱.

The Windows Explorer screen has two sections. The left-hand section shows all the resources available on the computer and the right-hand side shows the contents of the item selected on the left.

The single hard disk machine with a floppy drive and two CD/DVD drives would appear as follows in the left-hand section. See Figure 2.3 overleaf.

> The contents of the various items displayed may be viewed as follows:
>
> - ▣ the item in the left-hand side 🖱.
>
> The contents will be displayed in the right-hand pane.

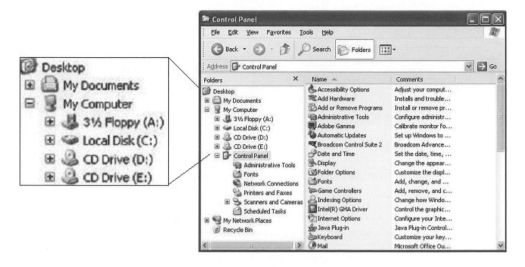

Figure 2.3

More information about the various items may be viewed as follows:

- ▲ Item (C:, D:, etc.) 🖱.

- ⊕ Properties 🖱.

The properties window will appear, showing all the information about the item selected.

The program is closed by simply pointing to the close icon ☒ in the top right-hand corner of the window and clicking the left mouse button.

Moving Backward and Forward

Both My Computer and Windows Explorer have a number of icons on the toolbar. The two most used are the Back and Forward icons. The Back icon ← allows the user to go back to previous selections one step at a time. After going back the Forward icon → allows the user to move forward one step at a time.

Task 2.1.3

(a) Load the Control Panel.
(b) Display the following information and adjust if necessary:

- Date/time.
- Regional settings.
- Volume control.
- Display properties.

- Keyboard properties.
- System properties, e.g. operating system, CPU type, amount of RAM, etc.

Note: Remember to close each window when you have finished with it.

(c) Close the Control Panel.

CONTROL PANEL

The Control Panel is used to manage most of the computer's functions. It can also be used to view the computer configuration information, such as processor and RAM size.

The Control Panel is accessed as follows:

- ▶ Start button ⬦. (*The start menu will appear.*)
- ⊕ Control Panel ⬦. (*The control panel window will appear.*)

The Control Panel is one of the options displayed when My Computer is loaded.

The Control Panel may be loaded from this window as follows:

- ▶ Control Panel (*in the left-hand pane*) ⬦.

The Control Panel is effectively a suite of programs that allows the user to control the resources attached to the computer. Some of the **Control Panel's** functions are shown below.

The Control Panel may be displayed in either of two settings, namely Category View or Classic View. For the purpose of the following notes it is assumed that Classic View is being used. The windows displayed for each task are the same regardless of how they are selected.

Date/Time

The date and time displayed on the computer may be viewed/changed as follows:

- ▶ Date and Time icon ⬦. (*The date and time window will appear.*)

This window allows the user to change the date and time on the computer clock.

Note: This window may also be accessed by pointing to the clock on the taskbar and double-clicking the mouse button.

Regional Settings

When Windows is installed on the computer the regional area (country) where the computer is being used should be designated.

The regional setting on the computer may be viewed/changed as follows:

- 🖱 Regional and Language Options icon 🖱.

  (*The regional and language options window will appear.*)

- Select the country from the list.

This option also allows the formats for other items to be set, such as numbers, currency, time and date.

Volume Control

The volume for the media player may be viewed/changed as follows:

- 🖱 Sounds and Audio Devices icon 🖱.

  (*The sounds and audio devices properties window will appear.*)

- 🖱 Volume tab 🖱. (*if not already selected*)

- Move the volume slider to adjust the volume.

Note: The volume may be quickly adjusted by pointing to the small speaker on the taskbar (if it is displayed) and clicking the left mouse button (once or twice). This will display a simple volume control on which the slider may be moved to adjust the volume.

Display

This option allows the user to set the various options for the monitor display.

The display option is selected as follows:

- 🖱 Display icon 🖱. (*The display window will appear.*)

- Select the tab required and set the various options as required.

Note: This option is used to set the desktop background, screen saver, colour settings and screen pixel resolution. The Display window may also be selected by pointing to any blank area of the desktop, clicking the right mouse button and selecting Properties.

Some of the display options are as follows:

Background Desktop

> The background of the desktop may be changed as follows:
> - ▣ Desktop tab 🖱.
> - Select the background and options required.

Screen Saver

Windows provides a screen saving device that may be activated. If the computer is left unattended for a short period of time, the screen saver blanks out the screen and displays a simple message, picture or motion clip. The work screen will return as soon as a key on the keyboard is pressed or the mouse is moved. The screen saver may be customised by using one of the screen savers provided by Windows or installing a custom screen saver.

> The screen saver is set as follows:
> - ▣ Screen Saver tab 🖱.
> - Select the screen saver and timings required.

Settings

> The screen colour configuration and pixel resolution may be changed as follows:
> - ▣ Settings tab 🖱.
> - Select the colour and resolution options required.

System

This is the option used to view the computer system configuration.

> The system option is selected as follows:
> - ▣ System icon 🖱. *(The system window will appear.)*

The General tab will list all the information about the computer's operating system, CPU, RAM, etc.

It is not a good idea to interfere with these settings as it could render the computer unusable. The various settings may be viewed without changing them.

Task 2.1.4

(a) Load an application program, e.g. Microsoft Word, using a desktop shortcut.
(b) Close the application program.
(c) Load an application program, e.g. WordPad, using the **Start** button.
(d) Restore the window to its previously restored size or maximise if already restored.
(e) Maximise the window or restore if already maximised.
(f) Close the application program.

APPLICATION PROGRAMS

Each application program used with Windows must be specially matched to the Windows environment. This means that all programs appear similar to the user.

Starting Programs

The simplest method of starting a program is to point to the program icon on the desktop and double-click the left mouse (click the button twice in quick succession).

Alternatively, a program may be started as follows:

- Start button . *(The start menu will appear.)*
- All Programs. *(Another menu will appear.)*
- (program required) .

As these menus are selected there may be a small arrow (▷) opposite some items on the menus. This indicates that this option contains another menu, which will be displayed by simply moving the mouse and resting it on that option.

Note: Remember that once a program is started it should always be shut down (exited) before shutting down the computer.

Shutting Down a Program

All programs should be shut down (exited) properly.

The correct procedure for shutting down a program is as follows:

- Save all files that are to be retained.

- Close all open files.

- ▲ File 🖰.

- ▲ Exit or Close 🖰

OR ▲ Close icon ☒ 🖰.

Task 2.1.5 (Additional)

Carry out the operations specified in **Task 2A-1** on the CD.

Task 2.2.1

(a) Load an application program, e.g. Microsoft Word.
(b) Examine the screen and locate the various parts mentioned in Figure 2.4.
(c) Display/hide the rules.
(d) Display/hide a toolbar.
(e) Reposition a toolbar.
(f) Add an icon to a toolbar.
(g) Remove an icon from a toolbar.
(h) Close the application program.

WINDOWS PROGRAMS

When a Windows program is loaded, the screen (with the exception of the work area) will appear similar to all other Windows programs.

The screen shown below is from Microsoft Word, but other applications have a similar layout.

The top row on the screen, called the **title bar**, displays the name of the present file being worked on together with the name of the program being used or vice versa, depending on the program.

In the case of Office **2007** the left-hand side of the top row will also have the Quick Access Toolbar with a number of icons which are used to perform certain operations. Icons can be added to this toolbar for performing frequent operations. The Office button is also located in the top left-hand corner.

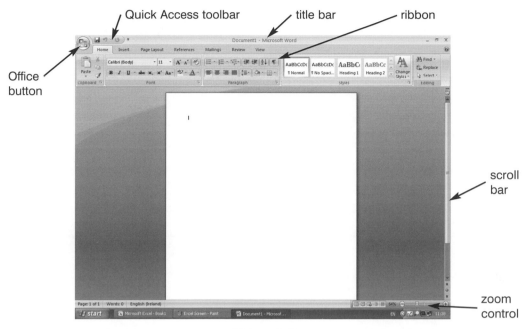

Figure 2.4

The next line, called the **menu bar**, consists of a number of words, each of which is the name of a menu or ribbon. When the mouse is pointed at one of these menu names and the left mouse button is clicked, a menu will appear to drop down under the heading or a ribbon of icons will appear. In the case of Office **2003**, these are called **pull-down** or **drop-down** menus. These menus may also have submenus, which appear as the mouse is pointed to each item on the menu with an arrow symbol after it. In the case of Office **2007**, each menu or tab displays a ribbon which contains icons which perform tasks simply by pointing to the icon and clicking the left mouse button.

In the case of Office **2003** there will be a row or number of rows of icons under the menu bar, called the **toolbar(s)**. Each icon performs a certain task simply by pointing to it and clicking the left mouse button. Some of these icons are standard to all programs, such as the printer, opening a file, saving a file, etc. – we will get to know each of these as we need to use them.

The centre portion of the screen is the work area where the operations are performed (typing text or figures, inserting pictures and charts, etc.).

The bottom portion of the screen contains some information about the program which is being used, such as the page number or sheet number, position on the page, printing, saving, special keys selected, etc. This is referred to as the **status bar**. Some programs may also have another toolbar at the bottom.

On the right-hand side and the bottom of the work area will be two bars with arrowheads on each end. These are referred to as **scroll bars** and are used to move the screen over the work in the direction of the arrow. Scroll bars may only appear when the work area is larger than the screen.

It is worth noting that the user may display the rules, status bar and a large number of toolbars on the screen. The more of these that are displayed, the smaller the work area will be.

We will examine the common functions of Windows programs and some setting and configuration options available. The following tasks may be performed using any Windows program.

DISPLAYING RULES

The screen may show rules at the top and left of the work area. These rules may be displayed or hidden depending on the setup.

Office 2003	Office 2007
Rules are displayed as follows: ➤ View menu. ➤ Ruler.	➤ View Ruler icon at the top of the vertical scroll bar.

TOOLBARS

Every program will automatically display a number of toolbars or ribbons, each of which will have a number of icons on them. The number of these toolbars or ribbons, their position and the icons on them are set by the program when it is installed on the computer. These settings are referred to as the **default** settings.

With Office **2007** the ribbons may be switched off or on, but the ribbon icons are set and may not be changed. However, in the case of Office **2003** it is possible to change the toolbars displayed and the icons on particular toolbars.

Displaying

Office 2003	Office 2007
Toolbars are displayed as follows: ➤ View menu. ➤ Toolbars. ➤ Toolbar required.	Ribbon display is changed as follows: ➤ Menu bar. ➤ Minimise the ribbon.

Note: A tick indicates that a toolbar or ribbon is set to be displayed.

Position

Office 2003

Toolbars may be repositioned as follows:

➤ Left-hand end of the toolbar. (*A four-headed arrow will appear.*)

➤ Drag the toolbar to the required position.

Note: Toolbars may be positioned at the top, bottom or sides of the screen. Two toolbars may be positioned on the same row.

Adding and Removing Icons on Toolbars

Toolbars are displayed with a number of icons on each toolbar. The icons displayed are normally the most popular icons for that toolbar. However, when using programs for a period of time the user may find that it would be advantageous to have an icon on the toolbar that is not there. Equally it may be found that some icons on a particular toolbar are never used. Icons may therefore be added or removed from toolbars.

Office 2003

Icons are added as follows:

➤ Tools menu.

➤ Customise. (*A customise window will appear.*)

➤ Commands tab.

➤ Icon in the window. (*The user may have to search through the various options in order to locate the icon in the customise window.*)

➤ Drag the icon onto the required position on a toolbar.

Office 2003

Icons are removed as follows:

➤ Tools menu.

➤ Customise. (*A customise window will appear.*)

➤ Icon on the toolbar.

➤ Drag the icon into the customise window.

Task 2.2.2

(a) Load an application program, e.g. Notepad.

(b) Restore the application to the previous restored size.

(c) Change the size of the program window so that it occupies the left half of the screen.

(d) Open another application program, e.g. Paint.

(e) Restore this application to the previous restored size.

(f) Change the size of the program window so that it occupies the right half of the screen.

(g) Minimise both programs.

(h) Open the first program from the taskbar and maximise.

(i) Close the program.

(j) Open the second program from the taskbar and maximise.

(k) Close the program.

WINDOW CONTROL

The individual windows that are being used at any time may be controlled using the window control icons in the top right-hand corner of each window. There are four icons, but only three of them will be visible at any one time. The middle icon alternates between maximise and restore, depending on the option selected. The icons are operated by simply pointing to them and clicking the left mouse button.

The control icons are as follows:

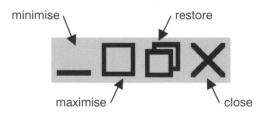

Figure 2.5

Minimise Removes the window from the screen and displays the filename on the taskbar. (The window appears on the taskbar only.) The window may be displayed again by simply pointing to the file on the taskbar and clicking the left mouse button.

Maximise Displays the window the full size of the screen. The maximise icon changes to the restore icon.

Restore   Changes the size of the window to a custom size. This size may be changed and the window repositioned on-screen. The restore icon changes to the maximise icon.

Close   Closes the window and shuts down the program.

Changing the Window Size

The size of a window may be changed as follows:

- ▮ Restore icon ⌔. (*If not already selected.*)

- ▮ Any side or corner of the window ⌔.

  (*The pointer changes to a resize icon* ↔ ↕ ⤢ ⤡ .)

- ⊕ Until the window is the required size ⌔.

Positioning a Window

A window may be positioned anywhere on-screen, provided it is not maximised.

A window is positioned as follows:

- ▮ Title bar of the window ⌔. (*The title bar is blue.*)

- ▮ Drag the window to the required position ⌔.

Task 2.2.3

(a) Load My Computer or Windows Explorer.
(b) Restore the window, if not already restored.
(c) Resize the window so that part of the desktop is visible.
(d) Locate a work folder containing one of your work files.
(e) Create a shortcut on the desktop to that file.
(f) Close My Computer or Windows Explorer.
(g) Change the icon which was created on the desktop. (Use any Windows icon.)
(h) Open the file using the icon on the desktop.
(i) Close the file.
(j) Close the program.
(k) Delete the shortcut from the desktop.

CREATING A DESKTOP SHORTCUT

Most programs automatically offer the option of placing an icon on the desktop to start the program when they are installed. However, it is possible to create a shortcut to any program. It is also possible to create a shortcut to a particular file that may be used quite frequently.

There are a number of methods of creating a shortcut on the desktop but the following is a simple method:

Locate the program file or work file using My Computer or Windows Explorer. (Ensure that the desktop is visible by resizing My Computer or Windows Explorer.)

- File to which the shortcut is to be linked.

- Drag the file to the desktop. (*A pop-up window will appear.*)

- Create shortcut(s) here.

CHANGING A SHORTCUT LABEL

When the shortcut is created on the desktop, Windows will create an icon with a label attached.

The label may be changed as follows:

- Label name. (*A pop-up menu will appear.*)

- Rename. (*The label text only will be highlighted.*)

- Type the new label.

CHANGING A DESKTOP SHORTCUT ICON

When a shortcut is created, Windows will automatically display an icon on the desktop.

It is possible to change the icon as follows:

- Icon. (*A pop-up window will appear.*)

- Properties. (*The properties window will appear.*)

- Shortcut tab.

- Change icon. (*The change icon window will appear.*)

continued

- ▣ The icon required 🖰.
- ▣ OK 🖰.
- ▣ OK 🖰.

The new icon will appear on the desktop.

Task 2.2.4 (Additional)

Carry out the operations specified in **Task 2A-2** on the CD.

FILE MANAGEMENT

Every item saved on a computer is saved in a file. This may be visualised as a suspension file into which a number of sheets of paper may be placed. Each file will have a name or label in the same way as a name tag would be placed on a suspension file. All of these files are stored on a magnetic disk in the machine. This storage disk is referred to as a hard disk and is capable of storing vast numbers of files. Computers may also have a CD/DVD or floppy disk drive into which a CD or floppy disk may be placed and files stored on that. However, the speed of these storage devices is relatively slow and the capacity is small.

In order to be able to locate files it is essential to have some structure on the hard disk. This structure consists of a system of folders and subfolders which are created in order to store files. The user may think of a folder as a drawer in a filing cabinet. This drawer may contain any number of files. A folder may also contain other folders (subfolders).

When programs are installed on the computer, they consist of a large number of files that are placed in folders. The user does not have to worry about the structure of these folders as the program takes care of this when it is installed. However, care should be taken not to disrupt the program files as this would cause a fault in the program and it would no longer operate.

VIEWING AND WORKING WITH FILES

When using a computer it is advisable to be able to perform certain housekeeping functions in order to store and locate files which have been created and to avoid running out of space on the hard disk. Windows provides two programs (My Computer and Windows Explorer) that allow the user to perform housekeeping functions. However, these are very powerful programs and it is easy to end up deleting or moving program files that may leave the computer unusable. Most housekeeping functions may also be performed from within the application program, e.g. Word or Excel.

Task 2.3.1

(a) Load the Windows Explorer program.

(b) Open a number of folders and view the contents.

(c) Identify the file types.

(d) Expand some folders and view the contents of subfolders.

(e) Contract the folders you expanded.

(f) Select a number of files and record the following information about five different files:

- The name of each file (including the file extension).
- The size of the file.
- The type of file.
- The date and time of last modification of each file.

(g) Select a folder and display the files in order of file size.

(h) Select a folder and display the files in order of date modified.

(i) Select a folder and display the files in order of file type.

(j) Select a folder and display the files in descending name order.

(k) Close the Windows Explorer program.

WINDOWS EXPLORER

When Windows Explorer is loaded (as described earlier) it will appear similar to the window shown in Figure 2.6.

The Windows Explorer window has two sections. The section on the left shows the various resources on the computer. It also allows the user to view all the folders that are on the hard disk, floppy disk, CD/DVD, etc. A folder is selected by simply pointing to the folder in the left section and clicking the left mouse button.

- An open folder will appear like this: 🗁

- A closed folder will appear like this: 🗀

The section on the right shows the contents of the selected (open) folder on the left. A folder may contain any number of files or it may contain other folders (subfolders). Folders may have a small or sign in front of the icon. Pointing to the + symbol and clicking the left mouse button causes that folder to expand and show all the subfolders in that folder and the + sign will change to a – sign. Subfolders may be expanded in the same way until there are no more folders to expand. Folders may be contracted by simply pointing to the – sign and clicking the left mouse button.

Note: Folders may also be expanded and contracted by pointing to the folder name and double-clicking the left mouse button.

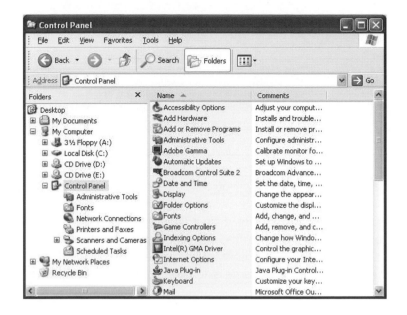

Figure 2.6

The way in which the folder contents are displayed is controlled by the views icon on the toolbar. There are five different ways in which the contents may be displayed (Thumbnails, Tiles, Icon, List and Details).

Note: The toolbar may have to be displayed, as described above.

FILE DATA

The following information will be displayed about each file:

- An icon associated with the type of file.

- The name of the file (may include the file extension).

- The size of the file.

- The type of file.

- The date and time of last modification of the file.

- Any other attributes associated with the file, e.g. read only, system, etc.

FILE STATUS

When viewing files, the Attributes column indicates the status of the file. When files are created and saved they are saved as **archive** files, which means that the file may be opened, modified and saved again. Sometimes the user may want to prevent a file from being modified, in which case it would need to have the status of **read only**.

The status of a file is viewed and/or changed as follows:

- ▮ File 🖱.
- ▮ Properties 🖱. (*The properties window will be displayed.*)
- Tick the property box required in order to change the status.
- ▮ OK or cancel 🖱.

FILE EXTENSIONS AND ICONS

When a program such as Word saves a file it attaches a full stop and a three-, four- or five-letter extension to the filename that has been given to the file. This extension is used by that program to recognise its own files.

Some of the more common filename extensions and icons are shown below.

Program	Extension	Icon
Word document	.doc (**2003**), .docx (**2007**)	
Rich text format (*one of the standard text formats*)	.rtf	
Text only file	.txt	
Excel workbook	.xls (**2003**), .xlsx **2007**	
Access database	.mdb (**2003**), .accdb (**2007**)	
PowerPoint presentation	.ppt (**2003**), .pptx (**2007**)	
Web page	.htm or .html	
Bitmapped picture (*pictures, but usually a large file size*)	.bmp	

Program	Extension	Icon
Jpeg picture (*pictures with smaller file sizes*)	.jpg or .jpeg	
Temporary file (*used by Windows while a file is open*)	.tmp or .tmpx	

Task 2.3.2 (Additional)

Carry out the operations specified in **Task 2A-3** on the CD.

SORTING FILES

It is sometimes helpful to be able to order (sort) a list of files displayed on-screen. The files may be ordered using Windows Explorer by simply pointing to the heading in the contents panel that is to be sorted and clicking the left mouse button. The list will be displayed in ascending order. Pointing to the same heading a second time and clicking the left mouse button will produce a list in descending order.

Task 2.4.1

(a) Insert a blank floppy disk, rewritable CD or memory stick into the computer.
(b) Load the Notepad or WordPad program.
(c) Type your name and address.
(d) Save this file, on the removable media, with the filename **Name** (in text-only format).
(e) Open a new file.
(f) Type the name and address of your school, college or institute.
(g) Save this file, on the removable media, with the filename **College** (in text-only format).
(h) Close (exit) the Notepad or WordPad program.
(i) Load the My Computer or Windows Explorer program.
(j) Copy a filename **Name** to the removable media.
(k) Rename the file named **Copy of Name** on the removable media, and give it the filename **Home**.
(l) Copy a file named **College** on the removable media.
(m) Rename the file named **Copy of College** on the removable media, and give it the filename **Work**.
(n) Copy the file named **Work** on the removable media.

(o) Rename the file named **Copy of Work** on the removable media and give it the filename **Institute**.

(p) Delete the file named **Work**.

(q) Close My Computer or Windows Explorer.

COPYING FILES

Within a Folder

This will produce a duplicate file in the folder. The procedure is as follows:	
Method 1	**Method 2**
Open the folder or disk containing the the the file. ▸ Filename 🖱 (*on the right*). ▸ Copy icon 📋 🖱. ▸ Paste icon 📋 🖱.	Open the folder or disk containing file. ▸ File to be copied 🖱 (*on the right*). ✛ Copy (*on the menu which appears*) 🖱. ▸ Anywhere in the right section 🖱. ✛ Paste (*on the menu which appears*) 🖱.

The new file with the name 'Copy of ... ' will appear in the list of files. The name of the file may then be changed as described later.

To Another Folder or Disk

This will produce a copy of a file in a different folder or on another disk (such as a floppy disk). The procedure is as follows:	
Method 1	**Method 2**
Open the folder containing the file. ▸ Filename 🖱 (*on the right*). ▸ Copy icon 📋 🖱. Scroll the left-hand section until the folder (or disk) into which the file is to go is visible.	Open the folder containing the file. Scroll the left-hand section until the folder (or disk) into which the file is to go is visible. Hold down the Ctrl key. ▸ Filename (*on the right*) 🖱.

continued

Disk/folder into which the file is to be copied 🖱.	Drag the file across to the left-hand section.
Paste icon 📋 🖱.	Folder (or disk) into which the file is to be copied 🖱.
	Release the Ctrl key.

The file will be copied into that folder. The folder must be opened in order to see the file.

Note: Copying files to floppy disks, CDs, memory sticks or zip disks at regular intervals is recommended in order to have a backup copy in case anything happens to the hard disk in the computer.

RENAMING A FILE

It may be necessary to change the name of a file. The file cannot be renamed if it is open.

Files may be renamed as follows:

- Select the file to be renamed.
- Filename 🖱.
- Rename 🖱. (*A box appears around the filename.*)
- Type the new filename ⌨.

The old filename will disappear and the new filename will appear in the list.

Note: When renaming a file the complete name, including the filename extension must be typed. If the extension is changed then the program will not be able to open that file again.

DELETING A FILE

A file may be deleted from the current folder as follows:

- Select the file to be deleted.
- File menu 🖱.

continued

- ⊕ Delete 🖱.

  (*A message asking for confirmation to delete the file will appear.*)

- ▸ Yes 🖱.

RECYCLE BIN

When files are deleted from the hard disk in the computer they are still stored in the recycle bin in that computer. If files were accidentally deleted and are still in the recycle bin they may be restored to their original folders.

Restoring Files

Files are restored using the desktop as follows:

- ▸ Recycle bin 🖱. (*On the desktop.*)

- ▸ File 🖱.

- ▸ File menu 🖱.   **OR**   ▸ Filename 🖱.

- ⊕ Restore 🖱.

Files are restored using Windows Explorer as follows:

- ▸ Recycle bin 🖱. (*In Windows Explorer.*)

- ▸ File 🖱. (*In the right-hand panel.*)

- ▸ File menu 🖱.   **OR**   ▸ Filename 🖱.

- ⊕ Restore 🖱.

Emptying the Recycle Bin

The recycle bin is emptied as follows:

- ▸ Recycle bin 🖱. (*Either on the desktop or in Windows Explorer.*)

- ⊕ Empty recycle bin 🖱.

Note: Folders, including contents, may be restored in the same way.

FILE COMPRESSION

It is possible to save space on the computer's hard disk by compressing files. This will have the effect of reducing the space used on the disk to store files while still retaining its integrity. The Windows operating system provides a compression agent that will compress all the files on a particular disk.

There are also special programs available, e.g. WinZip and WinRAR, which will perform extensive compression on files. The use of these programs is increasing as the use of the Internet grows. When sending or downloading large files over the Internet it is much more economical and time efficient to transfer small files rather than large ones.

Task 2.4.2 (Additional)

Carry out the operations specified in **Task 2A-4** on the CD.

Task 2.5.1

(a) Insert the floppy disk, rewritable CD or memory stick, used in **Task 2.4.1**, into the computer.

(b) Load the My Computer or Windows Explorer program.

(c) Create a new folder and label it **Letters**.

(d) Copy the file named **Name.txt** into the **Letters** folder.

(e) Move the file named **College.txt** into the **Letters** folder.

(f) Rename the file named **Name.txt** in the **Letters** folder to **Name.doc**.

(g) Create another folder on the removable media and label it **Reports**.

(h) Copy the file **College.txt** in the **Letters** folder into the **Reports** folder.

(i) Move the file named **Institute.txt** into the **Reports** folder.

(j) Move the **Letters** folder into the **Reports** folder so that it is a subfolder of the Reports folder.

(k) Delete the file named **Name.doc** from the Letters folder.

(l) Delete the **Letters** folder and all its contents.

Note: This task may be repeated by simply deleting all the files and folders from the removable media and repeating **Tasks 2.4.1** and **2.5.1**.

MOVING A FILE

The safest way to move a file is to first copy the file and then delete the file from its original folder.

However, there is a move command that may be performed as follows:	
Method 1	**Method 2**
Open the folder or disk containing the file.	Open the folder or disk containing the file.
Select the file to be copied. 🖰 Filename 🖱 (*on the right-hand side*). 🖰 Cut icon 📋 🖱. Scroll the left-hand section until the folder (or disk) into which the file is to go is visible. 🖰 Disk/folder into which the file is to be moved 🖱. 🖰 Paste icon 📋 🖱.	Scroll the left-hand section until the folder (or disk) into which the file is to go is visible. Hold down the Shift key. 🖰 Filename (*on the right-hand side*) 🖱. Drag the file across to the left-hand section. 🖰 Folder (or disk) into which the file is to be copied 🖱. Release the Shift key.

CREATING A NEW FOLDER

A new folder may be created as follows:

Select the folder into which the new folder is to be created. (The new folder will become a subfolder of the one selected.)

- 🖰 File menu 🖱.
- ⊕ New 🖱.
- ⊕ Folder 🖱. (*The new folder will appear in the right-hand section.*)
- Type the name for the new folder ⌨.

MOVING A FOLDER

A folder can be moved in the same way as a file. When a folder is moved, the contents of that folder (including subfolders) will be moved with the folder.

A folder is moved as follows:

- ⬚ Folder name 🖱.

  (Either cut and paste or drag the folder as described above for a file.)

DELETING A FOLDER

A folder can be deleted as follows:

- ⬚ Folder name 🖱.
- Press the Delete key. *(The confirm folder delete window will appear.)*
- ⬚ Yes 🖱.

Task 2.5.2

(a) Insert the floppy disk, rewritable CD or memory stick used in the previous tasks, into the computer.

(b) Examine the folder structure of the removable media.

(c) Create a new folder on the removable media and label it **Forms**.

(d) Create a new subfolder in the **Forms** folder and label it **Personal**.

(e) Create a new subfolder in the **Forms** folder and label it **Office**.

(f) Move the file named **Name** into the **Personal** folder.

(g) Move the file named **Home** into the **Personal** folder.

(h) Move the file named **Institute** into the **Office** folder.

(i) Copy the file named **Institute** in the **Forms** folder into the **Reports** folder.

(j) Rename the file named **Institute.txt** in the **Reports** folder to **Address.doc**.

(k) Make a diagram of the folder structure of the removable media.

Note: This task may be repeated by simply deleting all the files and folders from the removable media and repeating **Tasks 2.4.1**, **2.5.1** and **2.5.2**.

FOLDER STRUCTURE

Every disk, whether hard disk, floppy disk, zip disk, CD or memory stick, will have a structure of folders and subfolders in which files may be stored. (Floppy disks, because of their small size, may not have a structure; instead, all files may be just stored on the root of the disk.)

The folder structure starts at what is termed the **root** of the disk or stick. This is the position on the media where the first folders are created. If no folder is created and files are stored on the media, then these files will be stored in the root of that media.

A simple diagram is a good way of visualising the media structure. There are two common methods used to illustrate folder structures, as shown below.

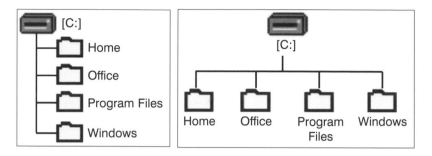

Figure 2.7

The structure shows the hard disk, labelled C:, with four folders. Each folder is a subfolder on the root of the C: drive.

Subfolders may be added to any folder, thus creating another level of folders. The structure below shows that the Office folder has two subfolders.

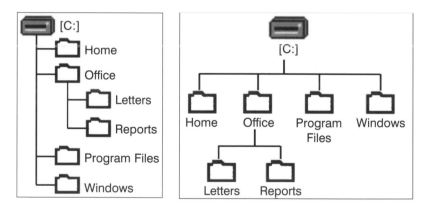

Figure 2.8

The folder structure can continue like this with new folders being added whenever required. There is no limit to the number of folders or subfolders on a storage media. There is also no limit to the number of levels of folders, but after two or three levels it becomes difficult to find the required folder in order to store or retrieve files.

The left panel of Windows Explorer shows the structure of the various storage media on the computer. The structure is displayed in a manner similar to the first diagrams above. The only additions in Windows Explorer is that when a folder has subfolders a small plus sign ⊞ appears in front of the folder and when a folder is open the open folder symbol 🗁 is shown.

Task 2.5.3

(a) Insert the floppy disk, rewritable CD or memory stick used in the previous tasks, into the computer.

(b) Load the Notepad or WordPad program.

(c) Type your parents' names and address.

(d) Save this file on the removable media with the filename **Parents** (in text-only format).

(e) Open a new file.

(f) Type the name and address of your friend.

(g) Save this file on the removable media with the filename **Friend** (in text-only format).

(h) Close (exit) the Notepad or WordPad program.

(i) Create a folder on the removable media and label it **Personal**.

(j) Move the **Name.txt**, **Home.txt**, **Parents.txt** and **Friend.txt** files into the **Personal** folder (in one operation).

(k) Create a new folder in the Personal folder and name it **Addresses**.

(l) Copy the files **Home.txt** and **Name.txt** in the **Personal** folder into the **Addresses** folder (in one operation).

Note: This task may be repeated by simply deleting all the files and folders from the removable media and repeating **Tasks 2.4.1**, **2.5.1**, **2.5.2** and **2.5.3**.

GROUPS OF FILES OR FOLDERS

When working with files and folders it is possible to select more than one file or folder in order to copy, move or delete them. The Ctrl key and the Shift key may be used when selecting files or folders in order to select more than one. The Shift key is used to select adjacent files or folders and the Ctrl key is used to select nonadjacent files or folders. When the files are selected they may be copied, moved or deleted in the normal way.

Selecting Adjacent Files or Folders	Selecting Nonadjacent Files or Folders
Open the folder or disk containing the file or folders.	Open the folder or disk containing the file or folders.
➤ First file (folder) name 🖱.	➤ First file (folder) name 🖱.

continued

Hold down the Shift key.

Last file (folder) name 🖱.

All the files (folders) between the first and last will be highlighted.

Hold down the Ctrl key.

Next filename 🖱.

Repeat the process until all the required files (folders) have been selected.

All the files (folders) selected will be highlighted.

Task 2.5.4 (Additional)

Carry out the operations specified in **Task 2A-5** on the CD.

Task 2.6.1

(a) Use the find/search facility to locate the following files on the CD supplied with this book:

- Prices.xls.
- Computers.doc.
- Shapes.jpg.
- Tennis Club.mdb.
- My Lecture.ppt.
- All .xls files.
- All .jpg files.

(b) Close the find/search facility.

LOCATING FILES

The simplest method of locating a file is to select the folder in which the user thinks the file may be located and then look at the contents of that folder.

However, the Windows operating system also provides a search facility that will search any storage media for a particular file or folder.

The search facility is operated as follows:

- Start button 🖱.

- Search 🖱. (*The search window will appear.*)

- Type the name of the file to be located in the 'Search for files or folders named' field.

continued

- Select the drive or folder to be searched in the 'Look in' field (*if the correct one is not displayed*).

- [▶] Search now 🖱.

The program will search the specified storage media or folder and all subfolders and display the results of the search in the right-hand side of the window. The window also displays the number of files that matched the specification. If the number is very large then a more precise name or location may be used in another search.

Note: The search may be limited to a particular folder, by using the browse option, at the bottom of the list of drives in the 'Look in' field, to select the starting folder for the search.

Wildcards

Wildcards are special characters used to replace one or more characters in the filename or folder name. When searching for files or folders there are two very useful wildcards that may be used. These wildcards are the * and the ? mark. The * may be used to replace either all or part of the filename or filename extension. The ? mark may be used to replace one character in a filename or extension.

*.doc Every file with a .doc extension, i.e. all Word(**2003**) files.

*report.doc Every file with a filename ending in 'report' and having an extension .doc.

report?.xls Every file with a filename 'report' plus one more character and an extension .xls.

report???.* Every file with a filename 'report' plus three more characters and any extension.

report.* Every file with the word 'report' anywhere in the filename and any extension.

.d Every file with a filename extension beginning with d, e.g. .doc, .dot.

. Every file with any extension, i.e. all files.

Note: When there is a space in a filename it is a good idea to insert a ? mark instead of the space to limit the number of files that will be displayed.

Other Search Options

The search facility provides a number of other options that may be used to locate files. These options are available on the Date Modified tab and the Advanced tab in the search window. These options include:

- Files/folders created or modified within the last number of months.

- Files/folders created or modified within the last number of days.
- Files/folders created or modified between certain dates.
- Files of specified types.
- Files containing specified text.
- Files greater than a specified size.
- Files less than a specified size.

Task 2.6.2 (Additional)

Carry out the operations specified in **Task 2A-6** on the CD.

Task 2.7.1

(a) Insert a blank floppy disk, rewritable CD or memory stick into the computer.
(b) Load My Computer.
(c) Check the contents of the disk.
(d) Format the disk.
(e) Close My Computer and remove the media from the computer.

FORMATTING A DISK

Formatting a disk will delete all data on the disk and reformat the disk for use again. The disk may be quickly formatted, in which case it simply clears the table containing the location of the data on the disk, or it may be completely formatted, in which case there will be no trace of previous data.

Any disk (with the exception of read-only CDs) may be formatted and therefore great care should be taken when formatting a disk to ensure that the correct disk is being formatted.

A floppy disk is formatted as follows:

- 🔳 Load My Computer.
- 🔳 3.5 inch floppy disk icon 🖱.
- 🔳 File menu 🖱.
- ⊕ Format 🖱. (*The format window will appear.*)
- 🔳 Start button 🖱. (*A warning message will appear.*)
- 🔳 OK 🖱.

The disk will be formatted and a progress window will appear as the disk is being formatted. When formatting is complete the Format Complete window will appear, then another disk may be formatted or the window closed.

Task 2.7.2

(a) Load a virus-scanning program.
(b) Scan a disk for viruses and clean/disinfect any infected files.
(c) Close the virus-scanning program.

VIRUSES

Viruses are spread by being carried on files that are moved from one computer to another. This can be done using floppy disks, CDs, in e-mail or even over the Internet. Most computer users invest in antivirus software in order to prevent infection.

A disk is checked for viruses as follows:

- ▪ Load the antivirus program.

- ▪ Select scan computer **OR** scan disk.

- ▪ Follow instructions on-screen.

The software may be configured to automatically clean or disinfect infected files, in which case the program will normally report the result. In other cases the user may have to select the operation to be performed on an infected file. The options are normally:

- Clean or disinfect.

- Quarantine.

- Remove or delete.

Task 2.7.3

(a) Install a new printer or uninstall and reinstall a printer on your computer.
(b) Change the default printer from the current one to any other installed printer.
(c) Open Notepad or WordPad.
(d) Type a short sentence.
(e) Restore the Notepad/WordPad window so that it occupies the top half of the screen.
(f) Display the printer information window for the new default printer.

(g) Restore the printer information window so that it occupies the bottom half of the screen.

(h) Print the document and observe the printer information window.

(i) Close all open windows.

INSTALLING NEW SOFTWARE (INCLUDING PRINTER DRIVERS)

When a new program is purchased it must be installed on the computer. When a new piece of equipment, such as a printer, scanner or modem, is attached to a computer it usually needs a software program, called a driver, to be installed on the computer in order for it to work.

Programs are installed as follows:

- Insert the CD in the DVD drive and wait for a few seconds (the program should AutoRun).

- When the program displays an installation screen, simply follow the instructions.

If the program does not AutoRun, then it is necessary to run the setup program as follows:

- Start button.

- Run.

- Type **D:\Setup** in the Open field (where D: is the DVD drive).

- When the program displays an installation screen, simply follow the instructions.

If the installation program is not called **setup** or is not in the root of the CD then it is necessary to browse the CD using the browse button on the run window to find the installation program.

SETTING A DEFAULT PRINTER

A computer may have access to a number of different printers attached to the computer or to the network to which the computer is attached. One of these printers will be set as the **default** printer and this is the printer that will be automatically used when printing. Other printers may be selected from the print window when printing individual documents.

Sometimes it is necessary to change the default printer, which is accomplished as follows:

- ▣ Start button 🖰. (*The start menu will appear.*)

- ⊕ Printers and Faxes 🖰. (*The printer window will appear.*)

- ▣ Required printer 🖰.

- ▣ File menu 🖰. (*The file menu will appear.*)

- ⊕ Set as Default Printer 🖰.

DISPLAYING PRINTING INFORMATION

When a document is sent to a printer it enters a queue for printing. This queue may be viewed using the printer information window, as follows:

- ▣ Start button 🖰.

- ⊕ Printers and Faxes 🖰. (*The printer window will appear.*)

- ▣ Printer required 🖰.

- ▣ File menu 🖰.   **OR** ▣ Printer required 🖱.

- ⊕ Open 🖰.

A document may be removed from the print queue as follows:

- ▣ Document 🖰.

- Press the Delete key.

Task 2.7.4

(a) Use the Windows Help facility to find information on how to set up a microphone.
(b) Print the information.
(c) Close the Help facility and any other open windows.

(d) Press the Print Screen button.

(e) Load WordPad or Word and maximise.

(f) Paste the screen into the WordPad or Word program.

(g) Resize the picture in the document so that the whole picture is visible.

(h) Print one copy of the document.

(i) Close the WordPad or Word program.

USING THE HELP FACILITY

Windows provides a Help facility, which offers information about various aspects of Windows.

The Help facility is operated as follows:

- Start button.

- Help and Support. (*The Help window will appear.*)

- Type a word or words which relate to what you want to find in the Search field.

- Select some matching words from the second section (if displayed).

- One of the options offered (*in the Search Results section*).

Information relating to the topic will appear on the right-hand side. The screen may have links (similar to web page links) to other topics. These links may be selected by simply pointing to the link and clicking the left mouse button. The window usually displays a link to related topics.

Information displayed in a window may be printed as follows:

- Print icon.

PRINT SCREEN FACILITY

Windows provides a facility that allows the complete screen to be copied and then pasted as a picture into a document, e.g. WordPad or Word.

The print screen process is as follows:

- Display the information on-screen, which you want to be in the document.
- Press the Print Screen button on the keyboard.
- Open the program.
- ▣ Paste icon 🖱.

Task 2.7.5 (Additional)

Carry out the operations specified in **Task 2A-7** on the CD.

3 Word Processing

SYMBOLS USED IN THIS CHAPTER

The symbols used in this chapter, and their meanings, are as follows:

Click the left mouse button.

Click the right mouse button.

Double-click the left mouse button.

Triple-click the left mouse button.

Hold down the left mouse button.

Release the mouse button.

Move the mouse to point to an item or to another area without clicking or holding any button.

Point to an item on the screen.

Press the Backspace key.

Hold down the Ctrl button.

Hold down the Ctrl button and click the left mouse button.

Hold down the Shift key.

Hold down the Shift key and press the number eight.

Press the Delete key.

Press the Enter key.

INTRODUCTION

Word processing has virtually replaced the typewriter as a method of producing typeface letters and documents. A word processor is a computer program which allows the user to type words, sentences, paragraphs and then enhance and manipulate text in order to produce a professional-looking typed document. Modern word processors also provide a wide range of other functions that allow the insertion of such features as tables, charts, Clip Art and drawings into a document. There are also a number of advanced features that are now incorporated into word processing programs such as mail merge, envelopes and labels, frames, as well as borders and shading.

LOADING THE WORD PROCESSING PROGRAM

The word processing program is loaded from the desktop as follows:

➤➤ 🖱️ Word processing shortcut icon 🖱️.

If the program is not available from the desktop then it may be loaded from the Start menu as follows:

➤➤ 🖱️ Start 🖱️.

➤➤ ✛ All Programs.

➤➤ ✛ Word processing program 🖱️.

(You may have to open a submenu to find the program.)

THE WORD PROCESSING SCREEN

When the word processing program is loaded the screen should look something like Figure 3.1.

A cursor, which is usually a short vertical or horizontal flashing bar, will appear in the work area. Anything typed on the keyboard will appear where the cursor is placed in the work area.

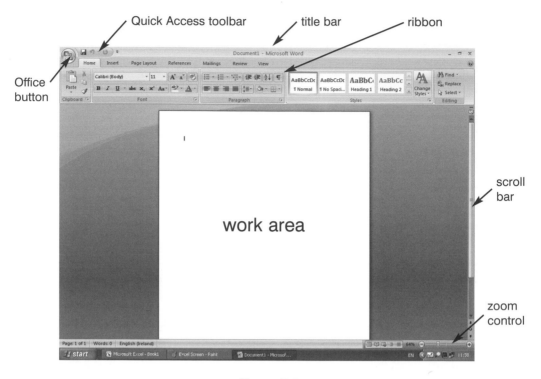

Figure 3.1

Task 3.1.1

(a) Load the word processing program (if not already loaded).
(b) Type the following text in a blank document (this text is available on the CD in the Documents folder with the filename **Computers.doc** or **Computers.txt**):

Computers are so popular today that it is surprising that the first computer was not produced until 1944. This computer was produced by a team of IBM engineers and measured 15 m long and 8 m high. The power of this computer was less than the smallest pocket calculator of today.

The first commercial computer was produced for a bakery in 1951, and this computer was 10 m long, 2.5 m high and 1.2 m wide.

The advent of the modern personal computer (PC) was not until 1971 with the development of the microprocessor by Intel. This chip, the Intel 4004, had a complete processor on a single chip. The power of this chip was not good by modern standards but it did set the pattern for future development.

CREATING A NEW DOCUMENT

When the Word program is loaded it will open with a blank document displayed.

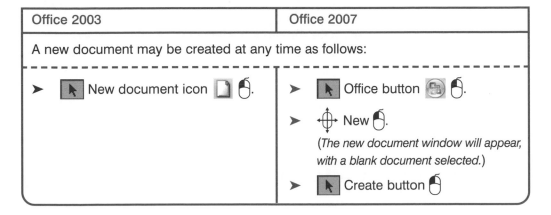

Office 2003	Office 2007
A new document may be created at any time as follows:	
➤ New document icon	➤ Office button ➤ New (*The new document window will appear, with a blank document selected.*) ➤ Create button

ENTERING TEXT

Text is entered into the work area by simply typing the text, letter by letter. When the end of a line is reached, there is no need to press the Enter key. The program has a function called Word Wrap that will automatically place the text on a new line when it reaches the end of a line. It will also carry any unfinished word onto the new line.

When the end of a paragraph is reached, the Enter key must be pressed in order to move onto a new paragraph, and pressed again to leave a blank line between paragraphs.

The following simple rules about entering text may be helpful at this stage:

- Continue to type text until the end of a paragraph is reached.

- Press the Enter key twice at the end of a paragraph before starting a new paragraph.

- Press the space bar twice after a full stop at the end of a sentence. (A single space is acceptable but the double space is used more frequently.)

- Hold down the Shift key and press the Enter key ( ) to go onto a new line while staying within the same paragraph.

Task 3.1.2

Edit the text that has been entered in Task 3.1.1 as follows:
(a) Insert the word 'select' before the word 'team' in the second sentence.
(b) Insert the word 'much' between the words 'was' and 'less' in the last sentence of the first paragraph.
(c) Change the word 'popular' to 'common' in the first sentence.
(d) Insert the word 'Computers' at the top of the document and leave a blank line between it and the first paragraph.

EDITING TEXT

Once text has been entered, the user may edit it at any time. The cursor appears as a flashing vertical or horizontal bar on the screen, whereas the mouse appears as an I-beam or an arrow. The cursor may be positioned anywhere on the screen by using the mouse to place the I-beam in the required position in the text and clicking the left mouse button. This will immediately position the cursor in that location. If the mouse is moved away from that position the cursor will not move unless the mouse button is clicked again.

Inserting text at the start of the document is the same as in any other part. Position the cursor to the left of the first letter and press the Enter key once (or twice) in order to create blank lines. It is then possible to move into the first blank line and type the text as normal.

It is possible to move the cursor small distances by using the arrow keys on the keyboard.

Text may be edited as follows:

➤➤   Simply type any additional text at the cursor position.

➤➤   Delete text to the left using the Backspace key ⬅.

➤➤   Delete text from the right using the Delete key Del.

The word processor will automatically move the rest of the text as required.

Task 3.1.3

Edit the text which has been entered in Tasks 3.1.1 and 3.1.2 as follows:
(a) Select the word 'modern' in the first sentence of the last paragraph and delete it (press the Delete key).
(b) Select the second paragraph and the blank line following it and delete them.
(c) Undo the last deletion in order to replace the second paragraph.
(d) Save the document with the filename **Computers1**.
(e) Close the document.

SELECTING TEXT

One of the major advantages of using a word processor is the ability to work on blocks of text at the same time. In order to work on a word, a number of words, a sentence, a paragraph or even more, then it is necessary for the word processor to know exactly what text to work with. The user tells the word processor what text to work with by selecting the text.

Text is selected as follows:

➤➤ [↖] Start of the text to be selected 🖱.

➤➤ ✛ Over the text to be selected 🖱. (*The selected text will be highlighted.*)

A complete word is selected as follows:

➤➤ [↖] Word 🖱.

A complete sentence is selected as follows:

➤➤ [↖] Anywhere in the sentence [Ctrl] 🖱.

A complete paragraph is selected as follows:

➤➤ [↖] Anywhere in the paragraph 🖱.

The text may be deselected by simply pointing the mouse anywhere on the work area and clicking the left mouse button.

Sometimes the user may wish to select a number of lines of text. This may be done in the same way as above; alternatively, it may be simpler to use the following procedure:

➤➤ [↖] Left margin opposite the first row 🖱. (*While the pointer is a white arrow.*)

➤➤ ✛ Down the rows until the required lines have been highlighted 🖱.

UNDOING A CHANGE

One very useful command in all programs is the Undo command. This allows the user to quickly undo whatever has just been done. It is helpful when something goes wrong or when something has been accidentally deleted.

The Undo command is operated as follows:

➤➤ [↖] Undo icon [↺] 🖱.

The Undo command may be performed a number of times to undo the last number of changes made to a document.

REDOING AN UNDO COMMAND

If after performing an Undo command the user would prefer to have the document the way it was before the undo, then it is possible to perform a Redo command.

The Redo command may be performed a number of times to redo any of the last undo changes made to a document.

The Redo command is operated as follows:

➤➤   Redo icon

SAVING A DOCUMENT

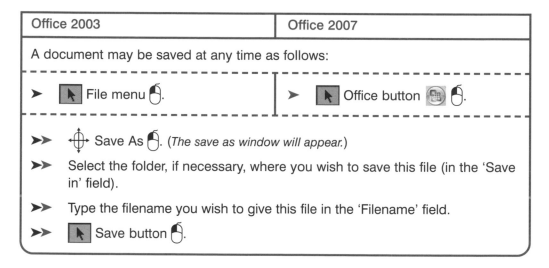

Office 2003	Office 2007
A document may be saved at any time as follows:	
➤ File menu.	➤ Office button.

➤➤   Save As. (*The save as window will appear.*)

➤➤   Select the folder, if necessary, where you wish to save this file (in the 'Save in' field).

➤➤   Type the filename you wish to give this file in the 'Filename' field.

➤➤   Save button.

The filename will appear on the title bar.

The procedure for saving a document, after giving it a name, is much simpler and is accomplished as follows:

➤➤   Save icon

Saving a Document as Another File Type

Every time the word processing program saves a file it will automatically save the document as a word processed document. Modern word processing programs allow documents to be saved as other types, e.g. .htm/.html (for publishing on a website), .txt (text only, with no formatting), or .rtf (standard for formatted text).

Office 2003	Office 2007
A document may be saved as another file type as follows:	
➤ ▣ File menu 🖱.	➤ ▣ Office button 🔲 🖱.

➤➤ ⊕ Save As 🖱.
(The save as window will appear.)

➤➤ Select the folder, if necessary, where you wish to save this file in the 'Save in' field.

➤➤ Type the filename you wish to give this file in the 'Filename' field.

➤➤ Select the file type in the 'Save as type' field.

➤➤ ▣ Save button 🖱.

Note: When using Office **2007**, files may need to be saved in the older format as the Office **2007** format is not compatible with older versions of Office.

Office 2007
Files may be saved in the older format as described above or the following, slightly simpler, method may be used:

➤ ▣ Office button 🔲 🖱.

➤ ⊕ Save As.

➤ ⊕ Word 97 – 2003 Document 🖱. *(The save as window will appear.)*

➤ Select the folder, if necessary, where you wish to save this file in the 'Save in' field.

➤ Type the filename you wish to give this file in the 'Filename' field.

➤ Save button 🖱.

CLOSING A DOCUMENT

Office 2003	Office 2007
A document that is no longer required to be open may be closed as follows:	
➤ ▣ File menu 👆. ➤ ⊕ Close 👆.	➤ ▣ Office button 🔘 👆. ➤ ⊕ Close 👆.

If the document has not been saved or if changes have been made to the document since last saving it, then a message will appear asking if changes to the document are to be saved. Select Yes or No as appropriate.

Task 3.1.4

(a) Open the document named **Computers1**, available in the Documents folder on the CD (if not already open).

(b) Add the following paragraphs at the end of the document.

The development of the computer has continued rapidly since the early 1980s, with new models appearing at least every year. These new models sometimes used the same processor as previous models and were simply an upgrade in terms of speed and processing power. In other cases a completely new processor was produced and this then became the standard for the next couple of years. The most popular generations of Intel processors are as follows:

4004
8086/8088
80286/386/486
Pentium/Pentium II/Pentium III/Pentium IV

The processing power of a modern computer is phenomenal in comparison to the early 1970s. The future will surely continue at the same speed or even faster and we can't really comprehend where developments will lead.

Note: Remember to use ⬛ ⇧ / ⬛ ↵ for a new line within a paragraph.

(c) Save the document with the Computers2. filename.
(d) Close the document.

Task 3.1.5 (Additional)

Perform the operations specified in **Tasks 3A-1** on the CD.

Task 3.2.1

(a) Open the document named **Computers2**, available in the Documents folder on the CD (if not already open).

(b) Select the letters 'IBM' in the first paragraph and apply bold enhancement. Apply the same enhancement to the letters 'PC' in the third paragraph.

(c) Select all the years (1994, 1951, etc.) then apply bold and italic enhancement to each.

(d) Select the word 'Computers' at the top of the document and perform the following operations on it:

- Apply bold enhancement.
- Apply underline enhancement.
- Centre the word over the document.
- Change the font to Arial.
- Change the font size to 14 pt.
- Change the font colour to blue.

(e) Save the document again with the filename **Computers3**.

OPENING A DOCUMENT

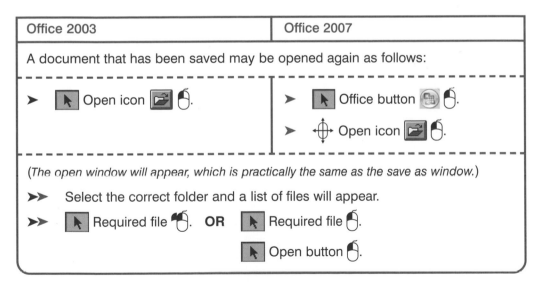

Office 2003	Office 2007
A document that has been saved may be opened again as follows:	
➤ [▶] Open icon 📂 🖱.	➤ [▶] Office button 🪟 🖱.
	➤ ✜ Open icon 📂 🖱.

(The open window will appear, which is practically the same as the save as window.)

➤➤   Select the correct folder and a list of files will appear.

➤➤   [▶] Required file 🖱. **OR** [▶] Required file 🖱.

       [▶] Open button 🖱.

More than one document may be open at the same time, however, only one of the documents will usually be visible on the screen at any one time. The various open documents may be displayed on the taskbar (usually at the bottom of the screen).

Switching between open documents is accomplished as follows:

➤➤ ▮ Document on the taskbar 🖱.

Alternatively:

Office 2003	Office 2007
➤ ▮ Window menu 🖱.	➤ ▮ Office button 🖱
➤➤ ▮ Document required 🖱.	

ENHANCING TEXT

Individual letters, words, sentences and paragraphs may be enhanced using the bold, underline and italics icons on the toolbar.

The appearance and colour of the text may be changed as follows:

Appearance

➤➤ Select the text to be enhanced. (**2007** – *Select the Home ribbon.*)

➤➤ ▮ Bold **B** 🖱.

AND/OR

➤➤ ▮ Italics *I* 🖱.

AND/OR

➤➤ ▮ Underline U 🖱.

Colour

➤➤ Select the text. (**2007** – *Select the Home ribbon.*)

➤➤ ▮ Arrow beside font colour icon **A**▾ 🖱. (*The colour pallet will appear.*)

➤➤ ▮ Colour required from the selection of colours offered 🖱.

FORMATTING TEXT

Text may be displayed in different fonts and font sizes. The text font and size may be set either before or after the text has been typed.

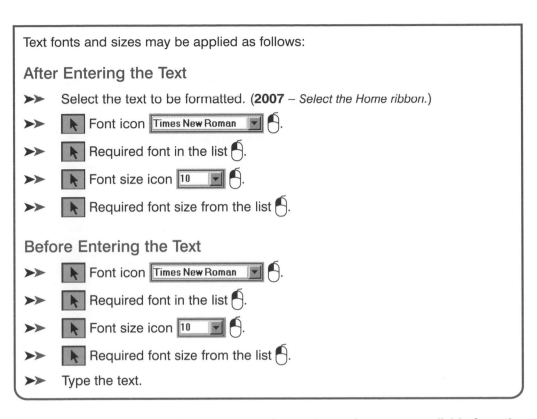

Text fonts and sizes may be applied as follows:

After Entering the Text

➤➤ Select the text to be formatted. (**2007** – *Select the Home ribbon.*)

➤➤ Font icon `Times New Roman` 🖱.

➤➤ Required font in the list 🖱.

➤➤ Font size icon `10` 🖱.

➤➤ Required font size from the list 🖱.

Before Entering the Text

➤➤ Font icon `Times New Roman` 🖱.

➤➤ Required font in the list 🖱.

➤➤ Font size icon `10` 🖱.

➤➤ Required font size from the list 🖱.

➤➤ Type the text.

Font formats, such as small caps, superscript, embossed, etc., are available from the format font menu and may also be applied either before or after typing the text.

In Office **2007**, some of these functions are available as icons on the Home ribbon.

Office 2003	Office 2007
Font Formats are applied as follows:	
➤ Format menu 🖱.	➤ Select the Home ribbon. ➤ Small arrow on the bottom right of the Font group ▣ 🖱.

➤➤ Font tab 🖱. (*if not already selected*)

➤➤ Select the effects required by ticking the required box(es).

➤➤ OK 🖱.

TEXT ALIGNMENT

There are four different text alignments, which may be set as follows:

➤➤ [pointer] Select the text to be aligned.

(**2007** – *Select the Home ribbon.*)

➤➤ [pointer] required text alignment icon [alignment icons] [mouse].

COPYING TEXT FORMATTING

The text formatting (enhancement, font, alignment, etc.) may be quickly applied to other text as follows:

(**2007** – *Select the Home ribbon.*)

➤➤ [pointer] Text with formatting applied [mouse].

➤➤ [pointer] Format painter icon [brush] [mouse] (one application).

OR [mouse] (multiple applications).

➤➤ Select the text to which the formatting will be applied.

If multiple applications were selected, then the application to other text may be repeated until the format painter is switched off, by clicking on the icon again.

Task 3.2.2 (Additional)

Perform the operations specified in **Task 3A-2** on the CD.

Task 3.3.1

(a) Open the document named **Computers3**, available in the Documents folder on the CD (if not already open).
(b) Split the fourth paragraph into two separate paragraphs so that the sentence beginning 'The most popular generations...' becomes the start of the new paragraph.
(c) Combine the first and second paragraphs to form one paragraph.
(d) Select the paragraph with the four lines of generations of Intel processors and place it in 1.5 line spacing.
(e) Select the last paragraph and position it to become the third paragraph.

(f) Copy the second paragraph and paste it as a new paragraph at the end of the document.

(g) Select the last paragraph (the one that has been copied) and delete it.

(h) Save the document again with the filename **Computers4**.

SPLIT AND JOIN PARAGRAPHS

An existing paragraph may be split into two separate paragraphs as follows:

➤➤   ▐▲▌ Position where the new paragraph is to start 🖰.

➤➤   ⌐⌐┘ To move the text onto a new line.

➤➤   ⌐⌐┘ To insert a blank line between the paragraphs.

Two separate paragraphs may be joined to form a single paragraph as follows:

➤➤   ▐▲▌ Position in front of the first letter of the paragraph to be moved up 🖰.

➤➤   ◀─ Twice (once to move up to the blank line and once to join the previous paragraph).

It may be necessary to insert a space or two between the words of the joined paragraphs.

SETTING LINE SPACING

When a new document is started the text will be entered in standard single-line spacing. However, it is sometimes necessary to alter the space between lines.

There are three standard line spacings that may be quickly applied as follows:

➤➤   Place the cursor anywhere in the text to be spaced.

➤➤   [Ctrl] [2] This will produce double-line spacing.

➤➤   [Ctrl] [5] This will produce 1.5 line spacing.

➤➤   [Ctrl] [1] This will produce single-line spacing.

Office 2003	Office 2007
A more comprehensive line spacing and paragraph indentation is available as follows:	

➤ ▐ Format menu 🖱.

➤ ⊕ Paragraph 🖱.

➤ Select the Home ribbon.

➤ ▐ Small arrow on the bottom right of the Paragraph group ▫ 🖱.

(The paragraph formatting window will appear.)

➤➤ ▐ Select the indentation and spacing required.

EDITING BLOCKS OF TEXT

A block of text, which may be anything from a word to a number of paragraphs, may be edited as follows:

Moving

➤➤ Select the required text.

➤➤ ▐ The selected text 🖱.

➤➤ Drag the text to the required position 🖱.

Copying

➤➤ Select the required text. (**2007** – *Select the Home ribbon.*)

➤➤ ▐ Copy icon 🗐 🖱.

➤➤ ▐ Position where the text is to be inserted 🖱.

➤➤ ▐ Paste icon 📋 🖱.

It may be necessary to adjust line spacing when the text is inserted.

Deleting

➤➤ Select the text to be deleted.

➤➤ Press the Delete key.

Copying/Moving Text to Another Document

It is possible to copy or move text, graphics, etc. from one document to another. The simplest method of doing this is to have both documents open at the same time.

Text is moved as follows:

➤➤ Select the text/graphic to be copied/moved.

➤➤ ⬛ Cut/copy icon ✂️ / 📋 🖱️.

➤➤ Select the second document.

➤➤ Select the position in the document for the insertion.

➤➤ ⬛ Paste icon 📋 🖱️.

Use the copy icon to copy an item and use the cut icon to move an item.

Task 3.3.2

(a) Open the document named **Computers4**, available in the Documents folder on the CD (if not already open).
(b) Spell check and proofread the document.
(c) Correct any errors found.
(d) Save the document again if any changes were made.
(e) Preview the document.
(f) Print one copy of the document.

SPELL CHECKING

Word processing programs provide a facility for spell checking documents. However, it must be remembered that this facility simply checks every word in the document to see if there is a matching word in one of the program's dictionaries. The whole document may be spell checked or individual words may be checked as they are typed.

The Whole Document

The spell checker will check every word in the document against every word in the dictionaries.

The procedure for spell checking is as follows:

➤➤ Position the cursor at the start of the document.

(**2007** – *Select the Review ribbon.*)

continued

➤➤ ▮ Spell check ▦ 👆. (*The spell check window will appear.*)

The window will display the first word that is not in the dictionaries together with a list of suggested correct words. One of a number of tasks may be performed:

(a) Select **Ignore Once** to leave this occurrence of the word as it is.
(b) Select **Ignore All** to leave all occurrences of the word as it is.
(c) Select the correct word from the list of suggestions and select **Change** or **Change All**.
(d) Type the word required and select **Change** or **Change All**.
(e) Select **Add to Dictionary** to add this new word to the custom dictionary.

Individual Words

As a document is typed, any unrecognised words will usually appear with a red line underneath. The spelling may be corrected before proceeding with typing in the same way as any editing.

Pointing to a misspelled word and clicking the right mouse button will cause a pop-up window to appear. This pop-up window may offer a number of options for the misspelled word. Simply point to the word required and click the left mouse button and the correction will be made.

PROOFREADING

If there is a word in the document which is not the correct word, but is a word in one of the dictionaries, then the spell checker will not register that word as incorrect. It is therefore necessary to proofread every document along with spell checking it. Proofreading involves reading the whole document and closely examining every word for spelling and also checking punctuation and grammar.

PREVIEWING A DOCUMENT

Before printing a document it is a good idea to preview it to see what each page will look like when printed.

Office 2003	Office 2007
A document is previewed as follows:	
➤ ▮ Preview icon ▤ 👆. (*One or more pages will appear as a preview.*)	➤ ▮ Office button ▦ 👆. ➤ ⊕ Print.

continued

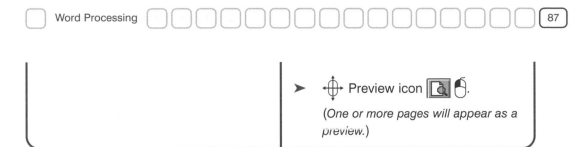

➤ ⊕ Preview icon 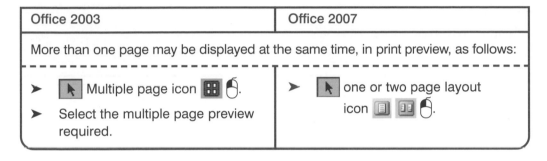.

(One or more pages will appear as a preview.)

Note: It is possible to place the preview icon on the Quick Access Toolbar in Office 2007.

The **scroll bar**, the **mouse scroll** or the **Page Up** and **Page Down** keys may be used to move from page to page.

Office 2003	Office 2007
More than one page may be displayed at the same time, in print preview, as follows:	
➤ 🔼 Multiple page icon ⊞ 🖱️. ➤ Select the multiple page preview required.	➤ 🔼 one or two page layout icon 📄 📑 🖱️.

It is possible to zoom in on part of a page as follows:

➤➤ 🔼 Area of the page to be enlarged 🖱️.

(The mouse pointer appears as a magnifying glass.)

It is possible to zoom out again by simply clicking the left mouse button a second time.

FORCING PAGE BREAKS

It is sometimes necessary to move onto a new page even though the present page is not full.

A new page may be created at any time as follows:

➤➤ 🔼 Position where the new page is to start 🖱️.

➤➤ Ctrl ⏎ .

The page break may be removed by positioning the cursor on the last active line on the previous page and pressing the Delete key.

SHOW/HIDE NONPRINTING CHARACTERS

Word processing programs provide a facility that allows the user to view the nonprinting characters the program uses to produce spaces, new lines, new paragraphs, etc. Viewing these characters is often helpful when laying out a document.

> Nonprinting characters may be displayed on-screen as follows:
>
> (**2007** – *Select the Home ribbon.*)
>
> ➤➤   Show/hide icon ¶ 🖱.
>
> (*The nonprinting characters will appear in the text.*)

Clicking the icon again will hide the characters.

The characters used for Office 2003 and Office 2007 are as follows:

•	One space
¶	New paragraph
↵	New line (within a paragraph)
→	Tab
·············Page Break················	New page

Deleting one of these characters will remove the space, paragraph, etc.

PRINTING A DOCUMENT

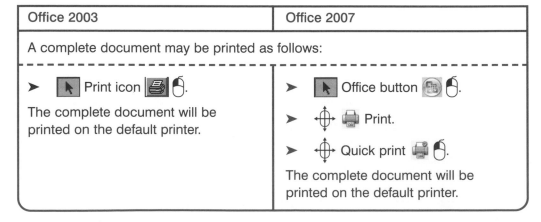

Office 2003	Office 2007
A complete document may be printed as follows:	
➤ 🖱 Print icon 🖶 🖱. The complete document will be printed on the default printer.	➤ 🖱 Office button 🪟 🖱. ➤ ⊕ 🖶 Print. ➤ ⊕ Quick print 🖶 🖱. The complete document will be printed on the default printer.

Note: It is possible to place the Print and Quick Print icons on the Quick Access Toolbar in Office 2007.

The printing process provides a range of options, which may be selected from the print window.

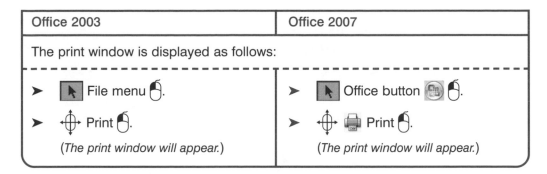

Office 2003	Office 2007
The print window is displayed as follows:	
➤ File menu.	➤ Office button.
➤ Print.	➤ Print.
(*The print window will appear.*)	(*The print window will appear.*)

Some of the options that may be selected from the print window are shown below.

Selecting a Printer

There may be more than one printer connected to the computer and it is therefore necessary to direct the output to the correct printer. This is accomplished as follows:

➤➤ Printer name icon.

➤➤ Printer required.

Selecting the Number of Copies

The program will normally print only one copy of a document, but any number of copies may be printed as follows:

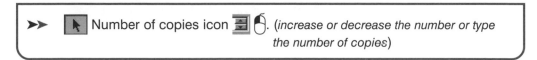

➤➤ Number of copies icon. (*increase or decrease the number or type the number of copies*)

Printing Current Page

It is sometimes only necessary to print the page being worked on. This is accomplished as follows:

➤➤ Current page (*in the page range*).

Printing Selected Pages

It is sometimes necessary to print specific pages from a document without printing the whole document. This is accomplished as follows:

➤➤ ▮ Pages field (in the page range) 🖱.

➤➤ Enter the pages to be printed.

(1,3 means pages 1 and 3, 5-12 means pages 5 to 12.)

Printing Selected Text

If a portion of a document is to be printed, then select (highlight) the portion to be printed before displaying the print window and then:

➤➤ ▮ Selection (*in the page range*) 🖱.

When all the options are correct ▮ OK and the document will be printed.

Task 3.3.3

(a) Open the document named **Computers4**, available in the Documents folder on the CD (if not already open).
(b) Replace all occurrences of the word 'long' with the words 'in length'.
(c) Replace all occurrences of the word 'high' with the words 'in height'.
(d) Replace all occurrences of the word 'wide' with the words 'in width'.
(e) Place a hanging indent of 1 cm on the last paragraph. (This should indent the generations of Intel processors by 1 cm.)
(f) Place a 2 pt blue border around the last paragraph, i.e. the paragraph with the generations of Intel processors.
(g) Place a 6 pt red line near the bottom of the page.
(h) Type your name underneath the line in 14 pt bold, green, Arial font.
(i) Save the document again with the **Computers5** filename.

FIND AND REPLACE

It is sometimes necessary to change a particular word (or a group of words) in a document. Word processing programs have a facility to automatically search for a word (or a group of words) and replace with another word (or a group of words).

Office 2003	Office 2007
The procedure to find and replace is as follows:	
➤ ▮ Edit menu 🖱.	➤ Select the Home ribbon.
➤ ▮ Replace 🖱.	➤ ▮  Replace 🖱.

continued

(*The find and replace window will be displayed.*)

➤➤ Type the word(s) to be replaced in the 'Find what' field.

➤➤ Type the new word(s) to be inserted in the 'Replace with' field.

➤➤ ▣ Find next 🖱. (*The first occurrence of the word will be displayed.*)

➤➤ ▣ **Replace** to change the word(s).

OR

➤➤ ▣ **Find next** to leave the word(s) unchanged and move to the next occurrence.

MULTIPLE COLUMNS

Text may be laid out in a number of columns across a page as follows:

(**2007** – *Select the Page Layout ribbon.*)

➤➤ ▣ Columns icon ▦ / ▥ 🖱.

➤➤ ▣ Number of columns required 🖱.

BORDERS AND SHADING

Office 2003	Office 2007
A border may be quickly placed around text as follows:	
➤➤ Select the text to be bordered, e.g. word(s), sentence(s) or paragraph(s).	
➤ ▣ Outside border icon ▦ 🖱.	➤ Select the Home ribbon. ➤ ▣ Borders and Shading icon ▢ 🖱.

The border placed around the text will be the type which was specified in the setup of the program or when the border was last set. This is referred to as the **default border setting**.

Office 2003	Office 2007
More control over borders may be achieved as follows:	
➤➤ Select the text to be bordered, e.g. word(s), sentence(s) or paragraph(s).	

continued

➤ 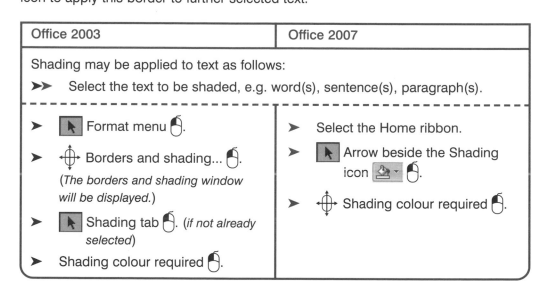 Format menu 🖱.

➤ Select the Home ribbon.

➤ Arrow beside the Border icon 🔲 ▾ 🖱.

➤➤ ⬩⊕⬩ Borders and Shading 🖱.

(The borders and shading window will be displayed.)

➤➤ Borders tab 🖱. *(if not already selected)*

➤➤ Select the border type, style, colour and size required.

This setting becomes the new default value and it is only necessary to click the border icon to apply this border to further selected text.

Office 2003	Office 2007
Shading may be applied to text as follows: ➤➤ Select the text to be shaded, e.g. word(s), sentence(s), paragraph(s).	
➤ Format menu 🖱. ➤ ⬩⊕⬩ Borders and shading... 🖱. *(The borders and shading window will be displayed.)* ➤ Shading tab 🖱. *(if not already selected)* ➤ Shading colour required 🖱.	➤ Select the Home ribbon. ➤ Arrow beside the Shading icon 🎨 ▾ 🖱. ➤ ⬩⊕⬩ Shading colour required 🖱.

TEXT FRAMES

Text frames into which text can be typed and positioned independently on the page may be inserted into a document.

Office 2003	Office 2007
Text frames are inserted as follows:	
➤ Text box 🖱. *(from the drawing toolbar)*	➤ Select the Insert ribbon. ➤ Text Box A☰ 🖱. *(A text box window will appear.)*

continued

➤ Place the cursor in the position where the graphic is to be inserted 🖱.

➤ Drag the mouse to draw the shape required 🖱.

➤ Select Draw Text Box (*at the bottom*).

➤ Place the cursor in the position where the graphic is to be inserted 🖱.

➤ Drag the mouse to draw the shape required 🖱.

Office 2003

If the Drawing toolbar is not on the Office 2003 screen then it may be displayed as follows:

➤ 🖱 View menu 🖱.

➤ ⊕ Toolbars.

➤ ⊕ Drawing 🖱. (*A tick indicates the toolbars which are active.*)

LINES, RECTANGLES, CIRCLES ETC.

Word processing programs provide a range of inbuilt graphics features, such as lines, rectangles, circles, text frames, etc. These features are quickly available from the drawing toolbar in Office 2003 and the Insert ribbon in 2007.

Office 2003	Office 2007
Simple graphics may be quickly inserted into a document as follows:	
➤ Display the drawing toolbar (*if not already displayed*). ➤ 🖱 the graphic to be inserted ╲ ╲ ☐ ○ (line, arrow, rectangle/square, oval/circle).	➤ Select the Insert ribbon. ➤ 🖱 Shapes icon 🔲 🖱. (*A selection of shapes will be displayed*) ➤ Select the graphic to be inserted (line, arrow, rectangle/square, oval/circle).

➤➤ Place the cursor in the position where the graphic is to be inserted 🖱.

➤➤ Drag the mouse to draw the shape required 🖱.

Holding down the Shift key before the mouse button will force a straight line, a square or a circle to be drawn, depending on the tool selected. (The mouse button must be released before the Shift key.) When the shape is drawn it will be displayed with small squares on the ends of lines or on the corners and sides of other shapes. These are referred to as **handles** and they indicate that the shape is active. In order to alter the graphic it must be active. A graphic may be made active by simply pointing to it and clicking the left mouse button.

When shapes are drawn, they will be solid and usually coloured white. There are a number of operations which may be carried out on these shapes in order to enhance them.

Office 2003	Office 2007
Shapes may be enhanced using the following icons on the Drawing toolbar:  Fill colour A shape may have no fill, in which case it is often used to create a border around a number of objects. Line colour This is the colour of a line or the line around the outside of the shape. Line thickness The thickness of a line or the thickness of the line around the outside of a shape. Clicking the selection arrow on the right-hand side of these icons will produce a selection of options.	Once the item has been drawn or is subsequently selected the Drawing Tools Format ribbon will be displayed. Shapes may be enhanced using the following icons on the Drawing Tools Format ribbon: Shape Fill ▾ Fill colour A shape may have no fill, in which case it is often used to create a border around a number of objects. Shape Outline ▾ Line colour This is the colour of a line or the line around the outside of the shape. Weight Line thickness This is selected from the Shape Outline icon. The thickness of a line or the thickness of the line around the outside of a shape. Clicking the selection arrow on the right-hand side of these icons will produce a selection of options.

INDENTING TEXT

The quickest method of indenting text is to use the indent markers on the rule bar. There are three separate parts to these markers, as shown below.

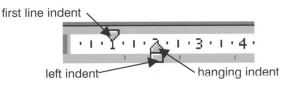

first line indent

left indent   hanging indent

Figure 3.2

First Line Indent   This is the position of the first line of text in a paragraph. This may be positioned in line with the rest of the paragraph or to the left or right.

Hanging Indent   This is the position of the remainder of the paragraph.

It will also be the position of any new lines (⬆ ⬅┘) within the same paragraph.

Left Indent   This is the position of the left side of the paragraph. If this marker is moved the first line will move with it in order to retain the relative position of the first line and the hanging indents.

Great care must be taken when moving these markers as they are quite small and the lower one has two separate parts in one.

The procedure for indenting text is as follows:

First Line Indent

➤➤   ▣ First line indent marker ▽ 🖱.

➤➤   Drag the indent marker to the required position 🖱.

Left Indent

➤➤   ▣ Left indent marker ⬠ 🖱. (*bottom half of marker*)

➤➤   Drag the indent marker to the required position 🖱.

Hanging Indent

➤➤   ▣ Hanging indent marker ⬠ 🖱. (*top half of marker*)

➤➤   Drag the indent marker to the required position 🖱.

Right Indent

➤➤   ▣ Right indent marker △ 🖱. (*on right-hand side of rule*)

➤➤   Drag the indent marker to the required position 🖱.

Office 2003	Office 2007
Indents may also be inserted using the menus as follows:	
➤ ▣ Format menu 🖱. ➤ ⊕ Paragraph 🖱. ➤ Enter the indents in the indents and spacing section.	➤ Select the Page Layout ribbon. ➤ Enter the indents in the indents section.

Task 3.3.4 (Additional)

Perform the operations specified in **Task 3A-3** on the CD.

Task 3.4.1

(a) Open the document named **Computers5** (if not already open).
(b) Set the page orientation to landscape.
(c) Set the page margins to top 2 cm, bottom 2 cm, left 3 cm and right 3 cm.
(d) Adjust the width of the red line to be the same width as the text.
(e) Save the document with the filename **Computers6**.

ADJUSTING MARGINS AND PAGE ORIENTATION

Margins

When the word processing program is started it opens each document with a default margin setting (usually top 2.54 cm, bottom 2.54 cm, left 3.17 cm and right 3.17 cm). However, it is often necessary to change these margin settings.

Office 2003	Office 2007
Margins are adjusted as follows:	
➤ ▣ File menu 🖱. ➤ ⊕ Page setup 🖱. ➤ ▣ Margins tab 🖱. (*this may already be selected*) ➤ Type the required margin sizes in the appropriate fields.	➤ Select the Page Layout ribbon. ➤ ▣ Margins icon ▥ 🖱. (*a selection of margins will be displayed*) ➤ Select one of the options offered or select Custom Options.

Orientation

The page orientation may also be changed using the Page Setup window.

Office 2003	Office 2007
The page orientation is selected as follows:	
➤ ▣ File menu 🖰. ➤ ⊕ Page setup 🖰. ➤ ▣ Margins tab 🖰. ➤ ▣ Portrait or landscape, as required 🖰.	➤ Select the Page Layout ribbon. ➤ ▣ Orientation icon ▣ 🖰. ➤ ⊕ Portrait or landscape, as required 🖰.

Task 3.4.2

(a) Open the document named **Computers6** (if not already open).

(b) Join up the second and third paragraph to form one paragraph.

(c) Add the following paragraphs (a separate paragraph for each maker) to the end of the document.

Intel are the largest makers of processors but there are others, some of whom are listed below.

AMD

Motorola

Cyrix

MIPS

Exponential Technology

(d) Bullet each of the manufacturers.

(e) Insert the header 'Computer Development' in the centre of the page in 10 pt font size.

(f) Insert a right-aligned footer 'Page #' (where # is the automatic page number) in 10 pt font size.

(g) Save the document again with the same filename.

(h) Print one copy of the document.

BULLETS

A list of items may have a number or bullet mark placed in front of each item.

> Numbers or bullets are inserted as follows:
>
> ➤➤   Select the list of items. (**2007** – *Select the Home ribbon.*)
>
> ➤➤   [🖱] Number icon ▤ or bullet icon ▤ 🖱.

The indents for the bullets may be adjusted by using the indent markers and tab stops.

Office 2003	Office 2007
A particular bullet style may be selected as follows:	
➤ [🖱] Format menu 🖱. ➤ ⊕ Bullets and numbering 🖱. ➤ [🖱] Bullet tab 🖱. (*if not already selected*) ➤ Select the style required.	➤ Select the Home ribbon. ➤ [🖱] Arrow beside the bullet icon ▤ ▾ 🖱. ➤ Select the style required.

HEADERS AND FOOTERS

Headers appear in the top margin and footers appear in the bottom margin. Anything may be placed in a header or footer, but the footer often contains the page number.

Office 2003	Office 2007
Headers and footers are inserted into a document as follows:	
➤ [🖱] View menu 🖱. ➤ ⊕ Header and footer 🖱. (*The header and footer window will appear.*) ➤ Type the text required in the header. ➤ [🖱] Switch between header and footer icon ▤ 🖱. ➤ Type the text required in the footer.	➤ Select the Insert ribbon. ➤ [🖱] Header icon ▤ 🖱. ➤ Select the header required. (*The Header and Footer Tools Design ribbon will be displayed.*) (*Select Edit Header to change a header already inserted.*) ➤ [🖱] Footer icon ▤ 🖱. ➤ Select the footer required. (*Select Edit Footer to change a footer already inserted.*)

Inserting Page Numbers in Header/Footer

These may be inserted in either the header or footer, but usually the footer.

Office 2003	Office 2007
Automatic page numbers are inserted as follows:	
➤ Select the position where the page number is to appear.	➤ Select the position where the page number is to appear.
➤ [↖] Insert page number icon [#] 🖰 (*on the Header and Footer toolbar*).	➤ [↖] Page Number icon [#] 🖰.
(*The page number will appear in the position.*)	➤ ⊕ Current Position 🖰.
	➤ Select the Page Number style required.
	(*The page number will appear in the position.*)

When the headers and footers are complete the user may return to the body of the text as follows:

Office 2003	Office 2007
➤ [↖] Close 🖰 (*on the Header and Footer toolbar*).	➤ [↖] Close the Header and Footer 🖰.

There are a number of other items on the header/footer toolbar that may be quickly inserted into headers and footers. The most popular of these are date, time and insert total number of pages. Other items such as filename, author may be inserted from the insert auto text option.

In order to see the headers and footers on the page it is necessary to select the print layout view [▣] (if not already selected at the bottom of the screen).

Office 2003	Office 2007
A simple number at the bottom of each page may be inserted as follows:	
➤ [↖] Insert menu 🖰.	➤ Select the Insert ribbon.
➤ ⊕ Page numbers 🖰.	➤ [↖] Page number [≡] 🖰.
	➤ ⊕ Top/Bottom of page 🖰.

continued

> ➤ Select the Page Number style required.
> ➤ Close the Header and Footer ribbon.

PAGE VIEWS

Most word processing programs allow the user to view pages in a number of different layouts. The most common are **normal**, **print layout**, **outline** and **web layout**.

The page view is selected as follows:

➤➤ Page layout required . (*at the bottom of the screen*)

Task 3.4.3 (Additional)

Perform the operations specified in **Task 3A-4** on the CD.

Task 3.5.1

(a) Start a new document.
(b) Set the following page margins: top 2.5 cm, bottom 2.5 cm, left 3 cm, right 3 cm.
(c) Type the following text (also available in the documents folder with the filename **Forecast.doc** or **Forecast.txt**):
The following figures indicate the projected worldwide sales for the next three months. These figures are the best estimates available at present, but are likely to be affected by the following conditions:
    Dollar/euro exchange rate.
    Rate of inflation in Ireland.
    Outcome of national wage negotiations.
    World oil prices.

Category	January	February	March
PC Computers	€128,000	€135,000	€142,000
Laptops	€56,000	€58,000	€62,000
Printers	€25,000	€28,000	€35,000
Peripherals	€18,000	€22,000	€28,000

(d) Use the following alignments for the figures:

Left indent (Category)	1 cm
1st tab (January)	5 cm, left align
2nd tab (February)	9 cm, left align
3rd tab (March)	13 cm, left align
Right indent	15 cm

(e) Bold the column headings (Category, January, February, March).

(f) Apply double-line spacing and an outside border to the figures and column headings.

(g) Bullet each of the conditions.

(h) Insert the following footnote, referenced after 'Dollar/euro exchange rate': 'Most components are purchased in US$.'

(i) Insert the words 'Sales Forecast' at the top of the document, in 14 pt bold print, small caps, blue and centred.

(j) Insert the header 'Forecast' in 10 pt, centred.

(k) Insert the following footer in 10 pt.

left	your name
centre	today's date
right	current time

(l) Save the document with the filename **Forecast1**.

TAB STOPS

Tab stops are used to align text in columns. Tabs may be set using four different alignments as indicated by the symbols on the left-hand side of the rule. The most popular alignments are left, right, centre and decimal (L ⌐ ⊥ ⊥.).

Before setting tabs it is a good idea to create a couple of blank rows underneath where the tabs are to be set. This provides space underneath the tabbed section with no tabs, which may be used to continue the document.

Setting Tab Stops

Tabs are set as follows:

➤➤ Select the alignment required.

➤➤ ▶ Position on the rule where the tab stop is required ⌐.

(The tab symbol will appear on the rule.)

Moving Tab Stops

Tab stops may be moved as follows:

➤➤ 　[▶] The tab stop on the rule 🖱.

➤➤ 　Drag the tab stop to the required position 🖱.

Removing Tab Stops

Tab stops are removed as follows:

➤➤ 　[▶] The tab stop to be removed 🖱.

➤➤ 　Drag the tab stop down, off the rule 🖱.

Alternative Method

Office 2003	Office 2007
Tabs may also be inserted using the Tab Stop window as follows:	
➤ [▶] Format menu 🖱. ➤ ⊕ Tabs... 🖱. *(The Tabs window will appear.)* ➤ Enter the position and alignment for each tab stop.	➤ Select the Home ribbon. ➤ [▶] Small arrow on the bottom right of the Paragraph group ▣ 🖱. *(The paragraph formatting window will appear.)* ➤ [▶] Tabs... button 🖱. *(The Tabs window will appear.)* ➤ Enter the position and alignment for each tab stop.

FOOTNOTES AND ENDNOTES

Footnotes and endnotes are references that appear at the bottom of a page or at the end of a document and are referenced in the text with a symbol, usually a small superscript number. Footnotes appear at the end of the page in which they are referenced, whereas endnotes appear at the end of the document.

Office 2003	Office 2007
Footnotes/endnotes are inserted as follows: ➤➤ Select the position for the reference in the text.	
➤ 🔺 Insert menu 🖱. ➤ ⊕ Reference 🖱. ➤ ⊕ Footnote 🖱. (*The footnote and endnote window will appear.*) ➤ Select footnote or endnote and the reference mark to be used. ➤ 🔺 Insert 🖱. (*The cursor will appear at the bottom of the page displaying a reference mark.*) ➤ Type the footnote/endnote.	➤ Select the Reference ribbon. ➤ 🔺 Footnote AB¹ or Endnote icon 🖱 Insert Endnote 🖱. (*The cursor will appear at the bottom of the page/document displaying a reference mark.*) ➤ Type the footnote/endnote.

After typing the footnote/endnote it is necessary to reposition the cursor back in the document using the mouse.

Task 3.5.2

(a) Open the document named **Forecast1** (if not already open).
(b) Add the following paragraph at the end of the document.
The projected income from other interests over the same period are listed below:
(c) Insert the following table, with enhancements and alignments shown, after the above paragraph:

Interest	January	February	March
Installations	€30,000	€25,000	€22,000
Repairs	€12,000	€10,000	€ 9,000
Consultations	€ 8,000	€ 9,000	€ 9,500
Software	€ 5,000	€ 8,000	€17,000

(d) Position the table and set column widths so that the table lines up with the figures above the table.
(e) Insert the following text below the table, setting a left indent at 1 cm, a hanging indent at 3 cm and a right indent at 15 cm.

Note: All computers are sold with the Windows™ operating system preinstalled. This affects the profit margin on all sales of computers as the licences for these operating systems are priced in US$.

(f) Save the document again with the filename **Forecast2**.

TABLES

Tables can be very useful for producing columns of data. As with tabs, it is a good idea to create a couple of blank rows underneath where the table is to be inserted to provide space to continue the document.

Office 2003	Office 2007
A table is inserted into a document as follows:	
➤ Table.	➤ Select the Insert ribbon.
➤ Insert.	➤ Table icon.
➤ Table. (*The insert table window will appear.*)	➤ Select the number of columns and rows required.
➤ Type the number of columns and rows required.	
➤ OK.	

A table will appear in the publication, something like the one shown below:

Moving the Table

The table may be moved around the page as follows:

➤➤ Position the cursor anywhere in the table.

➤➤ Four-headed arrow ⊞ (*outside the top left corner of the table*).

➤➤ Drag the table to the required position.

The complete table may be centred on the page as follows:

➤➤ ▮ Four-headed arrow ⊞ 🖱. (*The whole table will be highlighted.*)

➤➤ ▮ Centre icon on the toolbar/ribbon 🖱.

Changing Column Width

The width of columns may need to be changed to accommodate the data being entered into the table.

Column widths may be changed as follows:

➤➤ ▮ Line separating the columns 🖱.

(*A black double-headed arrow* ◄║► *appears.*)

➤➤ Drag the line to the required position 🖱.

Borders and Shading

Office 2003	Office 2007
Borders may be placed around cells and/or cells shaded as follows: ➤➤ Select the cell(s) to be bordered/shaded.	
➤ ▮ Format menu 🖱. ➤ ⊕ Borders and Shading... 🖱. (*The borders and shading window will be displayed.*) ➤ ▮ Borders/Shading tab 🖱. (*if not already selected*)	(*The table tools design ribbon will appear.*) ➤ ▮ Borders arrow ▢ Borders ▾ or Shading arrow ◆ Shading ▾ 🖱. (*The borders or shading selection window will appear.*)
➤➤ Select the border/shading type, style, colour and size required.	

Note: In Office 2007, the Borders and Shading window may be displayed by selecting the small arrow on the bottom right of the Draw Borders group ▣ or selecting Borders and Shading from the bottom of the Borders selection.

WORKING WITH TABLES

Apart from the items listed above there are a number of other common features associated with tables.

Selecting Cells/Rows/Columns

Cells are selected by simply placing the cursor in the cell and clicking the left mouse button. A number of adjacent cells may be selected by placing the cursor in the first cell, holding down the left mouse button and moving the mouse to highlight other adjacent cells and then releasing the mouse button.

Rows are selected by positioning the cursor to the left of the row to be selected (the cursor changes to a white arrow) and then clicking the left mouse button. A number of rows may be selected by holding down the mouse button and dragging it down or up to select the number of rows required.

Columns are selected by positioning the cursor above the columns to be selected (the cursor changes to a black arrow) and then clicking the left mouse button. A number of columns may be selected by holding down the mouse button and dragging it left or right to select the number of columns required.

Expanding Cells

A new paragraph may be created within a cell by simply pressing the Enter key. A new line may be created within a cell by holding down the Shift key and pressing the Enter key. Both operations will have the effect of expanding the row vertically. A height of a row may be altered by dragging the bottom of the cell vertically, but the row may not be reduced below the last line created in any of the cells on the row.

Text Direction in Cells

Along with the normal alignments on the toolbar, cells may have the direction of text altered.

Office 2003	Office 2007
Text direction may be altered as follows:	
➤ Select the cell to be formatted.	➤ Select the cell to be formatted.
➤ Format menu.	➤ Select the Table Tools Layout ribbon.
➤ Text direction.	➤ Text direction.
➤ Select the alignment required.	➤ Click the mouse many times until the required direction is displayed.

Inserting Rows/Columns

When working with tables, with the cursor positioned in the last cell, pressing the tab (⇥) key will automatically insert an extra row at the bottom of the table.

Office 2003	Office 2007
Extra rows or columns may be inserted in any position in a table as follows:	

➤ Select the position where the row or column is to be inserted.
➤ 🖱 Table menu 🖱.
➤ ⊕ Insert 🖱.
➤ Select one of the following, as required:
   • Column to the left.
   • Column to the right.
   • Row above.
   • Row below.
	➤ Select the position where the row or column is to be inserted.
	➤ Select the Table Tools Layout ribbon.
	➤ 🖱 one of the insert icons  🖱.

Deleting a Table/Rows/Columns

Deletions may involve the complete table, individual columns or rows. However it must be remembered that when a table, or part of a table, is deleted the contents will also be deleted.

Office 2003	Office 2007
A complete table, column or row may be deleted as follows:	
➤ Place the cursor anywhere in the table. ➤ 🖱 Table menu 🖱. ➤ ⊕ Delete. ➤ ⊕ Table/Columns/Rows 🖱.	➤ Place the cursor anywhere in the table. ➤ Select the Table Tools Layout ribbon. ➤ 🖱 Delete icon ⊠ 🖱. ➤ ⊕ Delete Columns/Rows/Table 🖱.

INSERTING SYMBOLS AND SPECIAL CHARACTERS

Word processing programs provide a large selection of symbols and special characters. These are not directly available on the keyboard but may be inserted into the document.

Office 2003	Office 2007
Symbols and special characters are inserted into text as follows: ➤➤ Select the position where the symbol or character is to be inserted.	
➤ 🔺 Insert menu 👆. ➤ ⊕ Symbol 👆. ➤ Select the symbol or special character tab as required. ➤ 🔺 Symbol/character required 👆. *(The symbol/character will appear in the text.)*	➤ Select the Insert ribbon. ➤ 🔺 Symbol Ω 👆. ➤ 🔺 the symbol required or More Symbols 👆. *(More Symbols will display the Symbols window.)*

Task 3.5.3 (Optional)

Perform the operations specified in **Task 3A-5** on the CD.

Task 3.6.1

(a) Start a new document.
(b) Set the following page margins: top 2 cm, bottom 2 cm, left 2.5 cm, right 2.5 cm.
(c) Type the following text (also available in the Documents folder with the filename **Cash Flow.doc** or **Cash Flow.txt**):
Cash flow is the lifeblood of every business. The living, beating, pulsing heart that keeps it flowing is the accounts software and its management of the debtors ledger and ability to warn and assist in taking action when accounts become due, overdue and seriously problematic. In fact, it is probably true to say that the success of any small business is going to depend in fairly large measure on the level of efficiency with which debtors and credit control generally are managed. It also has to be said that poor management of debtors is a major contributing factor in the failure of small businesses. For a start, it erodes working capital and pushes up the costs of banking and other financing.

Bad debts, whether they can be fairly judged to have been avoidable or not, can have a disproportionate and even devastating effect on the smaller business. Every single expert on credit management agrees that it is not rocket science and not even difficult. What it needs in the first place is that it actually gets done. Leaving it to the boss or management is generally not the best approach, because too many other apparent priorities will get in the way.

Human nature means that people with an eye on future sales are seldom the best at chasing payment for those already made. The other essentials for good credit control are method and consistency. Even hardened slow payers find it difficult when invoices are sent out promptly and accurately, statements are regular and follow-through phone calls politely but firmly ask, 'When?'.

(d) Insert the words 'Cash Flow' as a new paragraph at the start of the document.
(e) Insert a suitable Clip Art picture between the second and third paragraph.
(f) Insert a picture (which you have stored on disk) after the last paragraph.
(g) Resize the graphics so that they are 6 cm wide (maintaining the proportions).
(h) Centre the graphics on the page.
(i) Insert a suitable caption underneath each graphic.
(j) Place a 2 pt box around each graphic to surround the graphic and the caption.
(k) Save the document as **Cash Flow1**.

CLIP ART AND PICTURES

Clip Art

Clip Art are pictures which are supplied for use in a document. Some Clip Art is installed with the program but most Clip Art pictures are available online and it is therefore necessary to be connected to the Internet in order to insert them.

Office 2003	Office 2007
Any of the Clip Art pictures may be inserted into a document as follows:	
➤ Insert menu 🖰. ➤ Picture 🖰. ➤ Clip Art 🖰.	➤ Select the Insert ribbon. ➤ Clip Art 🖰.

(The clip art side window will appear.)

➤➤ Type a word in the 'Search for' field.

➤➤ Go 🖰. (*A selection of clip art will appear in the window.*)

continued

>> Clip Art picture required.

(The clip art will be inserted into the document.)

>> Close the Clip Art gallery.

Pictures

Office 2003	Office 2007
A picture that has been saved may be inserted into a document as follows:	
➤ Insert menu. ➤ Picture. ➤ From file.	➤ Select the Insert ribbon. Picture.

   (The insert picture window will appear.)

>> Select the correct folder and a list of files will appear.

>> The picture filename.

>> Insert button.

(The picture will be inserted into the document.)

Resizing a Graphic

Any graphic (Clip Art, picture, etc.) may be resized as follows:

>> Select the graphic. *(Eight handles will appear on the graphic.)*

>> Corner handle.

(Cursor changes to a double-headed arrow ⟋ OR ⟍.)

>> Drag the graphic in the direction of the arrow to the required size.

Text Wrap on a Graphic

When a graphic is inserted into a document it will normally be inserted in line with the text. This means that the graphic will match the alignment of the text. However, it is possible to change the way in which the graphic is placed in the document.

Office 2003	Office 2007
Text wrap is set as follows:	
➤ Select the graphic.	➤ Select the graphic.
➤ 🖰 Format menu 🖱.	➤ Select the Picture Tools Format ribbon.
➤ ✛ Picture 🖱.	➤ 🖰 Text Wrapping icon 🖼 🖱.
➤ 🖰 Layout tab 🖱.	➤ Select the text wrapping required.
➤ Select the text wrapping required.	

Moving a Graphic

Once a graphic has any wrapping other than in line with text, it may be moved to any position on the document as follows:

➤➤ Select the graphic.

➤➤ Position the cursor anywhere in the graphic 🖱.

(*The cursor becomes a four-headed arrow* ✛.)

➤➤ Drag the graphic to the position required 🖱.

A graphic may be moved or copied to another document by simply selecting the graphic and using the cut or copy icons and then pasting it into another document.

Any graphic may be deleted by simply selecting it and pressing the Delete key.

Task 3.6.2

(a) Open the document named **Cash Flow1** (if not already open).

(b) Create the following styles:

- Text – Times New Roman, 12 pt, justified.
- Heading – Arial, 14 pt, bold, centred, small caps, blue.
- Captions – Arial, 10 pt, bold, italics, underlined.

(c) Apply the styles to the appropriate text.

(d) Save the document with the filename **Cash Flow2**.

(e) Print one copy of the document.

STYLES

Styles are used to quickly apply formatting to text. Styles contain information about fonts, font sizes, alignments, enhancements, etc. and are stored with the document. Most word processing programs provide a number of predefined styles that are available for use in each document.

Applying Styles

Office 2003	Office 2007
Styles are applied to text, either before or after typing, as follows:	
➤ Select the text. (*if already typed*) ➤ [icon] Style arrow [icon] [mouse]. (*A list of styles will appear.*) ➤ ⊕ Style required [mouse].	➤ Select the text. (*if already typed*) ➤ Select the Home ribbon. ➤ [icon] Expand arrow [icon] [mouse]. (*beside the sample styles displayed*) (*The range of styles will be displayed.*) ➤ [icon] Style required [mouse].

The text will appear with the style selected.

When selecting text to apply a style to, it is only necessary to place the cursor in the paragraph required, as the style applies to whole paragraphs. If you wish to apply particular styles to individual words or sentences then this is normally done using the toolbar icons or the format font menu.

New Styles

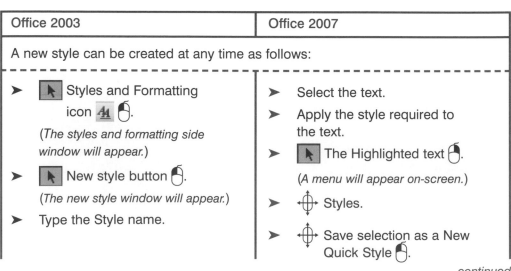

Office 2003	Office 2007
A new style can be created at any time as follows:	
➤ [icon] Styles and Formatting icon [icon] [mouse]. (*The styles and formatting side window will appear.*) ➤ [icon] New style button [mouse]. (*The new style window will appear.*) ➤ Type the Style name.	➤ Select the text. ➤ Apply the style required to the text. ➤ [icon] The Highlighted text [mouse]. (*A menu will appear on-screen.*) ➤ ⊕ Styles. ➤ ⊕ Save selection as a New Quick Style [mouse].

continued

➤ Select the font, font size, font effects, etc.

(*The Format button gives a full range of options.*)

➤ Select paragraph alignment, indents, spacing, etc.

➤ OK.

➤ Close the Styles and Formatting window.

➤ Type the Style name.

➤ OK.

Once the style has been created it will appear in the styles list and may be applied in the same way as the predefined styles.

Task 3.6.3 (Additional)

Perform the operations specified in **Task 3A-6** on the CD.

Task 3.7.1

(a) Start a new document using a memo template.

(b) Insert the following in the memo:

To: Mr James Hughes
CC: Ms Fiona Doyle
From: <your own name>
Date: <today's date>
Re: Revised price list
The revised price list for all products will not be available until Wed of next week.

(c) Save the document as **Price Memo**.

(d) Print one copy of the memo.

TEMPLATES

Word processing programs have a number of templates supplied with the program. Templates have predefined styles, layout, etc. which allows standardised documents to be quickly produced. Office **2003** has some templates supplied with the program and others are available online. Office **2007** has all of the pre-defined templates online and it is therefore necessary to connect to the Internet in order to use them.

Office 2003	Office 2007
New documents are produced using a template as follows:	

➤ 🖱 File menu 🖱. (*Do not use the new icon on the toolbar.*)

➤ ✛ New 🖱. (*The new document side window will appear.*)

➤ 🖱 On my computer 🖱. (*The templates window will appear.*)

➤ 🖱 Memo tab 🖱.

➤ Select a memo template.

➤ 🖱 OK 🖱.

➤ 🖱 Office button 📷 🖱.

➤ ✛ New 🖱. (*The new document window will appear.*)

➤ 🖱 Memos 🖱. (*on the left*)
(*Computer must be online, running a registered copy of Office 2007.*)

➤ Select a memo template.

➤ 🖱 Download 🖱.

➤➤ Type the necessary information in the template and save as a normal document.

Task 3.7.2

(a Start a new document.

(b) Insert the following in the document, leaving three blank lines underneath:

New Age Technologies

South Park Shopping Centre

Maynooth

Co Kildare

Phone: (01)6524816

(c) Format the company name in 24 pt, Arial, blue and centre.

(d) Format the address and phone number in 14 pt, Arial and bold.

(e) Place a suitable Clip Art graphic on the right side of the document opposite the address. Adjust the height of the graphic so that it is the same height as the address.

(f) Place a 3 pt line across the document underneath the address and graphic.

(g) Save the document as a document template with the filename **Letterhead**.

(h) Print one copy of the document.

CREATING A TEMPLATE

A new template may be created as follows:

- Start a new document.

- Set up all the formatting and styles required.

- Type any standard text which is to be on the template.

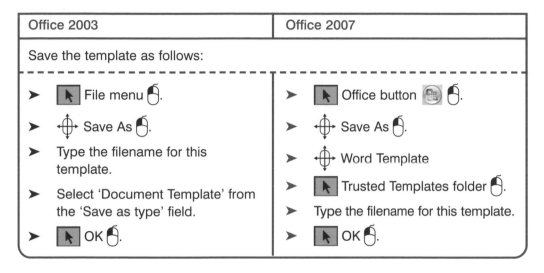

Office 2003	Office 2007
Save the template as follows:	
➤ File menu.	➤ Office button.
➤ Save As.	➤ Save As.
➤ Type the filename for this template.	➤ Word Template
➤ Select 'Document Template' from the 'Save as type' field.	➤ Trusted Templates folder.
	➤ Type the filename for this template.
➤ OK.	➤ OK.

The template will be saved in the general templates section and will be available any time the user wishes to create a new document using that template.

Task 3.7.3 (Additional)

Perform the operations specified in **Task 3A-7** on the CD.

MAIL MERGE

Mail merge is the process of producing a document and inserting data from a separate data source into specified locations in the document. Special placeholders are created in the document that are then linked with data items from the data source.

A simple example would be a letter that could be sent to all the members in a club. The individual names and addresses might be stored in a table (data source). The letter would be typed and the data from the table would be inserted into the letter, creating a separate letter for each member.

The process of producing a mail merge document is as follows:

- Create the data source (this may have been created already and it just needs to be accessed).

- Create the main document.

- Merge the document and data source.

Note: The data source may be a table in a word document, a spreadsheet or a table in a database. Where the Word program is used to create the data source as part of the mail merge process, it will create an Access database and table.

Task 3.8.1

(a) Start a new document.
(b) Set a left-aligned tab at 2 cm.
(c) Type the following text (press the tab key after typing **To:**, **Dept:** and **From:** in order to place the cursor away from the word):

    Memo

    To:
    Dept:
    From: Thomas Dunphy

    The IT meeting scheduled for this afternoon has been changed to Friday at 11:30 am.

(d) Save the document as **Memo**.
(e) Create a mail merge form letter to merge the memo with the following data source, which you will create and save as **Personnel**.

Name	Dept
Joan Healy	Sales
Michael Fleming	Production
Kathleen Lacey	Finance
Liam Griffin	Accounts

(f) Merge the data with the document, inserting the name after **To:** in the document and the department after **Dept:** in the document.
(g) View the merged data.
(h) Save the document again with the same filename.
(i) Print one copy of the memo to Kathleen Lacey.

MAIL MERGE FORM LETTER

The creation of a form letter involves three steps as mentioned above. Two methods of accomplishing this task will be explained.

Method 1   This method will use Word to create a table containing the data source and then merge that with the form letter. The first row of the table should contain the field names.

Method 2   This method will allow Word to create the data source (an Access database) while creating the form letter. The data source will then be merged with the form letter.

Method 1 – Using a Word Table

1 Create the data source as follows:

>> Start a blank document and produce the following table at the top of the document. Ensure that there are no blank rows (lines) above the table.

Name	Dept
Joan Healy	Sales
Michael Fleming	Production
Kathleen Lacey	Finance
Liam Griffin	Accounts

>> Save the document with the filename **Personnel**, and close the document.

2 Create the Form Letter as follows:

>> Start a new document and type the standard portion of the letter, leaving out the data which will be merged with the document afterwards.

>> Save the document with the filename **Memo**.

3a Create the mail merge in Office 2003, using the form letter, as follows:

Office 2003

➤ Open the form letter into the data to be merged.

➤ [cursor] Tools menu 🖰.

➤ ⊕ Letters and Mailings.

➤ ⊕ Mail merge 🖰. (*The mail merge side window will appear.*)

➤ Select document type (*Letters, in the side window*)

continued

➤ ⬚ Next: Starting document 🖱 (*at the bottom of the side window*)
   (*Use the current document will be selected.*)

➤ ⬚ Next: Select recipients 🖱 (*at the bottom of the side window*)

➤ Select 'Use an existing list' (*at the top of the side window*)

➤ ⬚ ▦ Browse 🖱. (*in the side window*)
   (*The select data source window will appear.*)

➤ ⬚ Select the location of the data in the 'Look in' field and select the file containing the data.
   (*The mail merge recipients list window will appear.*)

➤ ⬚ OK button 🖱.

➤ ⬚ Next: Write your letter 🖱 (*This step has just been done.*)

➤ ⬚ Select the position in the document where the data is to be inserted.

➤ ⬚ More items ▦ 🖱. (*The insert merge field window will appear.*)

➤ Select the field to be inserted.

➤ ⬚ Insert button 🖱.

➤ ⬚ Close button 🖱.

➤ Repeat the five previous steps for each field to be merged.

➤ ⬚ Next: Preview your letters 🖱. (*at the bottom of the side window*)

➤ Each separate document may be viewed by selecting the view buttons << >> (*in the side window*)

➤ ⬚ Next: Complete the merge 🖱. (*in the side window*)

➤ ⬚ Print 🖱. (*in the side window*)
   (*The merge to printer window will appear.*)

➤ ⬚ OK button 🖱, and print the documents.

3b Create the mail merge in Office 2007, using the form letter, as follows:

Office 2007
➤ Open the from letter into which the data is to be merged.
➤ Select the Mailings ribbon.

continued

➤ Select Recipients icon.

➤ Use Existing List. (*The Select Data Source window will appear.*)

➤ Select the location of the data in the 'Look in' field and select the file containing the data.

➤ Position the cursor in the position where the data is to be inserted.

➤ Insert Merge Field icon.

(*This icon has two sections. The top half displays the insert merge field window. The bottom half, or the little arrow, displays the recipient list of fields only.*)

➤ Field to be added.

➤ Repeat the previous three steps for each field to be merged.

➤ Preview Results icon.

(*The first merged document will be displayed.*)

➤ Each separate document may be viewed by selecting the view buttons ⏮ ◀ 1 ▶ ⏭ .

➤ Finish and Merge icon.

➤ Print Document.

➤ OK button and print the documents.

Method 2 – Create the Data Source as Part of the Process

Office 2003	Office 2007
1 Type the standard portion of the document.	**1 Type the standard portion of the document.**
This involves typing the complete document, leaving out the data which will be merged with the document afterwards.	This involves typing the complete document, leaving out the data which will be merged with the document afterwards.
2 Save the document in the normal way.	**2 Save the document in the normal way.**
3 Create the mail merge.	**3 Create the mail merge.**
This method will create the data source as an integral part of the process, as follows:	The mail merge is created as follows: ➤ Select the Mailings ribbon.

continued

➤   ▣ Tools menu 🖱.

➤   ✛ Letters and Mailings.

➤   ✛ Mail merge 🖱.
(The mail merge side window will appear.)

➤   Select document type.
(Letters, in the side window.)

➤   ▣ Next: Starting document 🖱.
(at the bottom of the side window)

(Use the current document will be selected.)

➤   ▣ Next: Select recipients 🖱.
(at the bottom of the side window)

➤   Select Type a new list. *(at the top of the window)*

➤   ▣ 🔲 Create 🖱. *(in the side window)*

(The new address list window will appear.)

➤   ▣ Customise button 🖱. *(in the side window)*

(The customise address list window will appear.)

➤   Delete the existing fields from the window by repeatedly clicking on the Delete button and confirming the deletion.

➤   ▣ Add button 🖱. *(A small add field window will appear.)*

➤   Type the first field name in the field provided.

➤   ▣ OK button 🖱.

➤   ▣ Select Recipients icon 🖾 🖱.

➤   ✛ Type New List 🖱. *(The new address list window will appear.)*

➤   ▣ Customise Columns button 🖱.

(The customise address list window will appear.)

➤   Delete the existing fields from the window by repeatedly clicking on the Delete button and confirming the deletion.

➤   ▣ Add button 🖱. *(A small add field window will appear.)*

➤   Type the first field name in the field provided.

➤   ▣ OK button 🖱.

➤   Repeat the three previous steps for each field to be added.

➤   ▣ OK button 🖱. *(when all the fields have been added)*

(The new address list window will now display the fields which have been added.)

➤   Enter the data in the each field, for the first entry.

➤   ▣ New Entry button 🖱.

OR

Press the Tab key ⇥.

➤   Repeat the two previous steps for each entry to be added.

➤   ▣ OK button 🖱. *(The save address list window will appear.)*

continued

➤ Repeat the three previous steps for each field to be added.

➤ ▣ OK button 🖱. (*when all the fields have been added*)

(*The new address list window will now display the fields which have been added*.)

➤ Enter the data in the each field, for the first entry.

➤ ▣ New Entry button 🖱.

➤ Repeat the two previous steps for each entry to be added.

➤ ▣ Close button 🖱. (*The save address list window will appear.*)

➤ Select the location to save the data in the 'Save in' field and type the filename for the data in the 'Filename' field.

Note: This will be an Access database table.

➤ ▣ Save button 🖱. (*The mail merge recipients list window will appear.*)

➤ ▣ OK button 🖱.

➤ ▣ Next: Write your letter 🖱. (*in the side window*)

➤ Select the position in the document where the data is to be added.

➤ ▣ ▦ More items 🖱. (*The insert merge field window will appear.*)

➤ Select the field to be inserted.

➤ ▣ Insert button 🖱.

➤ ▣ Close button 🖱.

➤ Select the location to save the data in the 'Save in' field and type the filename for the data in the 'Filename' field.

Note: This will be an Access database table.

➤ ▣ Save button 🖱.

➤ Select the position in the document where the data is to be added.

➤ ▣ Insert Merge Field icon 🖱.

(*This icon has two sections. The top half displays the insert merge field window. The bottom half, or the little arrow, displays the recipient list of fields only.*)

➤ ▣ Field to be added 🖱.

➤ Repeat the previous three steps for each field to be merged.

➤ ▣ Preview Results icon 🖱. (*The first merged document will be displayed.*)

➤ Each separate document may be viewed by selecting the view buttons ⏮◀ 1 ▶⏭ .

➤ ▣ Finish and Merge icon 🖱.

➤ ⊕ Print Document 🖱.

➤ ▣ OK button 🖱 and print the documents.

continued

➤ 🖱 Repeat the five previous steps for each field to be merged.

➤ 🖱 Next: Preview your letters 🖱. (*in the side window*)

➤ Each separate document may be viewed by selecting the view buttons ⬚<< ⬚>> . (*in the side window*)

➤ 🖱 Next: Complete the merge 🖱. (*in the side window*)

➤ 🖱 🖨 Print 🖱. (*in the side window*)

(*The merge to printer window will appear.*)

➤ 🖱 OK button 🖱. (*to print all the documents*)

➤ 🖱 OK button 🖱.

Task 3.8.2

(a) Open the document named **Personnel**.
(b) Adjust the column widths as necessary.
(c) Add the following names to the table. (Position the cursor after the last entry in the table and press the tab key ⇥.)

Name	Dept
Rita Dempsey	Complaints
Geraldine Burke	Warranty

(d) Save the table again with the same filename.

Task 3.8.3

(a) Open the document named **Memo**.
(b) View all the documents, in turn.
(c) Print the memo for Geraldine Burke.

Task 3.8.4 (Additional)

Perform the operations specified in **Task 3A-8** on the CD.

Task 3.9.1

(a) Start a new document.
(b) Create the following table (ensure that it is on the first line of the document and type the field names on the first row).

Name	Dept	Street	Town	County
Joan Healy	Sales	Main St	Naas	Co. Kildare
Michael Fleming	Production	Basin St	Naas	Co. Kildare
Kathleen Lacey	Finance	Cutlery Road	Newbridge	Co. Kildare
Liam Griffin	Accounts	Georges St	Kilcullen	Co. Kildare
Niall Jennings	Repairs	Newpark	Newbridge	Co. Kildare
Rita Dempsey	Complaints	Orchard Road	Clane	Co. Kildare
Geraldine Burke	Warranty	Dublin Road	Naas	Co. Kildare

(c) Save the document with the filename **Addresses**.
(d) Close the document.

Task 3.9.2

(a) Start a new document.
(b) Save the document with the filename **Labels Master**.
(c) Create mailing labels using the file **Addresses** as the data source. The layout of the labels should be as follows:

    <Blank Line>
    <Name>
    <Street>
    <Town>
    <County>
    <Blank Line>
    <Dept>

(d) Save the document again with the same filename.
(e) Print the labels (on plain paper will be OK).

MAILING LABELS

The process of producing mailing labels is very similar to the production of form letters and consists of the following two steps:

- Create the data source (this may be created already and it is only necessary to access it).
- Create the mail merge labels.

Note: The data source may be a table in a Word document, a spreadsheet or a table in a database. Where the Word program is used to create the data source as part of the mail merge process, it will create an Access database and table, and the first step is accomplished as part of the process.

1 Create the data source as follows:

➤➤ Start a blank document and produce the following table at the top of the document. Ensure that there are no blank rows (lines) above the table.

Name	Dept	Street	Town	County
Joan Healy	Sales	Main St	Naas	Co. Kildare
Michael Fleming	Production	Basin St	Naas	Co. Kildare
Kathleen Lacey	Finance	Cutlery Road	Newbridge	Co. Kildare
Liam Griffin	Accounts	Georges St	Kilcullen	Co. Kildare
Niall Jennings	Repairs	Newpark	Newbridge	Co. Kildare
Rita Dempsey	Complaints	Orchard Road	Clane	Co. Kildare
Geraldine Burke	Warranty	Dublin Road	Naas	Co. Kildare

➤➤ Save the document with the filename **Addresses**, and close the document.

2a Create the Mailing Labels in Office 2003 as follows:

Office 2003

➤ ▶ Tools menu 👆.

➤ ⊕ Letters and Mailings.

➤ ⊕ Mail Merge 👆.

➤ Select document type. (*Labels, in the side window*)

continued

➤ ⬚ Next: Starting document 🖱. (*at the bottom of the side window*)

➤ ⬚ Label Options 🖱. (*The label options window will appear.*)

➤ Select the label type being used.

➤ ⬚ OK 🖱.

➤ ⬚ Next: Select recipients 🖱. (*at the bottom of the side window*)

➤ Select 'Use an existing list' (*at the top of the side window*)

➤ ⬚ Browse ▦ . (*in the side window*)

(*The select data source window will appear.*)

➤ Select the location of the data in the 'Look in' field and select the file containing the data.

(*The mail merge recipients list window will appear.*)

➤ ⬚ OK button 🖱.

➤ ⬚ Next: Arrange your labels 🖱. (*at the bottom of the side window*)

➤ ⬚ ▦ More items 🖱. (*The insert merge field window will appear.*)

➤ Select the field to be inserted.

➤ ⬚ Insert button 🖱.

➤ ⬚ Close button 🖱.

➤ Insert a space or press the Enter key to move onto the next line.

➤ Repeat the five previous steps for each field to be merged.

➤ ⬚ Update all labels button 🖱.

➤ ⬚ Next: Preview your labels 🖱. (*at the bottom of the side window*)

➤ Each separate label may be viewed by selecting the view buttons
   ⟨<<⟩ ⟨>>⟩ (*in the side window*)

➤ ⬚ Next: Complete the merge 🖱. (*in the side window*)

➤ ⬚ 🖨 Print 🖱. (*in the side window*)

(*The merge to printer window will appear.*)

➤ ⬚ OK button 🖱 and print the documents.

2b Create the Mailing Labels in Office 2007 as follows:

Office 2007

➤ Select the Mailings ribbon.

➤ � Start Mail Merge 🖰.

➤ ⊕ Labels 🖰. (*The labels options window will appear.*)

(*Select the label type being used.*)

➤ � OK 🖰.

➤ � Select recipients icon 🖳.

➤ ⊕ Use Existing List 🖰. (*The select data source window will appear.*)

➤ Select the location of the data in the 'Look in' field and select the file containing the data.

➤ � Insert Merge Field icon 🖳 🖰.

(*This icon has two sections. The top half displays the insert merge field window. The bottom half, or the little arrow, displays the recipient list of fields only.*)

➤ � Field to be added 🖰.

➤ Repeat the previous two steps for each field to be merged.

➤ � Update labels icon 🖰.

➤ � Preview Results icon 🔍 🖰.

(*The first sheet of labels will be displayed.*)

➤ Print the labels.

Note: The process of creating the data source as part of the mail merge process is exactly the same as for a mail merge document.

Task 3.9.3 (Additional)

Perform the operations specified in **Task 3A-9** on the CD.

4 Spreadsheets

SYMBOLS USED IN THIS CHAPTER

The symbols used in this chapter, and their meanings, are as follows:

	Click the left mouse button.
	Click the right mouse button.
	Double-click the left mouse button.
	Hold down the left mouse button.
	Move the mouse to point to an item without clicking or holding any button.
	Release the mouse button.
	Point to an item on the screen.
Ctrl	Hold down the Ctrl button.
Ctrl ;	Hold down the Ctrl button and press the semicolon.
⇧	Hold down the Shift key.
⇧ 8	Hold down the Shift key and press the number eight.
	Press the Enter key.
=	Press the equals key.
+	Press the plus key.
–	Press the minus key.
*	Press the multiplication key.
/	Press the division key.
,	Press the comma key.
F4	Press the F4 function key.
(	Press the open bracket key (⇧ 9).
)	Press the close bracket key (⇧ 0).

INTRODUCTION

A spreadsheet is an electronic worksheet consisting of **rows**, which run **across** the page, and **columns**, which run **down** the page. This has the effect of producing a grid into which information can be placed and manipulated. Each rectangle in the grid is referred to as a **cell**. People sometimes have difficulty in remembering which is a row and which is a column. One way of remembering this is to think of a building with columns in the front – these are vertical structures. Another idea is to think of standing on a stage and looking out at the seating. The seats are in rows, which run across the theatre.

Each row and column is labelled. The rows are labelled with numbers at the left-hand side of the screen, with row one at the top and the last row at the bottom. The columns are labelled with letters. These letters appear at the top of the screen with column A to the left and the last column on the right.

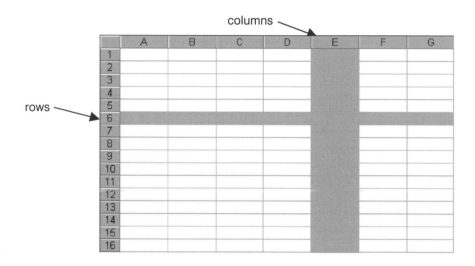

Figure 4.1

Spreadsheets are used where calculations have to be made and are widely used as an aid to modelling and planning. Some examples of the use of spreadsheets are household budgets, recording expenditure, wages calculations, analysis of capital budgets, making sales decisions, analysing product planning, planning investments, simulating mathematical models and much more.

Spreadsheet programs have an extensive graphics section that allows the production of bar charts, pie charts and many types of graphs in order to make it easier to interpret the data being presented on the spreadsheet.

The great power of a spreadsheet lies in the ability to carry out calculations on numbers. This is accomplished by building formulae that will automatically carry out calculations when numbers are inserted into cells on the spreadsheet. When numbers are changed in a spreadsheet the resulting effect on all other figures can be immediately seen, without the need for any other changes to the spreadsheet.

LOADING THE SPREADSHEET PROGRAM

The spreadsheet program may be loaded from the desktop, if there is an icon on the desktop, as follows:

➤➤ � Spreadsheet icon 🖱.

If the program is not available from the desktop then it may be loaded from the Start menu as follows:

➤➤ ▢ Start 🖱.

➤➤ ⊕ All Programs.

➤➤ ⊕ Spreadsheet program 🖱. (*You may have to open a submenu to find the program.*)

The program will then appear on-screen. The way in which the program appears is controlled by the various options, which may be set in the program to customise the layout. A common layout is shown in Figure 4.2.

THE SPREADSHEET SCREEN

When the spreadsheet program is loaded the screen should look something like Figure 4.2. The various sections are labelled in the diagram and explained below.

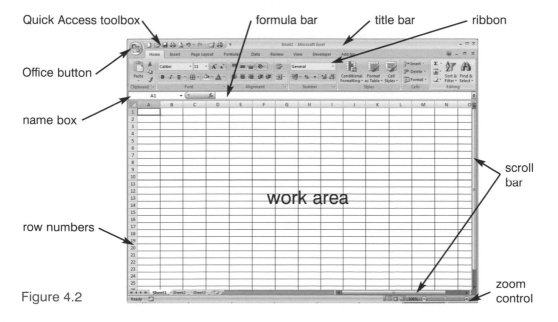

Figure 4.2

The spreadsheet screen consists of a number of different sections. The ones we are interested in at present are:

Title Bar
This is the top band and consists of the program title (Microsoft Excel) and the filename. The filename will usually be Book1, Book2, etc. until it is given it a name.

Quick Access Toolbar
This toolbar consist of icons (graphic representations of functions) that are available by simply pointing to them and clicking the left mouse button. When the program is installed there are only a couple of icons on this toolbar but other icons may be added.

Formula Bar
The next row indicates the active cell and also displays the contents of the active cell. In the case of a formula, the actual formula and not the result will be displayed on this bar.

Row Numbers
The row numbers appear down the left-hand side of the screen. The numbers continue far beyond those visible on the screen.

Column Labels
The column labels appear across the top of the work area. These labels continue far beyond those visible on the screen. When they reach the letter Z they continue with the letters AA, AB, etc.

Work Area
The work area takes up the major part of the screen and consists of rectangles, called **cells**, into which data can be entered. Each cell is referenced by the row/column labels, e.g. A1, D12, etc.

Scroll Bars
The scroll bars allow the screen to be moved over the worksheet in the direction of the arrow in order to view and work on large worksheets.

SELECTING CELLS

When using the program, the mouse may appear in different shapes on the screen (cross, pointer, I-beam, etc.) depending on the part of the screen in which it is positioned. For example, it appears as a cross when moved around the work area.

Each cell is selected as follows:

➤➤   Required cell. Place the white cross in the cell required and press the left mouse button.

A rectangle appears around the selected cell to indicate that it is the active cell. The arrow keys on the keyboard may be used to move from cell to cell – in this case the rectangle moves one cell at a time in the direction of the arrow.

The selected cell reference also appears in the name box on the left of the formula bar.

ENTERING DATA INTO CELLS

Data is entered into the active cell by simply typing the required data. The program is capable of distinguishing between numbers and words, but it is only possible to carry out calculations on numbers. When the data is being typed it appears in the active cell and also on the formula bar. Corrections can be made using the Backspace key while it is being typed. The data is entered into the cell by pressing the Enter key.

It is also possible to enter the data by moving to another cell using the arrow keys or the mouse. The use of the arrow keys is often a more efficient method, especially when entering rows of figures.

> **Task 4.1.1**
>
> Using a blank sheet, enter the data shown in Figure 4.3 into the cells indicated. Start typing the sentence in cell A12. Keep typing until you get to the end of the sentence and then press the Enter key.

	A	B	C	D	E	F	G
1	56						
2	89						
3	1457						
4							
5			45				
6			23				
7							
8	12	45	56	87	127	234	
9							
10	John		Linda		Kate		
11							
12	It is easy to enter data into cells in a spreadsheet						

Figure 4.3

When inputting data, numbers automatically line up on the right of the cell and words line up on the left of the cell. This alignment may be changed, but it is obvious from the fact that they lined up differently that the spreadsheet knows the difference between numbers and words. When the sentence was typed it automatically ran into the next cell when it got too long for the cell in which it was typed. This happens automatically, provided that the adjacent cells are empty.

STARTING A NEW SHEET

Each workbook may have up to 256 different sheets in it. (The setting is normally three to sixteen sheets.) The sheet numbers at the bottom of the work area will have 'Sheet1' in dark print (highlighted) and the other sheets will be on a grey tab. The highlighted sheet is the one being worked on.

Sheet2 is selected as follows:

➤➤ ▐▲▌ Sheet2 🖰. (*A blank sheet will appear on the screen.*)

Sheet1 may be selected again as follows:

➤➤ ▐▲▌ Sheet1 🖰. (*The work on Sheet1 will reappear.*)

Each sheet is very large, normally having about 65,000 rows and 256 columns in Excel 2003 and over one million rows and 16,000 columns in Excel 2007.

ADDING CELL CONTENTS

In order to perform a calculation on a spreadsheet it is necessary to enter a formula into a cell. The simplest formula we will be using is the addition formula. This is used to add the contents of a number of cells. It is worth noting at this stage that each formula is started by typing the = sign.

Task 4.1.2

(a) Select a new sheet and enter the data shown in Figure 4.4 into the cells indicated.
(b) Enter a formula into each shaded cell that will add the contents of the cells to the left.

	A	B	C	D	E	F	G
1							
2	12	25					
3							
4	14	24	46				
5							
6	56	87	124	149			
7							
8	127	581	248	1492	4278		
9							

Figure 4.4

Since this is our first formula, each step will be explained in detail in order to make the procedure as clear as possible. When working on spreadsheets it is good practice to use the number keypad for numbers, the + (add), the – (subtract), the * (multiply), the / (divide) symbols and the Enter key.

The procedure for addition is as follows:

For two numbers

➤➤ ⬚ Cell into which the answer is to go 🖱. | Place the cross in cell C2 using the mouse and click the left button.

➤➤ = | Press the equal sign (there is only one = sign on the keyboard). The = sign will appear in cell C2 and also in the formula bar.

➤➤ ⬚ First cell to be added 🖱. | Move the cross to the cell containing the number 12, i.e. cell A2, and click the left mouse button. A2 will appear beside the = sign in cell C2 and also in the formula bar.

➤➤ + | Press the + sign (on the right-hand number pad on the keyboard). The + sign will appear beside the A2 in cell C2 and also in the formula bar.

➤➤ ⬚ The cell with the second number 🖱. | Move the cross to the cell containing the number 25, i.e. cell B2, and click the left mouse button. B2 will appear beside the + sign in cell C2 and also in the formula bar.

➤➤ ⏎ | Press the Enter key. (There are two Enter keys on the keyboard, so either will do.) The number 37 will appear in cell C2.

The process for row 4 is exactly the same except that another + sign and the third number must be selected before pressing the Enter key. The procedure is shown below.

Any amount of numbers can be added as follows:

➤➤ ⬚ Cell in which the answer is to go 🖱.

➤➤ =

➤➤ ⬚ First cell to be added 🖱.

---

continued

➤➤ ⊞ +

➤➤ ◥ Next cell to be added 🖱.

➤➤ ⊞ +

➤➤ ◥ Next cell to be added 🖱.

➤➤ Continue the process until all additions have been done ⌨.

A common mistake is that people press the + key after selecting the last number and then press the Enter key. This produces an error message and the error has to be corrected before the formula will be accepted.

Task 4.1.3

(a) Enter more numbers on other rows and practise adding them.
(b) Continue until you are sure you are able to add any numbers.

WHAT IF

One of the major functions of a spreadsheet is the ability to change the values entered on the sheet and immediately see the results of the changes. This is commonly referred to as 'playing what if'. The number in a cell may be changed by simply pointing to the cell and clicking the left mouse button and typing the new number. There is no need to delete the old number as it will be replaced automatically.

Because the formulae are built into the spreadsheet, any time any of the values are changed the spreadsheet will automatically recalculate and display the new answer.

Care should be taken when playing 'what if' to ensure that a number is not entered into a cell containing a formula, as this will delete the formula and insert the number instead.

Task 4.1.4

Change some of the figures entered in the spreadsheet and check the new answers.

SUBTRACTION

Subtraction is practically the same as the addition function, except that the – sign is used instead of the + sign. There are two minus signs on the keyboard. One is located on the top row of the number keypad and the other is beside the number 0 on the top row of the main keyboard. Remember, it is better to get used to using the number keypad when working with spreadsheets.

Task 4.1.5

(a) Select a new sheet and enter the data shown in Figure 4.5 into the cells indicated.

(b) Enter a formula into each shaded cell that will subtract the contents of the cells to the left. All the numbers on the row should be subtracted from the first (biggest) number on that row.

	A	B	C	D	E	F
1						
2	12	8				
3						
4	25	17				
5						
6	136	97				
7						
8	168	59	16			
9						
10	657	128	246			
11						
12	348	124	56			
13						
14	845	241	58	121		
15						
16	2462	851	624	128		

Figure 4.5

Two numbers are subtracted as follows:

➤➤ 🔺 Cell in which the answer is to go 🖱.

➤➤ ☰

➤➤ 🔺 Cell with the larger number 🖱.

➤➤ ▭

➤➤ 🔺 Cell with the number to be subtracted 🖱.

➤➤ ▭

Any amount of numbers can be subtracted as follows:

➤➤   Cell in which the answer is to go .

➤➤   =

➤➤   Cell with the larger number .

➤➤   −

➤➤   Cell with the number to be subtracted .

➤➤   −

➤➤   Next cell to be subtracted .

➤➤   −

➤➤   Continue the process until all subtractions have been done .

Task 4.1.6

(a) Enter more numbers on other rows and practise subtracting them.
(b) Continue until you are sure you are able to subtract any numbers.

Task 4.1.7

(a) Change some of the numbers entered in the spreadsheet and check the new answers.
(b) Close the workbook and exit the spreadsheet program. (There is no need to save the workbook at this stage.)

CLOSING A WORKBOOK

Each workbook should be closed when the user is finished working on it. Several workbooks (files) may be open at any one time, but at this level it is probably better to have only one workbook open at a time.

Office 2003	Office 2007
A workbook is closed as follows:	
➤ ▣ File menu 🖱. ➤ ▣ Close 🖱.	➤ ▣ Office button 🔲 🖱. ➤ ▣ Close 🖱.

If the workbook (file) has not been saved then a warning message will appear, asking if changes to the workbook are to be saved. Select **Yes** or **No** as appropriate.

EXITING THE SPREADSHEET PROGRAM

Each time the user is finished with the spreadsheet program, it must be closed or exited.

Office 2003	Office 2007
The program is closed or exited as follows: ➤➤ Close all open files (workbooks).	
➤ ▣ File menu 🖱. ➤ ▣ Exit 🖱.	➤ ▣ Office button 🔲 🖱. ➤ ▣ Close 🖱.

The program may ask if changes to the workbook are to be saved. Select Yes or No as appropriate.

The program will close down and the Windows desktop will be displayed.

Task 4.1.8

(a) Load the spreadsheet program.
(b) Enter the data shown in Figure 4.6 into the cells indicated.
(c) Enter a formula into each shaded cell that will multiply the contents of the cells to the left.

	A	B	C	D	E
1					
2	2	7			
3					
4	5	8			
5					
6	12	14			
7					
8	23	45	67		
9					
10	54	48	24		
11					
12	248	25	59		
13					

Figure 4.6

MULTIPLICATION

The multiplication operator is the star (*) symbol, which is located on the top row of the number keypad and over the number eight (⇧ 8) on the main keyboard.

The procedure for multiplication is as follows:

➤➤   Cell in which the answer is to go 🖱.

➤➤   =

➤➤   First cell to be multiplied 🖱.

➤➤   *

➤➤   Next cell to be multiplied 🖱.

➤➤   *

➤➤   Next cell to be multiplied 🖱.

➤➤   Continue the process until all multiplications have been done ⌨.

Task 4.1.9

(a) Enter more numbers on other rows and practise multiplying them.
(b) Continue until you are sure that you are able to multiply any numbers.

Task 4.1.10

(a) Change some of the figures entered in the spreadsheet and check the new answers.

(b) Close the workbook (file). (There is no need to save the workbook at this stage.)

Task 4.1.11

(a) Start a new workbook (file).

(b) Enter the data shown in Figure 4.7 into the cells indicated on the first sheet (Sheet1).

(c) Enter a formula into each shaded cell that will divide the contents of the first cells on the row by the other number(s).

	A	B	C	D	E
1					
2	8	2			
3					
4	24	4			
5					
6	32	8			
7					
8	60	5			
9					
10	1536	24	16		
11					
12	4158	33	21		
13					

Figure 4.7

DIVISION

The division operator is the forward slash (/) symbol, which is located on the top row of the number keypad and beside the right-hand Shift key on the main keyboard.

The procedure for division is as follows:

➤➤   🔺 Cell in which the answer is to go 🖱.

➤➤   =

➤➤   🔺 Cell to be divided (the bigger number) 🖱.

continued

➤➤ /

➤➤ Cell to be divided by 🖰.

➤➤ /

➤➤ Next cell to be divided by 🖰.

➤➤ Continue the process until all divisions have been done .

Task 4.1.12

(a) Enter more numbers on other rows and practise dividing them.
(b) Continue until you are sure you are able to divide any numbers.

Task 4.1.13

Change some of the numbers entered in the spreadsheet and check the new answers.

MULTIPLE OPERATORS

The symbols used to perform the calculations (+, −, *, /) are called **mathematical operators**, or just operators. There are more operators that we will be using as we progress through the tasks in this section.

All the mathematical operators may be used together in a single formula. However, when using these operators together, it is good practice to write down the formula in normal maths format first and then as a single line formula using +, −, *, / operators in order to ensure that it is correct. In writing out the formula it is sufficient to use the numbers and not the cell references.

The rule of multiplication and division before addition and subtraction applies here – as it does in all mathematical calculations. However, brackets can be used to ensure that part of a calculation gets priority. A simple example may help to clarify this point.

Look at the following mathematical formula:

$\dfrac{6 + 4}{2}$ The answer to $\dfrac{10}{2} = 5$

When writing this on a single line the tendency is to write it as follows: 6 + 4/2
In this case the division will be performed first with the result 6 + 2 = 8.

This is obviously the wrong answer so brackets must be used to ensure that the addition is performed before the division. Therefore, this equation would be written as follows:

(6 + 4)/2 This will produce 10/2 = 5, the correct answer.

Task 4.1.14

Open a new workbook and enter the data shown below into cells on the rows indicated on the first sheet. Write out each equation that will be entered into the spreadsheet, using the numbers instead of the cell references (ensure that you use brackets where a calculation is to be performed before a multiplication or division). Enter a formula into the next cell on the right of the last figure on each row to perform the calculation.

(a) Row 2 $24 + 12 - 15$

(b) Row 4 $36 + 14 + 12 - 56$

(c) Row 6 $\dfrac{24 + 30}{6}$

(d) Row 8 $\dfrac{24 + 28}{10 + 14}$

(e) Row 10 $\dfrac{24 + 46 - 6}{12 + 20}$

(f) Row 12 $\dfrac{60 + 12 + 24}{6 - 4 + 16}$

(g) Row 14 $\dfrac{22}{44} + \dfrac{16 + 8}{26 - 4}$

(h) Row 16 $\dfrac{18 + 4}{4} \times \dfrac{24 - 8 - 4}{2 + 4}$

(i) Save the workbook with the filename **Task 4.1.14**.

(j) Close the workbook.

SAVING A WORKBOOK

Everything saved on a computer is saved as a file with a filename. The first time a workbook is saved it is necessary to give it a filename, which is done while saving it.

Office 2003	Office 2007
The procedure for saving a workbook and giving it a filename is as follows:	
➤ File menu.	➤ Office button .

➤➤   Save as. (*The save as window will appear.*)

➤➤   Select the folder into which the file is to be saved (if necessary) in the 'Save in' field.

continued

➤➤ Type a name for this file in the 'Filename' field. Simply type over Book# while it is still highlighted, and as soon as you type the first letter the old filename will disappear.

➤➤ 🖱 Save 🖱.

Any time the file is to be saved, after giving it a name, the procedure is as follows:

➤➤ 🖱 Save icon 💾 🖱.

Note: When using Office **2007**, files may need to be saved in the older format as the Office **2007** format is not compatible with older versions of Office. Files may be saved in the older format as described above or the following, slightly simpler method may be used.

➤ 🖱 Office button 🪟 🖱.

➤ ⬦ Save as.

➤ ⬦ Excel 97 – 2003 Workbook 🖱. (*The save as window will appear.*)

➤ Select the folder, if necessary, where you wish to save this file in the 'Save n' field.

➤ Type the filename you wish to give this file in the 'Filename' field.

➤ 🖱 Save button 🖱.

Task 4.1.15

(a) Open the workbook named **Task 4.1.14**.

(b) Add the following problem on row 18:

$$\frac{16 + 8}{15 - 3} \times \frac{26 + 18 - 8}{3 \times 2}$$

(c) Save the workbook again with the same filename.

(d) Close the workbook.

OPENING AN EXISTING WORKBOOK (FILE)

Every workbook that has been saved is saved as a file in a folder on a disk. Any saved file may be opened and worked on again.

Office 2003	Office 2007
The procedure for opening a file is as follows:	
➤ 🖙 Open icon 🖻 🖰.	➤ 🖙 Office button 🔘 🖰.
	➤ ✛ Open icon 🖻 🖰.

(The open window will appear, which is practically the same as the save as window.)

➤➤ 🖙 Select the correct folder and a list of files will appear.

➤➤ 🖙 Required file 🖰. **OR** 🖙 Required file 🖰.

🖙 Open button 🖰.

It may be necessary to select the drive and folder as for saving a file.

Task 4.1.16

(a) Start a new workbook and enter the data shown in Figure 4.8 on the first sheet.
(b) Rename the sheet to read 'Accounts'.
(c) Enter formulae into the shaded cells to calculate Mary's total income for each week. (Total = Allowance + Work)
(d) Save the workbook with the filename **Marys Accounts**.

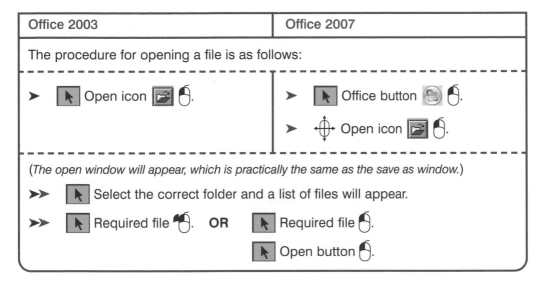

	A	B	C	D	E
1		Mary's Accounts			
2					
3		Week 1	Week 2	Week 3	Week 4
4	Income				
5	Allowance	25	25	25	25
6	Work	50	45	40	50
7	Total				
8					

Figure 4.8

RENAMING A SHEET

Instead of having each sheet in a workbook named Sheet1, Sheet2, etc., it is possible to give a specific name to each sheet.

A sheet is renamed as follows:

➤➤ 🖱 Sheet name, e.g. **Sheet1** 🖱. (*Sheet1 becomes highlighted.*)

➤➤ 🖱 Type the new name ⌨.

Task 4.1.17

(a) Add the data relating to Mary's expenses in Figure 4.9 to the spreadsheet.
(b) Enter formulae into the shaded cells to calculate Mary's total expenses for each week. (Total = Phone + Cinema + Sweets + Books)
(c) Save the workbook again with the same filename.

9	Expenses				
10	Phone	20	20	30	20
11	Cinema	12	6	8	15
12	Sweets	8	10	6	14
13	Books	6	9	10	7
14	Total				

Figure 4.9

Task 4.1.18

(a) Complete the sheet by adding the two words 'Savings' and 'Total' in the cells shown in Figure 4.10.
(b) Calculate Mary's savings for each week by entering formulae into each of the shaded cells on the savings row under each week. {Savings = Total (Income) – Total (Expenses)}
(c) Calculate the total for each row by entering formulae into the shaded cells in the column labelled 'Total'. (Total = Week 1 + Week 2 + Week 3 + Week 4)
(d) Save the workbook again with the same filename.

	A	B	C	D	E	F
		Mary's Accounts				
		Week 1	Week 2	Week 3	Week 4	Total
	Income					
	Allowance	25	25	25	25	
	Work	50	45	40	50	
	Total					
	Expenses					
	Phone	20	20	30	20	
	Cinema	12	6	8	15	
	Sweets	8	10	6	14	
	Books	6	9	10	7	
	Total					
	Savings					

Figure 4.10

Task 4.1.19

(a) What would Mary's total income and total savings be if her allowance went up to 27 per week?

(b) What would Mary's total savings be if she stopped buying sweets every week?

BLANKING OUT CELL CONTENTS

The contents of a cell, whether text, numbers or formulae, may be cleared or blanked out.

A cell is cleared as follows:

➤➤ 🖱 Cell to be cleared 🖱.

➤➤ Press the Delete key.

EDITING CELL CONTENTS

It is sometimes easier to simply type the new contents in a cell rather than editing it. However, if a cell contains a heading or a long word then editing (instead of replacing) may be more efficient.

The contents of a cell are edited as follows:

➤➤ 🖱 Cell to be edited 🖱.

➤➤ 🖱 Required position in the formula bar (the cursor changes to an I-beam) 🖱.

continued

> ➤➤ Delete characters to the left using the Backspace key.
>
> ➤➤ Insert characters by simply typing them.
>
> ➤➤ Press the Enter key when editing is complete.

Data in a Spreadsheet

When talking about data that is entered in a spreadsheet, it is useful to be able to identify the different types of data a spreadsheet may contain. The data may be divided into three basic types, as follows:

Constant Data   This is usually headings or labels but can be anything that is entered on the spreadsheet and will never change. It may be main headings, which run across a number of columns, or headings for columns or rows. Column and row headings are sometimes referred to as **labels**.

Variable Data   This is the numbers that are directly entered into the cells on the spreadsheet by typing the number in a particular cell.

Output Data   This is the numbers that appear in a spreadsheet as a result of a calculation, i.e. results produced by a formula.

When designing a spreadsheet it is necessary to identify what data types are involved. This is covered in more detail later in the spreadsheet design section.

Task 4.1.20 (Additional)

Produce the additional spreadsheets specified in **Task 4A-1** on the CD.

Task 4.2.1

(a) Enter the constant and variable data shown in Figure 4.11 into a blank workbook. Adjust column widths as necessary.

(b) Insert formulae into the shaded cells to calculate the following:

- The total income for each month.
- The total expenses for each month.
- All the totals for the six months in the Total column, i.e. column H.

(c) Save the workbook with the filename **Household Finances**.

(d) Insert the heading 'Savings' in cell A26.

(e) Insert formulae on the Savings row to calculate the following:

- The savings for each month.
- The total savings for the six months.

(f) Save the workbook again with the same filename.

	A	B	C	D	E	F	G	H
1			Household Finances					
2								
3		Jan	Feb	Mar	Apr	May	Jun	Total
4	Income							
5	Total Wage	1650	1824	1647	1842	1486	1643	
6								
7	Investment	56	0	0	72	0	0	
8								
9	Child Welfare	70	70	70	70	70	70	
10								
11	Total Income							
12								
13	Expenses							
14	Rent	250	250	250	250	250	250	
15								
16	Groceries	460	480	475	560	420	510	
17								
18	Bus Fares	98	110	88	112	96	148	
19								
20	Household Bills	84	394	46	847	88	245	
21								
22	Entertainment	240	125	96	280	320	186	
23								
24	Total Expenses							

Figure 4.11

ADJUSTING COLUMN WIDTHS

It is sometimes necessary to change the width of a column or several columns. There are a number of ways of doing this, but Method 1 below is generally the simplest.

Column widths are adjusted as follows:

Method 1

➤➤ ▌▶▏ Line between column labels ⌕.

(*The cursor changes to a black double-headed arrow* (✛) *and the width of the column will appear in the name box.*)

➤➤ ▌▶▏ Drag the line to the required width ⌕.

continued

Method 2

➤➤ 🖱 Line between columns 🖱.

(A black double-headed arrow appears.)

Method 3

Office 2003	Office 2007
➤ 🖱 Format menu 🖱. ➤ ✛ Column. ➤ ✛ Width 🖱.	➤ Select the Home ribbon. ➤ 🖱 Format icon ▦ 🖱. ➤ ✛ Column Width 🖱.

➤➤ Type the required width in the field labelled 'Column width'.

➤➤ 🖱 OK 🖱.

CHANGING CELL ALIGNMENT

As already mentioned the data in a cell will line up to the left or right depending on the type of data.

The alignment of a cell or group of cells is changed as follows:

➤➤ Select the cell(s) to be changed.

➤➤ 🖱 Required alignment icon on the toolbar ▤ ▤ ▤ 🖱.

Task 4.2.2

(a) Open the workbook named **Household Finances** (if not already open).

(b) Change the alignment of the column headings in Household Finances to centre align.

(c) Change the alignment of the row headings Total Income, Total Expenses and Savings to right align.

(d) Save the workbook again with the same filename.

(e) Enter your name in cell A28.

(f) Preview the sheet.

(g) Print one copy.

EDITING FORMULAE

At this stage the user will probably have begun to recognise formulae and may be able to recognise an error in one if it occurs. A formula may be edited in the same way as text or numbers.

A formula is edited as follows:

➤➤ 🖱 Cell containing the formula 🖱.

(The formula will appear in the formula bar.)

➤➤ 🖱 Required position in the edit line 🖱.

➤➤ Delete characters using the Backspace key.

➤➤ Insert characters by simply typing them.

➤➤ Press the Enter key when editing is complete.

USING SCROLL BARS

It is only possible to fit small spreadsheets on the screen. When viewing and working on larger spreadsheets it is necessary to move around the spreadsheet. There are two scroll bars, one located on the right and one on the bottom of the worksheet. These scroll bars allow the user to move the screen over the sheet in the direction of the arrow.

Scroll bars are operated as follows:

➤➤ 🖱 Arrow on the scroll bar 🖱.

(Each click of the mouse button will move the screen one row or column in the direction of the arrow.)

If the mouse button is held down (🖱) while pointing to the scroll arrow, the screen will scroll (keep moving) over the sheet in the direction of the arrow.

If your mouse has a scroll wheel then it is a simple matter of rotating the wheel in order to scroll up and down the sheet.

FREEZING THE TOP ROW(S) OR LEFT COLUMN(S)

When working on a large worksheet it may be useful to be able to keep the top row or rows (containing labels) while scrolling down the sheet. It is also possible to retain the first column or columns while scrolling across the sheet. The process of retaining the top row(s) and/or the left column(s) is called **freezing**.

Office 2003	Office 2007
Rows and columns are frozen as follows:	
➤➤ Select the cell below (or to the right of) the row/column to be frozen.	
➤ ▣ Windows menu 🖰.	➤ Select the View ribbon.
➤ ✛ Freeze panes 🖰.	➤ ▣ ▤ Freeze Panes.
	➤ ✛ Freeze panes 🖰.

As you scroll, the frozen row(s) and/or column(s) will remain in position.

Office 2003	Office 2007
The sheet may be unfrozen as follows:	
➤ ▣ Windows menu 🖰.	➤ Select the View ribbon.
➤ ✛ Unfreeze panes 🖰.	➤ ▣ ▤ Unfreeze Panes 🖰.

SPLIT SCREEN VIEWING

When working on a large worksheet it may be useful to be able to view two separate parts of the worksheet at the same time. This may be achieved by splitting the screen. When the screen is split it allows two different parts of the sheet to be viewed and scrolled independently. A worksheet may be split horizontally or vertically, using the split box handles at the top of the vertical scroll bar and the right of the bottom scroll bar.

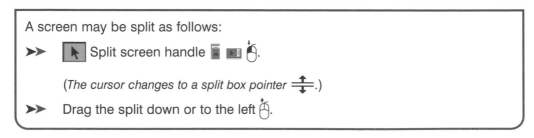

A screen may be split as follows:

➤➤ ▣ Split screen handle ▤ ▥ 🖰.

    (The cursor changes to a split box pointer ≑.)

➤➤ Drag the split down or to the left 🖰.

PREVIEW A SHEET

Previewing a sheet allows the user to see what it will look like when printed. A sheet may be previewed at any time but it is always a good idea to do so before printing.

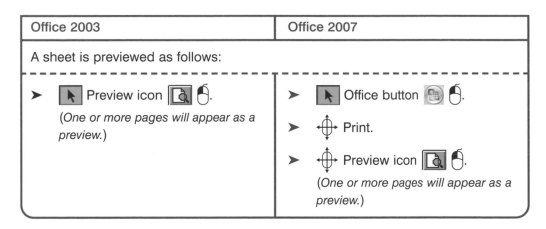

Office 2003	Office 2007
A sheet is previewed as follows:	
➤ Preview icon. (*One or more pages will appear as a preview.*)	➤ Office button. ➤ Print. ➤ Preview icon. (*One or more pages will appear as a preview.*)

It is possible to move from page to page using the right scroll bar or the **Page Up** and **Page Down** keys.

Note: It is possible to place the preview icon on the Quick Access Toolbar in Office **2007**.

PRINTING A SHEET

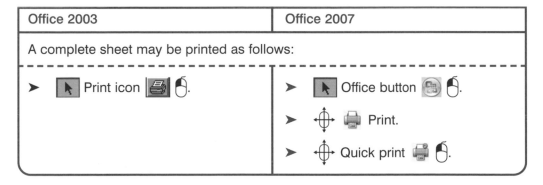

Office 2003	Office 2007
A complete sheet may be printed as follows:	
➤ Print icon.	➤ Office button. ➤ Print. ➤ Quick print.

The complete document will be printed on the default printer.

If the spreadsheet is larger than one page then it will automatically print the number of pages required, as seen in print preview.

We will examine more extensive printing options later.

Task 4.2.3 (Additional)

Produce the additional spreadsheets specified in **Task 4A-2** on the CD.

Task 4.3.1

(a) Enter the constant and variable data shown in Figure 4.12 into a blank workbook. Adjust column widths as necessary.

(b) Insert formulae into the shaded cells to calculate the following:

- The total marks for each student, using the SUM or AutoSum function (see SUM and AutoSum functions below).
- The average mark for each student. (The average is simply the total divided by the number of subjects. See the AVERAGE function below.)
- The average percentage for each student.

The average percentage is $\dfrac{\text{Total Mark}}{\text{Maximum Value}} \times 100$

= Total/640 * 100

Note: In this case we are actually typing in numbers in the formula as well as selecting the contents of cells.

(c) Display all figures as integers, i.e. no decimal places (see Controlling Decimal Places below).

(d) Save the workbook with the filename **Subject Results**.

	A	B	C	D	E	F	G	H	I
1		Subject Results for Computer Studies Class							
2									
3	Each subject is marked out of 80 marks								
4									
5	Subject	Mark	Jane	Mary	Paul	Rose	John	Peter	Kate
6									
7	Computer Theory	75	68	72	65	79	77	68	68
8	File Management	68	56	68	75	68	68	71	66
9	Word Processing	56	52	45	68	59	75	74	64
10	Spreadsheets	49	47	58	58	48	72	80	69
11	Databases	57	72	45	56	34	78	59	61
12	Presentation	72	77	67	56	78	45	67	60
13	Internet	74	56	76	36	49	63	77	71
14	E-Mail	68	49	62	41	59	80	59	64
15									
16	Total								
17									
18	Average Mark								
19									
20	Average Percentage								

Figure 4.12

THE SUM FUNCTION

So far we have used the addition operator to add up numbers, but spreadsheet programs provide a range of functions that may be used to perform calculations. The simplest function we will be using is the SUM function. This function is used to quickly find the sum of a number of figures that are in adjacent cells and can therefore be used instead of a number of addition operations. It must be remembered, however, that if the cells to be summed are not adjacent then it may be necessary to resort to the addition operator.

The SUM function is operated as follows:

➤➤ Select the cell into which the answer is to go.

➤➤ [=].

➤➤ Type **SUM**.

➤➤ [(]

➤➤ [↖] First cell of the group of figures 🖱.

➤➤ ⊕ To the last cell to be included 🖱. (*A dashed rectangle will appear around the selected figures.*)

➤➤ [)]. (*If this step is omitted, the spreadsheet will add the end bracket.*)

➤➤ [↵]

The formula should look like this: = **SUM(B7:B14)**

THE AUTOSUM FUNCTION

A quick way of operating the SUM function is to use the icon on the toolbar.

The AutoSum function is operated as follows:

(**2007** – *Select the Home ribbon.*)

➤➤ Select the cell into which the answer is to go.

➤➤ [↖] AutoSum icon (Σ) 🖱.

➤➤ [↖] First cell of the group of figures 🖱.

➤➤ ⊕ To the last cell to be included 🖱.

➤➤ [↵].

Note: (a) After the AutoSum function is selected, a dashed rectangle will appear around a suggested set of figures. If these are the required figures then simply press the Enter key. If they are not the correct set of figures then the required figures must be selected in the same way as for the SUM function. (b) The formula will be exactly the same as the SUM function above.

AVERAGE

The average of a group of numbers is simply the sum of the numbers divided by the number of numbers. In the above task the average can be calculated by simply producing a formula to divide the total by eight.

However, spreadsheet programs provide an AVERAGE function, which operates in the same way as the SUM function. Generally, it is preferable to use the AVERAGE function when finding averages.

The average function is operated as follows:

➤➤ Select the cell into which the answer is to go.

➤➤ | = |.

➤➤ Type AVERAGE. (**Note:** Some programs use AVG instead of AVERAGE.)

➤➤ | (|.

➤➤ ▶ First cell of the group of figures 🖱.

➤➤ ⊕ To the last cell to be included 🖱.

➤➤ |) |. (*If this step is omitted, the spreadsheet will add the end bracket.*)

➤➤ |◢|.

The formula should look like this: = **AVERAGE(B7:B14)**.

CONTROLLING DECIMAL PLACES

If a calculation results in a large number of figures after the decimal point, the number will be displayed with as many of these figures as will fit in the cell. If we wish to control the number of decimal places then there are two ways of doing so.

Decimal places are controlled as follows:

Method 1

(**2007** – *Select the Home ribbon.*)

➤➤ Select the cell with the number.

➤➤ ▶ Increase/Decrease decimal icon ⬚⬚ 🖱.

➤➤ Repeat the second step and the decimal places will increase/decrease by one place for each click of the mouse.

Method 2

Office 2003	Office 2007
➤ 🖱 Format menu 🖱. ➤ 🖱 Cells 🖱.	➤ Select the Home ribbon. ➤ 🖱 Small arrow on the bottom right of the Number group ▫ 🖱.

(The format cells window will appear.)

➤➤ 🖱 Number tab at the top, if not already selected 🖱.

➤➤ 🖱 Number 🖱. *(The number options will appear.)*

➤➤ 🖱 Decimal places adjusting arrows ▤ 🖱.

    (The up arrow increases decimal places – the down arrow decreases decimal places.)

➤➤ Repeat the last step and the decimal places will increase/decrease by one place for each click of the mouse.

➤➤ 🖱 OK 🖱.

Note: If a cell is not wide enough to display the number stored in it then the spreadsheet program will display the cell with hash marks (########). If the cell is widened then the number will be displayed.

SELECTING GROUPS OF CELLS

It is sometimes necessary to work on a group of cells at the same time. This is particularly useful when changing the alignment of cells, altering decimal places and performing any other formatting on cells. In order to carry out an operation on a group of cells, we must first select all the cells we wish to work on.

A group of cells is selected as follows:

➤➤ 🖱 First cell to be selected 🖱.

➤➤ ⊕ To the last cell to be included 🖱.

➤➤ The first cell will be white and the rest of the cells will be shaded.

An entire row or column may be selected as follows:

➤➤ ▮ Row number/column label 🖱.

(The row/column will appear shaded.)

A number of rows or columns may be selected as follows:

➤➤ ▮ Row number/column label of the first row/column to be selected 🖱.

➤➤ ✛To the last row/column to be included 🖱.

MOVING A GROUP OF CELLS

Once a group of cells has been selected they may be moved to any position on the sheet.

A group of cells are repositioned as follows:

➤➤ ▮ To the edge of the box surrounding the selection 🖱.

(The cross changes to a four headed arrow ✛.)

➤➤ Drag the selection to the required position 🖱.

Task 4.3.2

(a) Enter the constant and variable data shown in Figure 4.13 into a blank workbook. Adjust column widths as necessary.

(b) Align the column headings as shown.

(c) Align the headings 'Total:' and 'Average:' to the right.

(d) Insert formulae into the shaded cells to calculate the following:

- The total expenses for each month.
- The average expenses for each month.
- The average for each expense, i.e. Rent, wages, etc.

(e) Display all figures with two decimal places.

(f) Save the workbook with the filename **Office Expenses**.

(g) Move the main heading 'Office Expenses' to column B and then edit it to read 'Office Expenses for the First Six Months of the Year'.

(h) The rent was increased to 475.00 in June. Enter this on the sheet and note the results.

Note: The alteration of one figure changed three other figures. In actual practice there is no limit to the number of changes that may occur due to changing one figure.

(i) Save the workbook again with the same filename.

	A	B	C	D	E	F	G	H
1			Office Expenses for Six Months					
2								
3	Expense	Jan	Feb	Mar	Apr	May	Jun	Average
4	Rent	450.00	450.00	450.00	450.00	450.00	450.00	
5	Wages	720.00	740.00	720.00	750.00	720.00	720.00	
6	Electricity	125.36	134.28	122.48	105.80	98.50	88.60	
7	Telephone/Fax	248.45	267.45	302.48	238.18	246.27	221.45	
8	Internet	0.00	212.35	0.00	168.24	0.00	156.25	
9	Stationery	23.45	56.78	34.25	46.21	23.84	12.50	
10	Advertising	0.00	0.00	565.00	0.00	0.00	485.00	
11	Travel	124.00	150.00	148.00	135.00	187.00	206.00	
12								
13	Total:							
14								
15	Average:							

Figure 4.13

Task 4.3.3 (Additional)

Produce the additional spreadsheets specified in **Task 4A-3** on the CD.

Task 4.4.1

(a) Enter the constant variable data shown in Figure 4.14 into a blank workbook. Adjust column widths as necessary.

Note: Use the fill command to enter the Cleaning figures for weeks 2, 3 and 4.

(b) Align the column headings as shown.
(c) Align the heading 'Total:' to the right.
(d) Insert formulae into the shaded cells to calculate the following:

- The total expenses for each week.
- The total expenses for each category.
- The average for each category.

Note: produce each formula only once and then fill it into other cells.

(e) Display all figures with two decimal places.
(f) Save the workbook with the filename **Petty Cash**.

(g) Move the main heading 'Petty Cash Expenditure' to column B and then edit it to read 'Petty Cash Expenditure for January'.

(h) Insert a row between the column headings and the Post row. (Practise inserting and deleting rows and columns.)

(i) Display all figures in currency format.

(j) Save the workbook again with the same filename.

(k) Enter your name in cell A18. Preview the sheet and then print one copy.

	A	B	C	D	E	F	G
1			Petty Cash Expenditure				
2							
3		Week	Week	Week	Week		
4		Ending	Ending	Ending	Ending		
5	Category	07/01/05	14/01/05	21/01/05	28/01/05	Total	Average
6	Post	€ 56.25	€ 48.51	€ 65.21	€ 42.15		
7	Stationery	€ 25.00	€ 30.00	€ 20.00	€ 18.00		
8	Tea/Coffee	€ 10.00	€ 15.00	€ 10.00	€ 12.00		
9	Computer Accessories	€ 6.00	€ 8.00	€ 12.00	€ 9.00		
10	Cleaning	€ 10.00	€ 10.00	€ 10.00	€ 10.00		
11	Travel	€ 5.60	€ 6.20	€ 4.80	€ 8.75		
12	Office Supplies	€ 12.50	€ 8.60	€ 15.40	€ 12.60		
13	Miscellaneous	€ 3.50	€ 8.75	€ 12.00	€ 4.50		
14							
15	Total:						

Figure 4.14

FILLING (REPLICATING) CELL CONTENTS

Where the same data is repeated in a number of cells, it is possible to copy (fill or replicate) the data from one cell into a number of other cells.

Office 2003	Office 2007

Data is copied into other cells as follows:

Method 1

➤ Cell containing the data.

➤ Bottom right-hand corner of the selected cell.
(The fill cursor (+) appears.)

➤ To include the cells into which the data is to be copied.

Method 2

➤ Cell containing the data.

continued

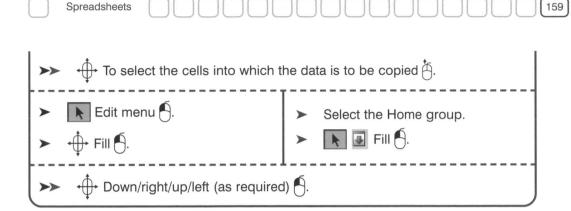

➤ Edit menu 🖱.	➤ Select the Home group.
➤ Fill 🖱.	➤ ▣ Fill 🖱.

➤➤ Down/right/up/left (as required) 🖱.

FILLING (REPLICATING) FORMULAE

If a cell contains a formula instead of data, then the formula will be copied (replicated) into other cells instead of the data in the cell. The spreadsheet will make all necessary adjustments to the formula in order to make the same calculation in the new row or column.

It is normal practice to only produce the formula in one cell, check that the answer is correct and then fill the formula into the other cells in the row/column where the same calculation is to be performed.

INSERTING EXTRA ROWS

One extra row is inserted by first selecting the position where the row is to be inserted. This is done by selecting any cell in the first row that will be moved down as a result of the insertion.

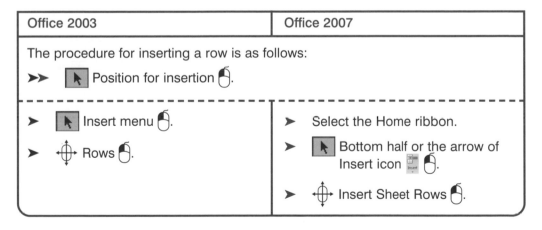

Office 2003	Office 2007

The procedure for inserting a row is as follows:

➤➤ Position for insertion 🖱.

➤ Insert menu 🖱.	➤ Select the Home ribbon.
➤ Rows 🖱.	➤ Bottom half or the arrow of Insert icon 🖱.
	➤ Insert Sheet Rows 🖱.

(The extra blank row will be inserted above the selected cell.)

INSERTING EXTRA COLUMNS

The procedure for inserting columns is similar to that for inserting rows. In this case the new column will be inserted on the left-hand side of the selected cell, i.e. the columns will move to the right.

Office 2003	Office 2007
The procedure for inserting a column is as follows: ➤➤ ▮ Position for insertion 🖱.	
➤ ▮ Insert menu 🖱. ➤ ✛ Columns 🖱.	➤ Select the Home ribbon. ➤ ▮ Bottom half or the arrow of Insert icon 🔲 🖱. ➤ ✛ Insert Sheet Columns 🖱.

(The extra blank column will be inserted on the left of the selected cell.)

DELETING A ROW OR COLUMN

The complete row or column can be deleted by first selecting the complete row or column and then deleting it.

Office 2003	Office 2007
A row or column is deleted as follows: ➤➤ ▮ Row/column label 🖱. *(The row/column will appear shaded.)*	
➤ ▮ Edit menu 🖱. ➤ ▮ Delete 🖱.	➤ Select the Home ribbon. ➤ ▮ Bottom half or the arrow of Delete icon 🔲 🖱. ➤ ✛ Delete Sheet Rows/Columns 🖱.

(The row or column will be deleted, including all its contents.)

CHANGING CELL FORMAT

There are a number of ways of displaying the contents of a cell. The most common format would be to display numbers as euros with a € sign in front of them. This is called the format of a cell and some of the most common formats are available as icons in the toolbar or ribbon. The full range of formats are available from the format menu or by selecting the small arrow on the bottom of the Number group. The formats we will be using are those on the toolbar.

The format of a cell or group of cells is adjusted as follows:

(**2007** – *Select the Home ribbon.*)

➤➤ Select the cell(s) to be formatted.

➤➤ ▐▲ Format icon required ▐ 🖳 ▐ % ▐ , ▐ 🖱.

Note: Once the format of a cell is changed, then even if the contents of the cell are deleted, the format will remain. This means that when another number is entered into the cell, it will be displayed with the € sign, % sign, or whatever format has been previously applied to the cell.

Office 2003	Office 2007

A cell may be restored to a general format as follows:

➤ Select the cell(s) to be formatted.	➤ Select the Home ribbon.
➤ ▐▲ Format menu 🖱.	➤ Select the cell(s) to be formatted.
➤ ✛ Cells 🖱. (*The format cells window will appear.*)	➤ ▐▲ Arrow beside the formatting applied ▐ Accounting ▾ ▐ 🖱.
➤ ▐▲ Number tab at the top, if not already selected 🖱.	(*The word in the icon may be different.*)
➤ ▐▲ General 🖱.	➤ ✛ General 🖱.
➤ ▐▲ OK 🖱.	

Task 4.4.2 (Additional)

Produce the additional spreadsheets specified in **Task 4A-4** on the CD.

Task 4.5.1

(a) Enter the constant and variable data shown in Figure 4.15 into a blank workbook. Adjust column widths as necessary.
(b) Align the row/column headings and data as shown.
(c) Align the two main headings across columns A to K. (See below for how to align across columns.)
(d) Align the 'Sales Quantity' heading across columns C to G.

(e) Insert formulae into the shaded cells to calculate the following:

- The Item Total for each item.
- The Profit per item on each item.
- The Total Profit per item on each item for the week.
- The Weekly Totals for each column.

(Remember to produce each formula only once and then fill it into other cells.)

(f) Format all money amounts as currency.

(g) Format the main heading 'Mini Company Report' to be 14 pt, bold.

(h) Format the second heading 'Accounts ... 14/02/2005' to be 12 pt, bold.

(i) Format all the column headings to be bold.

(j) Insert a row between the column headings and the first item.

(k) Sort the spreadsheet so that the items appear in alphabetical order.

(l) Save the spreadsheet with the filename **Mini Company**.

	A	B	C	D	E	F	G	H	I	J	K
1	Mini Company Report										
2											
3	Accounts for Week Ending 14/02/2005										
4											
5		Item	Sales Quantity					Item	Sales	Profit	Total Profit
6	Item	Cost	10/02/05	11/02/05	12/02/05	13/02/05	14/02/05	Total	Price	per Item	per Item
7	Plain Roll	€ 0.60	12	15	11	15	13		€ 0.95		
8	Cheese Roll	€ 1.15	24	26	32	26	28		€ 2.25		
9	Ham Roll	€ 1.95	15	24	12	16	18		€ 2.75		
10	Chicken Roll	€ 2.05	8	12	18	22	24		€ 2.85		
11	Cheese Sandwich	€ 0.95	11	9	15	18	17		€ 2.15		
12	Ham Sandwich	€ 1.65	14	24	18	24	22		€ 2.55		
13	Chicken Sandwich	€ 1.70	28	16	24	17	20		€ 2.65		
14	Chocolate Bars	€ 0.45	144	132	158	166	176		€ 0.80		
15	Crisps	€ 0.38	86	108	94	105	114		€ 0.75		
16	Water (Plain & Sparkling)	€ 0.55	156	134	124	115	108		€ 1.35		
17	Juices (All Flavours)	€ 1.10	32	46	56	68	75		€ 1.95		
18	Tea	€ 0.70	154	168	158	164	176		€ 2.20		
19	Coffee	€ 0.85	86	92	82	79	87		€ 2.50		
20											
21	Weekly Totals:										

Figure 4.15

ENHANCING

Bold, italics and underlining are used to add emphasis to such things as headings and important figures on the spreadsheet.

Bold, italics and underlining are applied as follows:

(**2007** – *Select the Home ribbon*.)

Method 1

This method is used with text/data which has already been typed.

➤➤ Select the cell containing the text/data to be enhanced.

continued

➤➤  required icon **B** *I* <u>U</u> 🖱.

Method 2

This method is used to set the emphasis before entering the text/data.

➤➤ Select the cell into which data is to be entered.

➤➤ 🔼 required icon **B** *I* <u>U</u> 🖱.

➤➤ Type text/data as required.

CENTRING ACROSS COLUMNS

It is possible to centre items across a number of columns in a spreadsheet. This is particularly useful when dealing with headings.

Items are centred across a number of columns as follows:

(**2007** – *Select the Home ribbon.*)

➤➤ Enter the data in one of the columns (usually the first column).

➤➤ Select the cells across which the data is to be centred.

➤➤ 🔼 Merge and centre icon 🔳 🖱.

SORTING A SPREADSHEET

Sometimes it is necessary to sort the data in a spreadsheet in order to produce an output in a desired order, whether alphabetical or numeric. This process is called organising or sorting.

Office 2003	Office 2007
The data in a spreadsheet is sorted as follows: ➤➤ Select the data to be sorted (*ensure that the data in all the columns is selected*).	
➤ 🔼 Data menu 🖱. ➤ ✛ Sort 🖱. (*The sort window will appear.*) ➤ Select Header row **OR** No header row as required.	➤ Select the data ribbon. ➤ 🔼 Sort icon 🔡 🖱 (*The sort window will appear.*) ➤ Tick the box 'My data has headers' if required.

continued

> ➤ Icon in the first 'Sort by' field ▾.
>
> *(The list of labels or headings for this field will be displayed.)*
>
> ➤ Required column label/heading.
>
> ➤ Ascending or descending (as required).
>
> ➤ OK.

> ➤ Icon in the Column 'Sort by' field ▾.
>
> *(The list of labels or headings for this field will be displayed.)*
>
> ➤ Required column label/heading.
>
> ➤ Icon in the Order 'A to Z' field ▾.
>
> ➤ Ascending (A to Z) or descending (Z to A).
>
> ➤ OK.

Note: If all the columns are not selected, then a warning window will appear. It is best to close this window and reselect the data.

Quick Sort

If the data is to be sorted on the first column, then the procedure is simpler and is as follows:

➤➤ Select the data to be sorted (ensure that the data in all the columns is selected).

➤➤ Quick sort icon ᴬᶻ↓ **OR** ᶻᴬ↓.

Task 4.5.2

(a) Open the file **Mini Company**, if not already open.
(b) Sort the spreadsheet on the 'Item Total' column so that the item with the smallest value in this column is at the top.
(c) Preview the sheet (you will notice that the sheet does not fit on one page).
(d) Set the page orientation to be landscape and preview again.
(e) Set the page margins to be 2 cm all around.
(f) Set the printout to appear horizontally centred on the page.
(g) Insert a footer to display Page # (where # is the page number).
(h) Set the printout to display gridlines and preview again.
(i) Save the spreadsheet again with the same filename.
(j) Insert your name on the spreadsheet and print one copy.

PRINTED PAGE SETTINGS

The page setup allows various options regarding the layout of the printed page to be set.

Office 2003
The page setup is selected as follows: ➤ �N File menu 🖰. ➤ ⊹ Page setup 🖰. (*The page setup window will appear.*)

The most common options to be set here are as follows:

Setting Page Orientation

Office 2003	Office 2007
➤ �N Page tab 🖰 (if not already selected). ➤ �N Portrait or landscape, as required 🖰.	➤ Select the Page Layout ribbon. ➤ �N Orientation icon 📄 🖰. ➤ �N Portrait or landscape, as required 🖰.

Setting Margins and Position on Page

Office 2003	Office 2007
➤ �N Margins tab 🖰. ➤ Enter margin sizes as required. ➤ Tick the horizontally and/or vertically boxes as required.	➤ Select the Page Layout ribbon. ➤ �N Margins icon ▥ 🖰. (*A selection of margins will be displayed.*) ➤ Select one of the options offered or select Custom Options.

Displaying Headers and/or Footers

Office 2003	Office 2007
➤ Headers/Footers tab.	➤ Select the Insert ribbon.
➤ Select one of the headers and/or footers provided as follows:	➤ Header and Footer. *(The cursor will appear in the header area, and the header and footer tools design ribbon will be displayed.)*
● Icon in the header/footer field.	➤ Type the header required **OR** Header icon. One of the header options offered.
● One of the header/footer options offered.	➤ Footer icon.
Specific headers/footers may be produced by selecting custom header/footer and entering the data required.	➤ Type the footer required **OR** one of the footer options offered.
	➤ Any cell in the main worksheet.
	➤ Select the View ribbon.
	➤ Normal.

Specific headers/footers may also be produced by simply inserting the desired text and/or graphics into the header and/or footer area.

Displaying Gridlines and Row/Column Headings

Office 2003	Office 2007
➤ Sheet tab.	➤ Select the Page Layout ribbon.
➤ Tick the box(es) as required.	➤ Tick the box to Print Gridlines.
	AND/OR
	➤ Tick the box to Print Headings.

Displaying Column Heading on Each Page

Office 2003	Office 2007
➤ ⬚ Sheet tab ⬚.	➤ Select the Page Layout ribbon.
➤ ⬚ Rows to repeat at top icon ⬚ ⬚.	➤ ⬚ Print Titles icon ⬚ ⬚.
➤ Select the rows on the sheet.	
➤ Close the Page Setup window.	
➤ ⬚ OK ⬚.	

PRINTER SETTINGS

There are a number of options that may be selected from the print window.

Office 2003	Office 2007
The print window is selected as follows:	
➤ ⬚ File menu ⬚.	➤ ⬚ Office button ⬚ ⬚.
➤ ⬚ Print ⬚. (*The print window will appear.*)	➤ ⬚ Print ⬚. (*The print window will appear.*)

The options that we will examine are as follows.

Selecting a Printer

There may be more than one printer connected to the computer and it is therefore necessary to direct the output to the correct printer. This is accomplished as follows:

➤➤ ⬚ Printer name icon ⬚.

➤➤ ⬚ Printer required ⬚.

Selecting the Number of Copies

The program will normally print only one copy of a sheet, but multiple copies may be printed as follows:

➤➤ ▣ Number of copies icon (increase/decrease) ▤ 🖱.

Printing Certain Portions of the Sheet

It is sometimes necessary to only print a certain section of the sheet. This is accomplished as follows:

➤➤ Select the portion of the sheet to be printed (before selecting the print window).

➤➤ Tick the selection box in the print window.

Printing Certain Pages of the Sheet

It is sometimes necessary to only print certain pages of the sheet This is accomplished as follows:

➤➤ ▣ Pages in the page range section 🖱.

➤➤ Type the page numbers in the 'From' and 'To' fields.

COPY AND PASTE COMMAND

Data that is entered on the sheet may be required in another part of the sheet. Instead of retyping this data it is possible to copy the data and paste it into another part of the sheet.

The procedure for copying and pasting is as follows:

(**2007** – *Select the Home ribbon.*)

➤➤ Select data to be copied.

➤➤ ▣ Copy icon 📋 🖱.

➤➤ ▣ Select the cell where the insertion is to start 🖱 (top left-hand corner).

➤➤ ▣ Paste icon 📋 🖱.

CUT AND PASTE COMMAND

Data that is entered in a sheet may be in the wrong place. Instead of deleting the text/data and retyping, it is possible to cut it out of its present position and paste it into a new position.

The procedure for cutting and pasting is as follows:

(**2007** – *Select the Home ribbon.*)

➤➤   Select the text/data to be cut.

➤➤   ▮▸ Cut icon ✄ 🖰.

➤➤   ▮▸ Select the cell where the insertion is to start 🖰. (*top left-hand corner*)

➤➤   ▮▸ Paste icon 📋 🖰.

Task 4.5.3 (Additional)

Produce the additional spreadsheets specified in **Task 4A-5** on the CD.

Task 4.6.1

(a) Enter the constant and variable data shown in Figure 4.16 into a blank workbook. Adjust column widths as necessary.
(b) Align the row/column headings and data as shown.
(c) Align the top and second headings across columns A to I.
(d) Insert formulae into the shaded cells to calculate the following:

- The total income for each month.
- The total expenditure for each month.
- The profit for each month.
- The profit as per cent of income. (*See below for calculating and displaying percentages.*)
- Totals in column H.
- Averages in column I.

(*Remember to produce each formula only once and then fill it into other cells.*)

(e) Format all money amounts as currency, with no decimal places.
(f) Format the main heading font to be 14 pt, bold.
(g) Format the second heading font to be 12 pt, bold.
(h) Format all the column headings to be bold.
(i) Format row headings 'Income' and 'Expenditure' to be bold and centre aligned.

(j) Insert a row between the column headings and the Other Sales and move down the Income heading one cell.

(k) Sort the Income section of the spreadsheet on the Total column so that the highest total sales appears on top.

(l) Sort the Expenditure section of the spreadsheet on the Total column so that the lowest total appears on top.

(m) Insert the following centre-aligned header: 'Income and Expenditure'.

(n) Save the spreadsheet with the filename **Mc Dermot**.

(o) Print the spreadsheet horizontally centred on a landscape page, with gridlines and row and column headings.

	A	B	C	D	E	F	G	H	I
1	Mc Dermot Trading Group								
2									
3	Income and Expenditure Report for first six months								
4									
5	Income	Jan	Feb	Mar	Apr	May	Jun	Total	Average
6	Other Sales	€ 2,840	€ 3,480	€ 3,570	€ 8,640	€ 18,570	€ 20,870		
7	European Sales	€524,980	€ 651,430	€ 684,120	€ 721,300	€ 752,410	€ 725,450		
8	North American Sales	€ 65,200	€ 67,300	€ 69,420	€ 78,500	€ 89,100	€ 102,540		
9	Home Sales	€285,380	€ 305,874	€ 315,890	€ 328,470	€ 315,640	€ 318,460		
10									
11	Total Income:								
12									
13	Expenditure								
14	Materials	€245,840	€ 287,620	€ 354,850	€ 428,410	€ 432,830	€ 398,400		
15	Transport	€ 89,500	€ 78,560	€ 82,470	€ 85,640	€ 76,420	€ 85,470		
16	Wages and Salaries	€ 28,650	€ 27,540	€ 29,840	€ 28,450	€ 27,900	€ 28,460		
17									
18	Total Expenditure:								
19									
20	Profit:								
21									
22	Profit as % of Income:								

Figure 4.16

DISPLAYING PERCENTAGES

As mentioned earlier, percentage is calculated as $\dfrac{\text{Actual Value}}{\text{Maximum Value}} \times 100$.

However, the spreadsheet program provides a % icon, which will automatically multiply by 100 and display the result with a % sign.
When using the percent formatting it is only necessary to calculate $\dfrac{\text{Actual Value}}{\text{Maximum Value}}$.

In the case of 'Profit as % of Income' above, the **actual value** will be the profit and the **maximum value** will be the total income. Once the value has been calculated it will be a figure less than 1, e.g. 0.59. The cell must then be formatted to display %.

Percentages are displayed as follows:

(**2007** – *Select the Home ribbon.*)

➤➤ Select the cell(s) to be formatted.

➤➤ [▶] % icon [%] 🖱. (*The figure will be multiplied by 100 and the % sign added, e.g. 59%.*)

Task 4.6.2

(a) Open the file **Mc Dermot** (if not already open).
(b) Insert today's date into cell A4.
(c) Increase the height of row 2 to 18.
(d) Save the workbook with the filename **Mc Dermot I&E**.

INSERTING DATE OR TIME

Today's date and/or the present time may be inserted from the computer clock into a cell.

Today's date is inserted as follows:

➤➤ Select the cell into which the date is to be displayed.

➤➤ [Ctrl] [;]

The current time is inserted as follows:

➤➤ Select the cell into which the time is to be displayed.

➤➤ [Ctrl] [⇧] [;]

Date and time are inserted as follows:

➤➤ Select the cell into which the date and time is to be displayed.

➤➤ Enter =NOW( ).

Calculations may be carried out on dates and times in the same way as if they were numbers, e.g. two dates may be subtracted in order to calculate the number of days between the two dates. Similarly, two times may be subtracted in order to find out how long something took.

ADJUSTING ROW HEIGHT

The height of a row may be altered in the same way as a column.

Row height is altered as follows:

➤➤   ▶ Line between the row numbers 👆.

➤➤   Drag the line to the required height 👆.

Task 4.6.3

(a) Enter the constant and variable data shown in Figure 4.17 into a blank workbook. Adjust column widths as necessary.

(b) Insert formulae into the shaded cells to calculate the following:

   ● The VAT on each item (Cost × VAT Rate).
     (**Note:** Use absolute cell referencing for the VAT rate.)
   ● The total for each item (Cost + VAT).

(c) Save the workbook with the filename **Prices**.

	A	B	C	D
1	Price List			
2				
3	VAT Rate:	21%		
4				
5	Item	Cost	VAT	Total
6	14" Portable TV	€ 145.00		
7	16" Portable TV	€ 165.00		
8	Four Head VCR	€ 125.00		
9	DVD Player	€ 165.00		
10	Mini Disc Player	€ 180.00		
11	Mini Disc Recorder/Player	€ 250.00		

Figure 4.17

ABSOLUTE CELL REFERENCE

In all the work we have done so far on building formulae, we simply clicked a cell to include the contents of that cell in a calculation. Consequently when we copied (replicated) these formulae into other cells, the program incremented the cell reference by one row or column when it was copied into the next cell.

For example, if we entered the formula **=A6+B6** into cell C6 to add the numbers in A6 and B6, filling (copying) that formula into cell C7 will cause it to change to **=A7+B7** in order to add the numbers in A7 and B7. Selecting cells in this way is referred to as **relative cell referencing**. This is convenient because it allows us to copy formulae into other cells and the program will increment the rows and/or columns as it copies (fills) each formula into another cell.

It is sometimes necessary to refer to a particular cell even when a formula is copied into other cells. When it is necessary to keep a cell reference from changing, even when the formula is filled or copied, it is necessary to specify that cell as **absolute**.

A cell reference is specified as absolute by placing the $ sign in front of the column letter and in front of the row number. An absolute cell reference would look like the following: **$B$3**.

The simplest method of producing a formula with an absolute cell reference is to produce the formula with relative cell references and then to edit the formula. Select the cell with the formula and it will appear in the formula bar. Place the $ signs where required and press the Enter key. The formula may then be filled into other cells. The finished formula should look like the following: **=B6*$B$3**.

Some programs use the F4 function key to produce absolute cell references. Pressing the F4 function key immediately after the cell (or cells in some cases) has been selected will automatically place the $ signs in the correct places.

Task 4.6.4 (Additional)

Produce the additional spreadsheets specified in **Task 4A-6** on the CD.

Task 4.7.1

(a) Enter the constant and variable data shown in Figure 4.18 into a blank workbook. Adjust column widths as necessary. Align headings and data as shown. Format data as shown.

(b) Insert formulae into the shaded cells to calculate the following:

- The bonus for each salesperson.
  Calculated as follows: If the sales are greater than €50,000 then the bonus is €800, otherwise the bonus is €500.

Note: See IF function below:

- The total salary (Bonus + Basic Salary).
- The total for each column.
- The average for each column.

(c) Save the workbook with the filename **O'Rourke Simple**.

	A	B	C	D	E
1			O'Rourke Computers		
2					
3			Salaries and Bonuses Report January 2005		
4					
5				Basic	Total
6	Salesperson	Sales	Bonus	Salary	Salary
7					
8	James Murphy	€ 56,482.00		€ 2,526.00	
9	Pauline Flynn	€ 64,872.00		€ 2,425.00	
10	Jacinta Murray	€ 45,812.00		€ 2,861.00	
11	Kevin Hughes	€ 75,148.00		€ 3,125.00	
12	Phylis O'Brien	€ 89,248.00		€ 2,574.00	
13	Thomas Galvin	€ 65,712.00		€ 2,615.00	
14	Geraldine Ryan	€ 48,241.00		€ 2,943.00	
15	Liam Mulhall	€ 35,214.00		€ 2,457.00	
16	Harry Lonergan	€ 23,614.00		€ 3,124.00	
17	Orla Walsh	€ 78,451.00		€ 3,208.00	
18	0				
19	Total:				
20					
21	Average:				

Figure 4.18

SIMPLE IF FUNCTION

The simple IF function is used to compare the contents of a cell with a value in another cell or an actual value entered from the keyboard. Depending on the result of the comparison the spreadsheet will enter one of two values into the cell.

The IF function is operated as follows:

➤➤ 🖱 Cell into which the answer is to go 🖱.

➤➤ =

➤➤ 🖱 Type IF.

➤➤ (

➤➤ 🖱 Cell to be compared 🖱.

➤➤ Press the appropriate operator (=, >, <, >=, <=.)

➤➤ Type the value to be compared to   **OR**   🖱 To the cell containing the compared value 🖱.

➤➤ Press the comma key , .

➤➤ Enter the value to be displayed in the cell if comparison is true.

➤➤ Press the comma key , .

➤➤ Enter the value to be displayed in the cell if comparison is false.

continued

In this case, if the value in cell B8 is less than 50,000, i.e. **true**, then the value entered into the cell with the formula will be 800. If the value in cell B8 is 50,000 or less, i.e. not greater than 50,000 or **false**, then the value entered into the cell with the formula will be 500.

The value entered into a cell as a result of an IF function does not have to be a number. Text may be entered into the cell by simply placing the word(s) in quote marks.

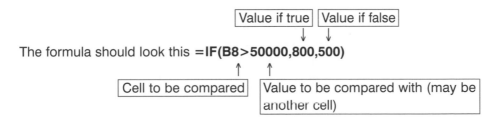

Figure 4.19

Operators

The operators used with IF functions are:

=	is equal to.
<	is less than, smaller than or before (will not include the value).
>	is greater than, bigger than or after (will not include the value).
<=	is less than or equal to (will include the value).
>=	is greater than or equal to (will include the value).

Task 4.7.2

(a) Open the workbook **O'Rourke SImple**, if not already open.

(b) Modify the formula for the bonus based on the following data:
If the sales are less than €20,000 then the bonus is €100. If the sales are between €25,000 and €50,000 then the bonus is €400. If the sales are €50,000 or more then the bonus is €700.

(c) Sort the data so that the largest sales figure is on top.

(d) Save the workbook again with the filename **O'Rourke Multiple**.

MULTIPLE IF FUNCTION

It is possible to use more than one IF function in the same formula. The structure of the formula for a multiple IF function is the same as the simple IF, but in this case the value, if false, is another IF function instead of an actual value. There can be a number of IF functions included in a single formula. The format of a multiple IF function is as follows:

=IF(C4<20000,100, IF(C4<50000,500,800))

In the above example, if the first IF function is true, the value of 100 will be entered in the cell and the remainder of the IF statements will not be checked. However, if the first IF function is not true then the program checks the second IF function, and if this is true then it enters the value 500 into the cell. If the second IF function is not true then that means that the value in cell C4 is not less than 50,000, i.e. 50,000 or more, and enters the value 800 into the cell.

In fact, it is possible to keep replacing the false value with another IF function up to the maximum number allowed by the program. The program will keep checking the IF functions until it finds one which is true, and failing that it will enter the last value which indicates that all the IF functions are **false**.

Task 4.7.3 (Additional)

Produce the additional spreadsheets specified in **Task 4A-7** on the CD.

Task 4.8.1

(a) Enter the constant and variable data shown in Figure 4.20 into a blank workbook. Adjust column widths as necessary. Align headings and data as shown. Format data as shown.

(b) Insert formulae into the shaded cells to calculate the following:

- The increase for each type, displayed with a % sign. If the growth is less than 5% OR the risk is high then the increase is 20%, otherwise the increase is 10%.
- This year's base. This year's base is equal to last year's base plus last year's base multiplied by the increase.
- The maximum growth.

   Note: See MAX function below.

- The minimum base for this year.

   Note: See MIN function below.

(c) Save the workbook with the filename **Complete Cover**.

	A	B	C	D	E	F
1			Complete Cover Insurance			
2						
3			Base Rates for 2006			
4						
5					Last Year's	This Year's
6	Type	Growth	Risk	Increase	Base	Base
7	House	5%	Low		€ 250.00	
8	Industry	4%	High		€ 325.00	
9	Building	8%	Low		€ 275.00	
10	Farm	1%	High		€ 260.00	
11	Motor	6%	High		€ 345.00	
12	Personal	7%	Low		€ 245.00	
13	Travel	12%	High		€ 420.00	
14	Life	2%	Low		€ 295.00	
15						
16	Maximum:				Minimum:	

Figure 4.20

IF FUNCTION WITH LOGICAL OPERATORS (OR, AND)

The IF function may be used to compare a number of values at the same time. This will require the use of a logical operator. The most common logical operators are **OR** and **AND**. When using these operators, the user must remember that the operator comes before the two (or more) values to be compared. The use of the OR operator would look as follows:

$$=IF(OR(C8=9,C8<12),450,650)$$

This function would be **true** if the value in cell C8 was equal to 9 **OR** the value in cell C8 is less than 12, in which case the value 450 will be entered into the cell containing the formula. For all other values the result will be **false** and will therefore enter the value 650 into the cell.

The following are further examples of the use of the IF function with logical operators.

Example 1

$$=IF(OR(C8=9,D9<50),2\%,5\%)$$

In this example the statement will be **true** if the value in C8 = 9 **OR** the value in D9 < 50 and therefore enter a value of 2%. All other conditions will render the statement **false** and therefore enter a value of 5%.

Example 2

$$=IF(AND(H18<=20,J18>50),"Invest","Bad Risk")$$

In this example the statement will be **true** if the value in H18 is less than or equal to 20 **AND** the value in J18 is greater than 50 and therefore enter the word 'Invest'. All other conditions will render the statement **false** and therefore enter the words 'Bad Risk'. (Note the use of quote marks to return words rather than numbers.)

Example 3

=IF(OR(A6<50,B6>A6),15%,10%)

In this example the statement will be **true** if the value in A6 is less than 50 **OR** the value in B6 is greater than the value in A6 and therefore enter a value of 15%. All other conditions will render the statement **false** and enter a value of 10%.

Example 4

=IF(OR(B8<500,C8>A8,D8="High"),25%,20%)

In this example the statement will be **true** if the value in B8 is less than 500 **OR** the value in C8 is greater than the value in A8 **OR** the word in D8 is 'High' and therefore enter a value of 25%. All other conditions will render the statement **false** and return a value of 20%.

MAX, MIN, COUNT AND OTHER FUNCTIONS

These functions are used to display the maximum and minimum values from a group of figures or to count the number of figures in a group. The structure of each function is exactly the same and they are as follows:

=MAX(B7:B14)
=MIN(F7:F14)
=COUNT(B6:F16)

The MAX, MIN and COUNT functions are produced as follows:

➤➤   Select the cell where the result is to appear.

➤➤   ▨

➤➤   ▣ Type MAX/MIN/COUNT as appropriate.

➤➤   ▣

➤➤   ▣ First cell of the group of figures 🖱.

➤➤   ⬦ Last cell to be included 🖱.

➤➤   ▣

➤➤   ▣

There are a number of other functions that may be useful, such as DB (fixed declining balance depreciation), DDB (double declining balance depreciation), PV (present value) and NPV (net present value). The structure of these functions is not dealt with here, but more information about them may be found in the Help function of the program.

Task 4.8.2

(a) Open the workbook **Complete Cover** (if not already open).

(b) Insert a blank column between the Risk and Increase columns. Insert the column heading 'Comment' in this new column.

(c) Enter formulae that will insert the word 'Poor' or 'Good' in the comment column, based on the following:

If the growth is less than 5% **AND** the risk is high then enter 'Poor', otherwise enter 'Good'.

(d) Save the worksheet again with the same filename.

(e) Display all formulae. (See below.)

(f) Adjust page layout, margins and column widths so that all the data and formulae will fit on a single page.

(g) Print one copy of the sheet, showing all formulae, gridlines and row/column identifiers.

DISPLAYING FORMULAE

It is sometimes useful to be able to print out the formulae and examine them. There is great variation in the method of displaying formulae in various spreadsheet programs, so it is necessary to find out how the program displays formulae.

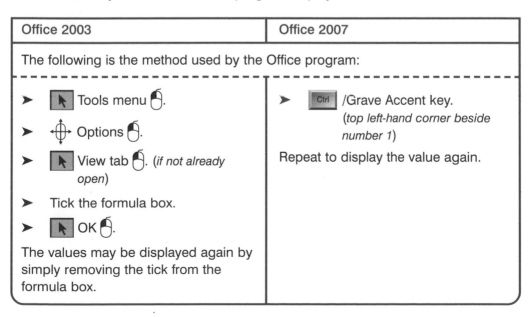

Office 2003	Office 2007
The following is the method used by the Office program:	
➤ 🔺 Tools menu 🖰.	➤ Ctrl /Grave Accent key. *(top left-hand corner beside number 1)*
➤ ⊕ Options 🖰.	Repeat to display the value again.
➤ 🔺 View tab 🖰. (*if not already open*)	
➤ Tick the formula box.	
➤ 🔺 OK 🖰.	
The values may be displayed again by simply removing the tick from the formula box.	

Task 4.8.3

(a) Enter the constant and variable data shown in Figure 4.21 into a blank workbook. Adjust column widths as necessary. Align headings and data as shown. Format data as shown.

(b) Insert formulae into the shaded cells to calculate the following:

- The **mark-up** for each model, displayed with the % sign and calculated as follows:

  If the **materials** is greater than 50 **AND** the **materials** is less than **the machining AND** the **demand** is high then the mark-up is 50%, otherwise the **mark-up** is 40%.

(c) Sort the spreadsheet so that the models are in alphabetical order.

(d) Save the workbook with the filename **Classic Furniture 1**.

	A	B	C	D	E
1	Classic Furniture Company				
2					
3	Model	Materials	Machining	Demand	Mark Up
4	Verona	€ 35.00	€ 25.00	High	
5	Milan	€ 45.00	€ 30.00	Low	
6	Roma	€ 54.00	€ 60.00	High	
7	Piza	€ 66.00	€ 55.00	Low	
8	Venice	€ 78.00	€ 64.00	High	
9	Florence	€ 57.00	€ 62.00	Low	
10	Palermo	€ 85.00	€ 54.00	Low	
11	Turin	€ 58.00	€ 62.00	High	
12	Brindisi	€ 36.00	€ 48.00	Low	

Figure 4.21

Task 4.8.4

(a) Open the file **Classic Furniture 1** (if not already open).

(b) Insert rows, columns and headings as shown in Figure 4.22.

(c) Insert formulae to calculate the following:

- The labour as the labour rate × hours. (See Absolute Cell Reference above.)
- The total cost as the materials + machining + labour.
- The selling price as the total cost + total cost × mark-up.

(d) Save the worksheet again with the filename **Classic Furniture 2**.

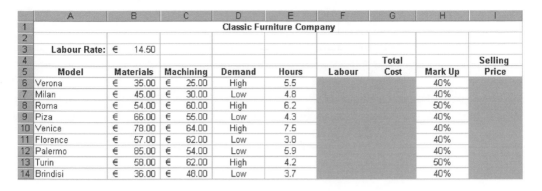

	A	B	C	D	E	F	G	H	I
1				Classic Furniture Company					
2									
3	Labour Rate:	€ 14.50							
4								Total	Selling
5	Model	Materials	Machining	Demand	Hours	Labour	Cost	Mark Up	Price
6	Verona	€ 35.00	€ 25.00	High	5.5			40%	
7	Milan	€ 45.00	€ 30.00	Low	4.8			40%	
8	Roma	€ 54.00	€ 60.00	High	6.2			50%	
9	Piza	€ 66.00	€ 55.00	Low	4.3			40%	
10	Venice	€ 78.00	€ 64.00	High	7.5			40%	
11	Florence	€ 57.00	€ 62.00	Low	3.8			40%	
12	Palermo	€ 85.00	€ 54.00	Low	5.9			40%	
13	Turin	€ 58.00	€ 62.00	High	4.2			50%	
14	Brindisi	€ 36.00	€ 48.00	Low	3.7			40%	

Figure 4.22

Task 4.8.5 (Additional)

Produce the additional spreadsheets specified in **Task 4A-8** on the CD.

Task 4.9.1

(a) Enter the constant and variable data shown in Figure 4.23 into a blank workbook. Adjust column widths as necessary. Align headings and data as shown. Format data as shown.

(b) Insert formulae into the shaded cells to calculate the following:
Use the HLOOKUP function to insert the charge in column C from the array.

(c) Save the workbook with the filename **Charge Price**.

Figure 4.23

	A	B	C	D
1		Charge Price		
2				
3				
4	Model	Type	Charge	
5	MC1024	A		
6	PH2041	B		
7	LG3427	A		
8	KG4572	C		
9	MT1473	B		
10	NW1054	A		
11	BT2481	C		
12	CU1047	B		
13	KJ2371	A		
14				
15				
16		Array		
17	Type	A	B	C
18	Charge	€ 25.00	€ 30.00	€ 35.00

THE LOOKUP FUNCTION

This function is used to search an array and return a value from the array. The array may be horizontal, in which case the HLOOKUP function is used. If the array is vertical then the VLOOKUP function is used.

Let us look at a simple example in order to understand this function. The array in Figure 4.23 has three types, A, B and C. For each type there is a corresponding charge. What we want to do is to get the program to look at the type in column B for each model and then pick the correct charge from the array at the bottom.

The LOOKUP function is made up of the following parts:

=	The start of each formula.
HLOOKUP or VLOOKUP	The function.
( )	Required to contain the elements of the function.
A6	The control value (this is the value – A, B or C – which will be looked for in the array).
, (comma)	Used to separate the different elements.
$B$17:$D$18	The range of cells in the array containing the control values and the lookup values as absolute cell references.
2	The number of rows down the array containing the lookup values.

The formula should look like the following:

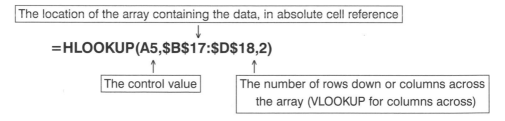

The $ signs are used to indicate absolute cell references to the array. If the absolute cell references were not used when the formula was filled into other cells, the formula would be looking for the array in a different location.

The formula in cell C5 in Figure 4.23 above would be produced as follows:

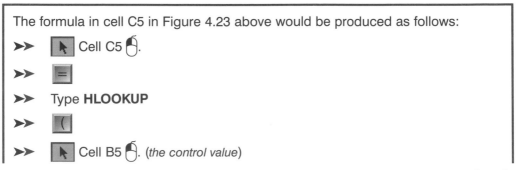

continued

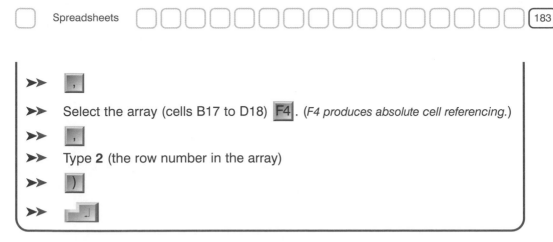

➤➤ Select the array (cells B17 to D18) F4 . (*F4 produces absolute cell referencing.*)

➤➤

➤➤ Type **2** (the row number in the array)

➤➤

➤➤

In the above example in Figure 4.23, the figure in cell C5 will be taken from the second row of the array in the type **A** column.

This formula is then filled (copied) down the column in the normal way.

Note: When using the LOOKUP function, the control values in the table must be sorted in ascending order.

Task 4.9.2

(a) Enter the constant and variable data shown in Figure 4.24 into a blank workbook. Adjust column widths as necessary. Align headings and data as shown. Format data as shown.

(b) Insert formulae into the shaded cells to calculate the following:

- Use the HLOOKUP function to insert the Trade in column C from the array.
- Use the HLOOKUP function to insert the Retail Extra in column D from the array.

(c) Sort the spreadsheet so that the models are in alphabetical order.
(d) Save the workbook with the filename **Tutty**.

	A	B	C	D
1		**Tutty's Car Sales**		
2				
3		**Price Mark-Up Guidelines**		
4				
5				Retail
6	Model	Category	Trade	Extra
7	Micra	A		
8	Astra	B		
9	Fiesta	A		
10	Stilo	C		
11	Corolla	B		
12				
13		**Array**		
14	Category	A	B	C
15	Trade:	15%	13%	12%
16	Retail:	€ 650	€ 785	€ 965

Figure 4.24

Task 4.9.3

(a) Open the file **Tutty** (if not already open).
(b) Insert additional labels and data as shown in Figure 4.25.
(c) Insert formulae into the shaded cells to calculate the following:

- The duty (use the lookup function to calculate the percentage and multiply by the basic price). Display in currency format with no decimals.
- The trade price (basic price + duty). Display in currency format with no decimals.
- The retail price (trade price + retail extra). Display in currency format with no decimals.

(d) Protect all formulae (see Protecting a Sheet below).
(e) Save the worksheet again with the filename **Tutty 2**.

				Retail	Basic		Trade	Retail
4								
5				Retail	Basic		Trade	Retail
6	Model	Category	Trade	Extra	Price	Duty	Price	Price
7	Fiesta	A	15%	€ 650	€ 15,450			
8	Corolla	B	13%	€ 785	€ 17,640			
9	Micra	A	15%	€ 650	€ 14,980			
10	Stilo	C	12%	€ 965	€ 14,750			
11	Astra	B	13%	€ 785	€ 16,240			
12								
13			**Array**					
14	Category	A	B	C				
15	Trade:	15%	13%	12%				
16	Retail:	€ 650	€ 785	€ 965				
17	Duty:	22%	27%	33%				

Figure 4.25

PROTECTING A SHEET

When formulae have been entered in a sheet it is a good idea to prevent them from being accidentally deleted or overwritten. Formulae may be protected or locked by protecting the workbook or sheet. The process varies from one program to another, so it is necessary to find out the method used by your program.

In the following method the program requires the user to first select the cells that are NOT to be locked and then lock the sheet. This means that all cells will be locked with the exception of the cells that were selected as unlocked.

Office 2003	Office 2007

The procedure for protecting a sheet involves two steps, as follows:

1 Unlock cells to be left unlocked (these will usually be the cells containing variable data).

➤➤ Select cells to be left unlocked.

➤ 🖱️ Format menu 🖱️.	➤ Select the Home ribbon.
➤ ⊕ Cells 🖱️.	➤ 🖱️ Format icon 🖾 🖱️.
	➤ ⊕ Format cells 🖱️.

(*The Format Cells window will appear.*)

➤➤ 🖱️ Protection tab 🖱️.

➤➤ Untick the locked box. This means that these cells will not be locked when the sheet is protected. You may have to repeat this process for various sections of the sheet if you are not able to select all the sections at once.

Note: A number of groups of cells may be selected by holding down the Ctrl key while selecting the various groups.

2 Protect the sheet.

➤ 🖱️ Tools menu 🖱️.	➤ Select the Review ribbon.
➤ ⊕ Protection.	➤ 🖱️ Protect Sheet icon 🖾 🖱️.
➤ ⊕ Protect sheet 🖱️	

(*The Protect Sheet window will appear.*)

➤➤ Add a protection password, if required (*this will mean that the sheet may not be unprotected without this password*).

➤➤ 🖱️ OK 🖱️.

Task 4.9.4 (Additional)

Produce the additional spreadsheets specified in **Task 4A-9** on the CD.

186 ◻◻◻◻◻◻◻◻◻◻◻◻◻ Step by Step Computer Applications ◻

Task 4.10.1

(a) Enter the headings and constant data shown in Figure 4.26 into a blank workbook. Adjust column widths as necessary. Align headings and data as shown. Format data as shown.

(b) Insert a Clip Art picture under the totals row (resize the picture, if necessary).

(c) Insert formulae into the shaded cells to calculate the following:

- The in-stock quantity as purchased – sold.
- The totals for purchased, sold and in stock.

(d) Create a column chart on the same sheet and position it underneath the picture. The chart should contain the following:

- The product as the X-axis identifier.
- A column for purchased and a column for sold.
- The chart title 'Product Report'.
- X-axis label 'Product' and the Y-axis label 'Quantity'.

(e) Save the workbook with the filename **Kennedy 1**.

(f) Print one copy of the sheet in the horizontal centre of the page with gridlines.

	A	B	C	D
1	Kennedy Engineering			
2				
3	Bolt Report for Week Ending 21/06/2005			
4				
5				
6	Product	Purchased	Sold	In Stock
7	10mm M6	6250	5560	
8	15mm M6	5620	5120	
9	20mm M6	7520	6450	
10	10mm M8	4820	4285	
11	15mm M8	5425	4250	
12	20mm M8	3520	3500	
13	10mm M10	4250	3645	
14	15mm M10	5685	4750	
15	20mm M10	6250	5820	
16				
17	Totals:			

Figure 4.26

INSERTING CLIP ART AND PICTURES

Clip Art

Clip Art are pictures which are supplied for use in a document. Some Clip Art is installed with the program but most Clip Art pictures are available online and it is therefore necessary to be connected to the Internet in order to insert them.

Office 2003	Office 2007
Any of the Clip Art pictures may be inserted into a document as follows:	
➤➤ Select the cell where you want the Clip Art to start.	
➤ 🖱 Insert menu 🖱. ➤ ⊕ Picture. ➤ ⊕ Clip Art 🖱.	➤ Select the Insert ribbon. ➤ 🖱 Clip Art 🖱.

(The Clip Art side window will appear.)

➤➤ Type a word in the Search for field.

➤➤ 🖱 Go 🖱. *(A selection of clip art will appear in the window.)*

➤➤ 🖱 Clip Art picture required 🖱.

➤➤ The Clip Art will be inserted into the document.

➤➤ Close the Clip Art gallery.

Pictures

Office 2003	Office 2007
A picture that has been saved may be inserted into a document as follows:	
➤➤ Select the cell where you want the Picture to start.	
➤ 🖱 Insert menu 🖱. ➤ ⊕ Picture. ➤ ⊕ 🖼 From file 🖱.	➤ Select the Insert ribbon. ➤ 🖱 Picture 🖼 🖱.

(The insert picture window will appear.)

continued

➤➤ Select the correct folder and a list of files will appear.

➤➤ [cursor] the Picture filename [mouse].

➤➤ [cursor] Insert button [mouse].

The Picture will be inserted into the document.

The graphic is positioned by simply pointing to the graphic, holding down the left mouse button and dragging the picture to the required position on the sheet.

The graphic may be resized by selecting the graphic and then pointing to a handle (one of the small squares on the corners), holding down the left mouse button and dragging the graphic to the required size.

GRAPHS AND CHARTS

Graphs or charts are produced using the data on the spreadsheet. When selecting the range of cells to be included in the graph/chart, the row/column labels to be used in the chart should be included in the selection. If the data is in nonadjacent cells then hold down the Ctrl key between selecting the various rows/columns of data. If more than one row/column is selected, then the first row/column will become the identifiers for the X-axis.

Office 2003	Office 2007
➤ Select the data for the chart.	➤ Select the data for the chart.
➤ [cursor] Chart wizard icon [icon] [mouse]. *(The chart wizard window will appear.)*	➤ Select the Insert ribbon.
➤ Select the chart type (*from the options offered*).	➤ [cursor] Chart icon [icon] [mouse].
➤ [cursor] Next [mouse].	➤ Select the chart type required.
➤ Select the data range (*this should be correct because you have already selected it*).	*(The chart will be inserted and the chart tools ribbons – Design, Layout, Format – will appear. These ribbons appear each time a chart is selected and may be used to label the chart.)*
➤ [cursor] Next [mouse].	
➤ Insert labels for:	
• Chart title.	
• X-axis.	
• Y-axis.	
➤ [cursor] Next [mouse].	

continued

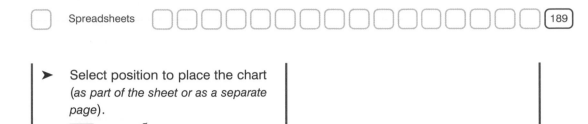
➤ Select position to place the chart (*as part of the sheet or as a separate page*).

➤ ⬚ Finish 🖱.

If the chart is placed on the sheet then it may be repositioned by dragging it to the required position. The chart may also be resized by dragging a corner handle to produce the required size.

Altering a Chart Title, Legend and Data labels

Office 2003	Office 2007
After the chart is created the user may wish to change the title, the legend or the data labels. This may be accomplished as follows:	
➤ Select the chart.	➤ Select the chart. (*The Chart Tools ribbon will be displayed.*)
➤ ⬚ Chart menu 🖱.	➤ Select the Chart Tools Layout ribbon.
➤ ⊕ Chart options 🖱.	
• Select title and type **title** for chart (if required).	➤ Use the icons on this ribbon to insert labels for:
• Select **legend** (if required).	• Chart title.
• Select **data labels** (if required).	• Axis titles – X-axis.
	• Axis titles – Y-axis.

Changing the Chart Type

Office 2003	Office 2007
If it is necessary to change the chart type, then this is accomplished as follows:	
➤ Select the chart. (*The Chart toolbar will appear.*)	➤ Select the chart.
	➤ Select the Chart Tools Design ribbon.
➤ ⬚ Chart type icon arrow ▭▾ 🖱.	➤ ⬚ Change Chart Type icon ▭ 🖱.
➤ ⊕ chart type required 🖱.	➤ ⬚ Chart type required 🖱.
	➤ ⬚ OK 🖱.

Changing the Chart Colours

Office 2003	Office 2007
The colours of the various chart sections may be changed as follows:	
➤ ▣ The section to be changed 🖱.	➤ ▣ The section to be changed 🖱.
➤ ▣ Format Data Series icon 🖼 🖱. (*on the chart toolbar*)	➤ Select the Chart Tools Format ribbon.
➤ ▣ Patterns tab 🖱. (*this will probably already be selected*)	➤ ▣ Shape Fill icon arrow 🖱.
➤ ▣ Colour required 🖱.	➤ ✛ Colour required 🖱.
➤ ▣ OK 🖱.	

Changing Size and Position of a Chart

Once the chart has been created it may be resized, moved and the proportions changed in the same way as a graphic (see above).

Task 4.10.2

(a) Open the file **Kennedy 1** (if not already open).

(b) Delete the Clip Art and the chart.

(c) Insert additional columns, labels and data as shown in Figure 4.27. Format and align labels and data as shown. Move the 'Totals:' label to the new position shown.

(d) Place a border around the Price List array as shown.

(e) Use the VLOOKUP function to insert the values in the Price column from the Price List array.

(f) Use formulae to calculate the following:

  • The stock value as the in-stock quantity multiplied by the price.
  • The total stock value.

(g) Insert a header and footer as follows:

Header: Kennedy Engineering Ltd, centre aligned.
Footer: (i)   Your name, left aligned.
             (ii) Today's date from the computer clock, centre aligned.
             (iii) The word 'Page' followed by the page number, right aligned.

(h) Save the workbook with the filename **Kennedy 2**.

(i) Print one copy of the sheet on a landscape page with gridlines.

(j) Create a bar chart on a separate sheet containing the following:

- The product as the X-axis identifier.
- A bar for purchased, sold and in stock.
- The chart title 'Bolt Sales 21/06/2005'.
- X-axis label 'Product' and the Y-axis label 'Quantity'.

(k) Print one copy of the bar chart.

(l) Create a 3-D pie chart on a separate sheet containing the following:

- The product as the X-axis identifier.
- A segment for the quantity in stock.
- The chart title 'In Stock'.

(m) Print one copy of the pie chart.

(n) Save the workbook again with the same filename.

	A	B	C	D	E	F	G
1			Kennedy Engineering				
2							
3			Bolt Report for Week Ending 21/06/2005				
4							
5							
6	Product	Category	Price	Purchased	Sold	In Stock	Stock Value
7	10mm M6	A		6250	5560		
8	15mm M6	A		5620	5120		
9	20mm M6	B		7520	6450		
10	10mm M8	A		4820	4285		
11	15mm M8	B		5425	4250		
12	20mm M8	C		3520	3500		
13	10mm M10	B		4250	3645		
14	15mm M10	C		5685	4750		
15	20mm M10	D		6250	5820		
16							
17			Totals:				
18							
19			Price List				
20			Category	Price / 100			
21			A	€ 12.65			
22			B	€ 13.75			
23			C	€ 15.95			
24			D	€ 17.25			

Figure 4.27

BORDERS

As we have already discovered, it is possible to print a spreadsheet with or without gridlines. Sometimes we may wish to place borders around certain cells.

A border is placed around a cell or number of cells as follows:

➤➤ Select the cell or cells.

continued

➤➤ Borders button selection arrow .

(The selection of borders will be displayed.)

➤➤ Option required .

Note: The option selected will become the default option and it is only necessary to click on the borders button if the same border is to be applied again.

More extensive borders may be obtained by selecting the format cells option (see below).

SHADING

Sometimes we may wish to shade certain cells.

Cells may have shading applied to them as follows:

➤➤ Select the cell or cells.

➤➤ Fill colour selection arrow .

(The fill colour window will be displayed.)

➤➤ Colour required .

Note: The option selected will become the default option and it is only necessary to click on the fill colour button if you want the same colour again.

More extensive shading options may be obtained by selecting the Patterns tab from the Format Cells option (see below).

FORMAT CELLS

So far the icons on the toolbar have been used to format the cell contents. However, there is a range of other formats that may be applied to cells.

Office 2003	Office 2007
➤ Format menu . ➤ Cells .	➤ Select the Home ribbon. ➤ Arrow beside the borders icon . ➤ More Borders .

continued

(*The format cells window will be displayed.*)

The following options will be available from the various tabs in the window:

- More extensive cell formatting, other than currency, per cent, comma, etc.
- More extensive borders.
- More extensive shading (patterns).
- Cell contents orientation.
- Font styles.

Task 4.10.3 (Additional)

Produce the additional spreadsheets specified in **Task 4A-10** on the CD.

Task 4.11.1

(a) Start a blank workbook.

(b) Record a macro, named *Start*, which will perform the following:

- Insert the heading 'Young & Jones Finance Ltd' in cell A1.
- Apply bold format to the heading.
- Align the heading between columns A and H.
- Insert today's date in cell A3 {**=now()**}.
- Format cell A3 to display date only, in format dd/mm/yyyy.
- Insert the heading 'Product' in cell A5.
- Insert the heading 'Jan' in cell B5.
- Fill the heading 'Jan' to the right for five more columns.(If your program does not fill the months, then you will have to enter the months Feb, Mar, Apr, May, Jun).
- Insert the heading 'Total' in cell H5.
- Centre align headings Jan to Total.
- Set column widths as appropriate.

Stop recording the macro.

(c) Select Sheet2.

(d) Run the macro on Sheet2.

(e) Edit the macro if it did not perform the tasks correctly.

(f) Save the workbook with the filename **Jones**.

CREATING A MACRO

Spreadsheet programs provide a facility called a macro for automating tasks that are to be performed repeatedly on a sheet. A macro is a series of commands and functions that are stored with the workbook and can be run whenever it is necessary to perform the task. When a macro is recorded, the spreadsheet program stores information about each step taken as the series of commands is performed. The macro is then run to repeat or play back the commands.

The simplest method of producing a macro is to record it on a copy of the spreadsheet on which the macro is to be executed.

Office 2003	Office 2007
A macro is recorded as follows:	

Office 2003	Office 2007
➤ Tools menu.	In Office 2007 the macro functions are on the Developer ribbon, which is not normally displayed. Therefore the first step is to display the Developer ribbon as follows:
➤ Macro.	
➤ Record New Macro. (*The record macro window will appear.*)	➤ Office button.
➤ This window allows you to:	➤ Excel Options button. (*The popular options will be displayed.*)
• Type the macro name.	➤ Tick the box to 'Show Developer tab in the ribbon'.
• Create a shortcut. (Type a letter in the shortcut box and the macro can then be executed by simply selecting `Ctrl` + the letter.)	➤ OK.
• Store the macro. (The macro may be stored either with the sheet or in a personal macro folder where it will be available every time you use the spreadsheet program.)	The Developer ribbon will be available until it is switched off again by un-ticking the box.
➤ OK.	The macro is recorded as follows:
• Perform the tasks to be repeated by the macro.	➤ Record Macro icon. (*The record macro window will appear.*)
➤ Stop Recording icon.	➤ This window allows you to:
	• Type the macro name.
	• Create a shortcut. (Type a letter in the shortcut box and the macro can then be executed by simply selecting `Ctrl` + the letter.)

continued

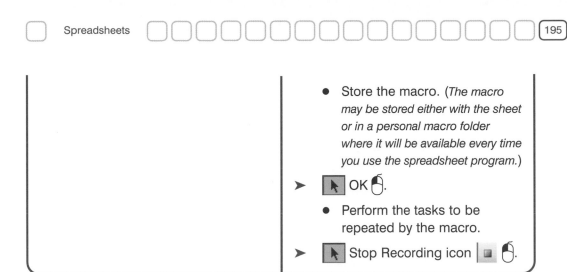

- Store the macro. (*The macro may be stored either with the sheet or in a personal macro folder where it will be available every time you use the spreadsheet program.*)

➤ [pointer] OK [mouse].

- Perform the tasks to be repeated by the macro.

➤ [pointer] Stop Recording icon [■] [mouse].

RUNNING (EXECUTING) A MACRO

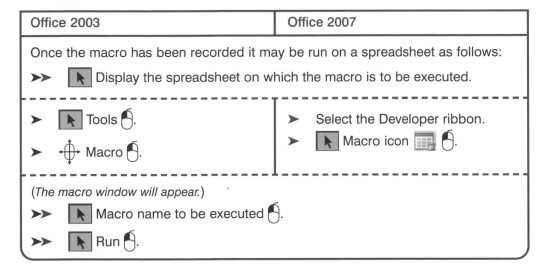

Office 2003	Office 2007
Once the macro has been recorded it may be run on a spreadsheet as follows:	
➤➤ [pointer] Display the spreadsheet on which the macro is to be executed.	
➤ [pointer] Tools [mouse].	➤ Select the Developer ribbon.
➤ ✛ Macro [mouse].	➤ [pointer] Macro icon [icon] [mouse].
(*The macro window will appear.*)	
➤➤ [pointer] Macro name to be executed [mouse].	
➤➤ [pointer] Run [mouse].	

EDITING A MACRO

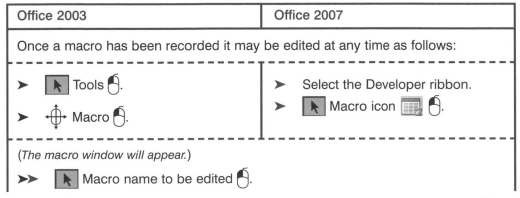

Office 2003	Office 2007
Once a macro has been recorded it may be edited at any time as follows:	
➤ [pointer] Tools [mouse].	➤ Select the Developer ribbon.
➤ ✛ Macro [mouse].	➤ [pointer] Macro icon [icon] [mouse].
(*The macro window will appear.*)	
➤➤ [pointer] Macro name to be edited [mouse].	

continued

➤➤ ▣ Edit 🖰.

➤➤ Carry out any editing required.

➤➤ Close the macro editor and return to the sheet.

The lines of the macro will be displayed in script format and may be edited as with any text editor or word processor. One item that very often needs to be edited is the command to insert the date from the computer clock. If the ⌨Ctrl ⌨; command is used to insert the date when recording the macro, it inserts the actual date and not the command **{=NOW()}**. The use of relative cell references is often used when recording a macro, which may need to be changed to absolute cell reference.

Task 4.11.2 (Additional)

Produce the additional spreadsheets specified in **Task 4A-11** on the CD.

SAVING SPREADSHEETS AS OTHER FILE TYPES

Every time a spreadsheet is saved, it will be saved as a spreadsheet with a filename extension corresponding to your spreadsheet program, e.g. .xls, xlsx. However, it is possible to save a worksheet as another file type, such as web page (.htm or .html), template, text only, etc.

Office 2003	Office 2007
A spreadsheet is saved as a different file type as follows:	
➤ ▣ File menu 🖰. ➤ ▣ Save as 🖰.	➤ ▣ Office button 📋 🖰. ➤ ▣ Save as 🖰.

(The save as window will appear.)

➤➤ Select the folder into which the file is to be saved (if necessary) in the 'Save in' field.

➤➤ Type a name for this file in the 'Filename' field.

➤➤ Select the type of file from the 'Save as type' field.

➤➤ ▣ Save 🖰.

DELETING A SHEET

> A complete sheet may be deleted from a workbook as follows:
>
> ➤➤   🔲 Sheet# 🖱. (*a pop-up menu will appear*)
>
> ➤➤   ✛ Delete 🖱.

REARRANGING SHEETS

The order of sheets in a workbook may be changed by moving a sheet to a new position at the bottom of the screen.

> Sheets are rearranged as follows:
>
> ➤➤   🔲 Sheet name, e.g. Sheet1 🖱.
>
> ➤➤   Drag the sheet left or right to the new position 🖱.

DUPLICATING (COPYING) A SHEET

It is possible to duplicate an entire worksheet and retain all column widths and formatting.

Office 2003	Office 2007
A sheet is duplicated as follows:	
➤ 🔲 Edit menu 🖱.	➤ Select the Home ribbon.
➤ ✛ Move or Copy Sheet 🖱.	➤ 🔲 Format icon 🔳 🖱.
	➤ ✛ Move or Copy Sheet 🖱.

(*The move or copy window will appear.*)

➤➤   Select the position in which the duplicate is to be placed.

➤➤   Tick the create a copy box.

➤➤   🔲 OK 🖱.

SPREADSHEET DESIGN

When producing simple spreadsheets it is not normally necessary to go through the design process. However, when dealing with larger projects the design process becomes invaluable in the production of a working spreadsheet. We will examine the individual steps of the design process and then apply the process to a simple example project.

STAGES

The production of a spreadsheet may be divided into the following stages:

- Design.

- Production or implementation.

- Evaluation.

If these steps are diligently followed then the final outcome should be successful in meeting the needs for which the spreadsheet was intended.

DESIGN

The design stage is the most important stage in the production of a spreadsheet. However, it is also the stage that is often neglected or only given a token attempt. The production of a spreadsheet normally begins with a need. This need may originate from an existing system that is not meeting its current requirements or from a new situation that needs a spreadsheet to produce specific results.

The design stage may be divided into a number or specific steps, as follows:

- Overview and aims.

- Input and output data identified.

- Data processing identified.

- Specification of data.

- Layout.

Overview and Aims

The design process will generally begin with a brief overview of the present situation or the needs to be addressed by the spreadsheet. This helps to set the project in context and focus the attention on a specific situation.

The aims of the spreadsheet should be clearly identified and stated. This will generally involve two specific steps.

1 A list of *specific* problems to be addressed by this spreadsheet. These problems must be very specific and should be items that a spreadsheet is capable of

addressing. Problems such as speed, presentation, accuracy, etc. would more correctly be identified in the overview and not in this section. Examples of problems that might be identified here are:

- Find total sales for each day/week/month.

- List the students who obtained a pass mark.

- Find percentage profit margin on each item.

2 A list of solutions to the problems listed. This list will be expressed in very general terms at this stage, as the layout of the spreadsheet will not have been attended to yet. The identification of formulae would not be part of this section, but general reference to some spreadsheet function may be appropriate. Examples of solutions that might be identified here are:

- The total sales may be obtained by entering the sales for each day and then using the spreadsheet to calculate the total sales.

- Finding the students who obtained a pass mark may be accomplished by inputting the marks obtained in each subject and then calculating a total. The spreadsheet can then use the IF function to identify the students who obtained a pass mark.

- The percentage profit margin may be obtained by using the cost price and the selling price and then using a formula to calculate the percentage profit margin.

Input and Output Data Identified

This stage may be divided into the two distinct categories of input and output data.

Input Data

This step involves the identification of each piece of data that will be input into the spreadsheet. The input data is raw data (variable data), i.e. data that is collected or taken from an existing system. The data is simply listed at this stage as individual pieces. Examples of input data are:

- Cost price of item.

- Quantity of CDs sold on Monday.

- Mark obtained for English.

The method used to collect this data should be specified at this stage. The methods used to collect data vary greatly and some examples are:

- Taking data from an existing system.

- Using a survey form.

- Records of sales and purchases.

- Membership records.

In any event a data capture form should be produced that will clearly identify the input data. The data capture form may be a form that is specially produced for the purpose of collecting the data – such as a survey form. Another type of data capture form would be the existing manual records that contain all the data that will be input into the spreadsheet.

Output Data

This step involves the identification of each piece of data that will be produced as a result of a calculation by the spreadsheet. The data is simply listed at this stage as individual pieces, with no attempt to identify the formulae that will be used to produce the output. Examples of output data are:

- Profit on each CD.

- Average quantity of each CD sold for the week.

- Grade obtained by each student.

Data Processing

The data processing stage identifies the formulae and/or functions that will be used in manipulating the input data to produce the required output data. The formulae or functions that are identified at this stage will be expressed in general format. The actual cells will not be included, as these will not have been identified at this stage. The processing will be listed as general English statements or as sample formulae, which would include dummy cell references. Examples of data processing might be:

- Profit on each item = selling price – cost price.

- Average quantity sold =AVERAGE(Sales Column).

- Grade obtained: Use the IF function to determine the grade, as follows:

    - If the mark is less than 50 then grade is Fail.

    - If the mark is 50 or greater then grade is Pass.

Specification of Data

The specification stage involves identifying each piece of data and specifying the way in which it will appear on the spreadsheet, such as type, format, alignment, colour, protection (if necessary), etc. Examples of data specification are:

- Cost price: currency.

- Profit on each item: number, centre align, protected.

- Grade obtained: text, right align, bold, protected.

The identification and specification of constant data such as main headings, row headings and column headings would also be done at this stage.

Layout

The final step in the design stage is to produce a layout for the spreadsheet. This will usually be a diagram of the screen showing the various sections, either in colour or different shadings, and clearly identifying each section as containing constant data, input data or output data. An example of a simple spreadsheet layout is shown below.

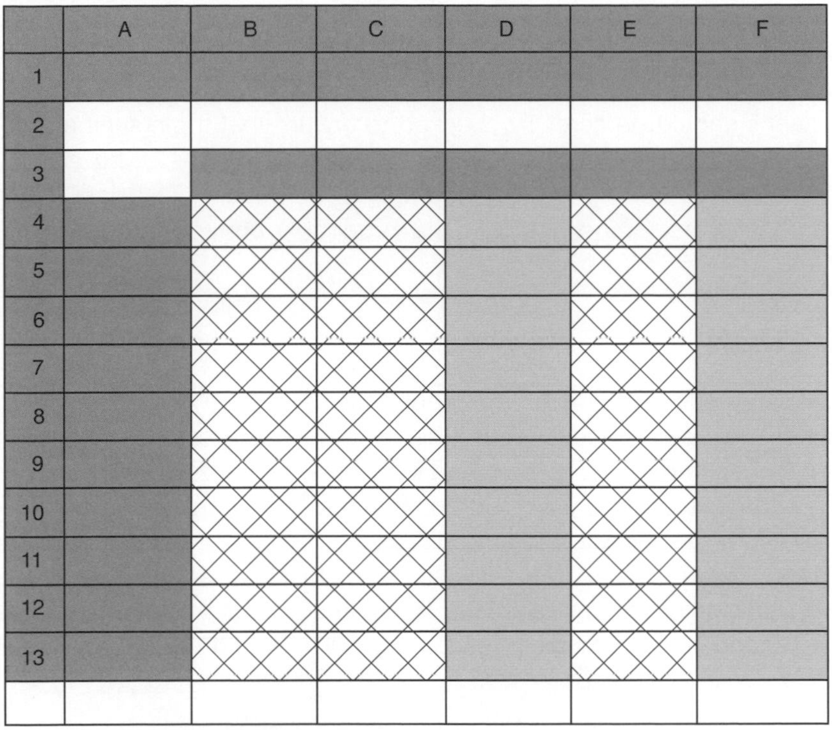

Colour	Data Type
	Constant Data
	Input Data
	Output Data

Figure 4.28

The diagram will have an accompanying specification that details the constant data, the variable data and the output data. This specification would detail each main heading(s), each row/column heading, variable data locations and output data locations. The actual variable and output data will have already been specified, as described above, so at this stage it is only necessary to specify the exact positioning of the data.

PRODUCTION OR IMPLEMENTATION

Once the spreadsheet has been designed it is then time to go to the computer and produce the spreadsheet as designed. If the design stage has been performed adequately it should be possible to hand the design to someone else and he or she should be able to implement the spreadsheet from the design specification.

This production stage simply involves inputting the constant and variable data and then producing the formulae and/or functions that have been specified in the processing step of the design stage. The output will then be produced and the results will appear on the spreadsheet.

Calculations should be carefully checked to ensure that the results are correct for all variable data. This will usually mean checking calculations using a calculator to ensure that the spreadsheet is producing the correct results. Test data may be used to ensure that formulae and functions are producing correct results for all variable data values.

EVALUATION

This is probably one of the most important aspects of the whole process. Once the spreadsheet has been produced and it has been carefully tested to ensure that it is producing the desired results as specified in the design stage, it is time to examine the overall spreadsheet and see if it could be improved. Items that could be re-examined would be listed and suggestions for modifications noted.

The actual implementation of modifications would involve going back to the design stage and redesigning the spreadsheet. This alteration would be carried through the process to produce an updated spreadsheet, which would then be evaluated and if necessary redesigned again.

EXAMPLE

The following is a simple example of using the design process to produce a spreadsheet. This is a very simple example intended to demonstrate the steps described above. In practice the spreadsheet would be much larger and consequently the individual steps of the design would be correspondently larger.

The presentation of the final project would be in a folder with the various sections clearly separated and labelled. (This has not been done here due to space restrictions.)

Overview and Aims

Thomas Murphy is a teacher of Computer Science in Muckross Community College. He keeps the results of all his examination assessments on paper, and whereas the results are always correct it involves a large amount of time and effort in ensuring that marks are entered correctly, calculations performed accurately and finally the correct grade awarded to each student.

Thomas has approached me and asked if I could help him in simplifying the whole process, making it easier and faster while still retaining the accuracy. I suggested that he use a spreadsheet and he immediately asked if I could produce one for him.

We discussed the situation and identified the following requirements:

- Produce a percentage for each student from an actual mark received in each assessment.

- Produce an overall total mark for each student for all assessments.

- Produce an overall average mark for each student.

- Produce a grade for each student.

- Produce an average mark and percentage for each assessment.

- Display the results in order, with the student who obtained the highest overall mark listed first.

In order to produce the requirements listed above the following output will be required from the spreadsheet:

- The percentage for each student for each assessment.

- The overall total mark for each student for all assessments.

- The overall percentage for each student.

- The grade obtained by each student (Pass or Fail).

- The average mark for each assessment.

- The average percentage for each assessment.

- A sorted list of students in result order, highest first.

Input Data

In order to collect the data for each student from Thomas, a data capture form was required. The following form records the marks obtained for each assessment.

Subject: Computer Studies		
Student Name: _____	Max Mark	Student Mark
Mark Assessment 1		
Mark Assessment 2		
Mark Assessment 3		

Figure 4.29

The following data was obtained from the data capture forms for Thomas's Computer Studies class.

Computer Studies Results			
	Max 55	Max 65	Max 75
Student Name	Mark	Mark	Mark
Doyle Kevin	45	64	68
Byrne Mary	42	62	72
Lawlor Keith	38	58	48
Kennedy Liam	40	47	69
Hughes Joan	39	39	65
Greene Irene	30	31	35
Jennings Brian	28	25	33
Galvin Patrick	33	47	72
Earley Hannah	37	61	67
Power Julie	47	62	71
Finn Michael	29	58	70
O'Rourke Noel	38	47	59
Collins Jane	31	28	30
O'Connor Kate	46	61	67
Higgins Helen	48	62	73

Figure 4.30

This is the data that will be input into the spreadsheet.

Output Data

The following output data will be required from the spreadsheet:

- The percentage for each student for each assessment.
- The overall total mark for each student for all assessments.
- The overall percentage for each student.
- The grade obtained by each student (Pass or Fail).
- The average mark for each assessment.
- The average percentage for each assessment.

Once the spreadsheet has been produced it will be sorted so that the students are listed in total mark order, with the highest mark on top.

Processing Required

- The percentage for each student for each assessment will be calculated as follows: Percentage will be the mark obtained by the student divided by the maximum mark for that assessment. This may be displayed with a % symbol so there is no need to multiply by 100.

- The overall mark for each student will be calculated as follows: Overall mark will be the addition of the individual marks for each assessment.

- The overall percentage will be calculated as follows:
  1 Calculate the total maximum mark. This will be the addition of the maximum mark for each assessment.
  2 The percentage will be the mark obtained divided by the total maximum mark. It will be necessary to use absolute cell reference for the total maximum mark.

- The grade obtained by each student will be calculated as follows:
  Use an IF statement to calculate the grade as follows:
  1 If the percentage is less than 50 then the grade is Fail.
  2 If the percentage is 50 or greater then the grade is Pass.

- The average mark for each assessment will be calculated as follows:
  Calculate the average mark for the various assessment marks using the AVERAGE function.

- The average percentage for each assessment will be calculated as follows:
  Calculate the average percentage for the various assessment percentages using the AVERAGE function.

Specification of Data

The following table shows the specification for each data item.

Data Item	Type	Allignment	Other	Protected
Student Name	Text	Left		No
Mark Assessment 1	Number	Centre		No
Mark Assessment 2	Number	Centre		No
Mark Assessment 3	Number	Centre		No
Max Mark Assessment 1	Number	Centre	Green, Bold	No
Max Mark Assessment 2	Number	Centre	Green, Bold	No
Max Mark Assessment 3	Number	Centre	Green, Bold	No
Max Mark Total	Number	Centre	Green, Bold	No
Percentage Assessment 1	Percentage	Centre		Yes
Percentage Assessment 2	Percentage	Centre		Yes
Percentage Assessment 3	Percentage	Centre		Yes
Overall Percentage	Percentage	Centre		Yes
Grade	Text	Centre		Yes
Average Assessment Mark	Number	Centre		Yes
Average Assessment Percentage	Percentage	Centre		Yes

Figure 4.31

Fonts

- All data will be 10 pt Arial.
- Main heading will be 14 pt Arial, bold, coloured.
- Second heading will be 12 pt Arial, bold, coloured.
- Other headings will be 10 pt Arial, bold.

Layout

The following is the layout for the spreadsheet as it will appear on-screen.

		Main Heading								
			Second Heading							
	Assessment 1			Assessment 2			Assessment 3			
	Max Mark			Max Mark			Max Mark		Max Total	
Name	Mark	%		Mark	%		Mark	%	Total	Avg %	Grade
Average										

Colour	Data Type
	Constant Data
	Input Data
	Output Data

Figure 4.32

Production

The process of producing the spreadsheet was relatively simple and the following shows the spreadsheet.

	A	B	C	D	E	F	G	H	I	J
1			Muckross Community College							
2										
3				Computer Studies Results						
4										
5			Assess 1		Assess 2		Assess 3			
6			Max Mark	50	Max Mark	65	Max Mark	75	Max Total	195
7										
8		Student Name	Mark	%	Mark	%	Mark	%	Total	Total %	Grade
9		Byrne Mary	42	84%	62	95%	72	96%	176	93%	Pass
10		Collins Jane	31	62%	28	43%	30	40%	89	47%	Fail
11		Doyle Kevin	45	90%	64	98%	68	91%	177	93%	Pass
12		Earley Hannah	37	74%	61	94%	67	89%	165	87%	Pass
13		Finn Michael	29	58%	58	89%	70	93%	157	03%	Pass
14		Galvin Patrick	33	66%	47	72%	72	96%	152	80%	Pass
15		Greene Irene	30	60%	31	48%	35	47%	96	51%	Pass
16		Higgins Helen	48	96%	62	95%	73	97%	183	96%	Pass
17		Hughes Joan	39	78%	39	60%	65	87%	143	75%	Pass
18		Jennings Brian	28	56%	25	38%	33	44%	86	45%	Fail
19		Kennedy Liam	40	80%	47	72%	69	92%	156	82%	Pass
20		Lawlor Keith	38	76%	58	89%	48	64%	144	76%	Pass
21		O'Connor Kate	46	92%	61	94%	67	89%	174	92%	Pass
22		O'Rourke Noel	38	76%	47	72%	59	79%	144	76%	Pass
23		Power Julie	47	94%	62	95%	71	95%	180	95%	Pass
24										
25		Average:	38.1	76%	50.1	77%	59.9	80%	148.1	78%	

Figure 4.33

When the spreadsheet was produced Thomas noticed that the max mark for Assessment 1 should be 55, not 50. I changed this figure and the printout of the corrected spreadsheet is shown below.

	A	B	C	D	E	F	G	H	I	J
1				Muckross Community College						
2										
3				Computer Studies Results						
4										
5		Assess 1		Assess 2		Assess 3				
6		Max Mark	55	Max Mark	65	Max Mark	75	Max Total	195	
7										
8	Student Name	Mark	%	Mark	%	Mark	%	Total	Total %	Grade
9	Byrne Mary	42	76%	62	95%	72	96%	176	90%	Pass
10	Collins Jane	31	56%	28	43%	30	40%	89	46%	Fail
11	Doyle Kevin	45	82%	64	98%	68	91%	177	91%	Pass
12	Earley Hannah	37	67%	61	94%	67	89%	165	85%	Pass
13	Finn Michael	29	53%	58	89%	70	93%	157	81%	Pass
14	Galvin Patrick	33	60%	47	72%	72	96%	152	78%	Pass
15	Greene Irene	30	55%	31	48%	35	47%	96	49%	Fail
16	Higgins Helen	48	87%	62	95%	73	97%	183	94%	Pass
17	Hughes Joan	39	71%	39	60%	65	87%	143	73%	Pass
18	Jennings Brian	28	51%	25	38%	33	44%	86	44%	Fail
19	Kennedy Liam	40	73%	47	72%	69	92%	156	80%	Pass
20	Lawlor Keith	38	69%	58	89%	48	64%	144	74%	Pass
21	O'Connor Kate	46	84%	61	94%	67	89%	174	89%	Pass
22	O'Rourke Noel	38	69%	47	72%	59	79%	144	74%	Pass
23	Power Julie	47	85%	62	95%	71	95%	180	92%	Pass
24										
25	Average:	38.1	69%	50.1	77%	59.9	80%	148.1	76%	

Figure 4.34

Evaluation

When the spreadsheet was completed I presented it to Thomas. We discussed the use of the spreadsheet and he quickly found that it was of tremendous value and he was able to process his results much faster.

After using the spreadsheet for a short time Thomas made the following suggestions:

- His computer studies group is assembled from a number of different classes. He would like to have the class that each student belongs to included in the spreadsheet.

- When he was entering the marks he found that he accidentally awarded marks greater than the maximum mark. He wondered if there was some way of showing this error if it occurred.

- Thomas would like to be able to quickly see the maximum and minimum mark achieved in each assessment.

I examined the three problems listed above and made the following suggestions:

- The class could easily be included by adding an extra column for class.

- The other two problems could be solved by displaying the maximum and minimum mark obtained in each assignment. If the maximum mark displayed here was greater than the maximum mark for the assignment then this indicated an error.

⑤ Databases

SYMBOLS USED IN THIS CHAPTER

The symbols used in this chapter, and their meanings, are as follows:

Click the left mouse button.

Double-click the left mouse button.

Click the right mouse button.

Hold down the left mouse button.

Release the mouse button.

Move the mouse to point to an item without clicking or holding any button.

Point to an item on the screen.

Press the Enter key.

Press the equals key.

INTRODUCTION

A database is a collection of structured data that's related to a particular topic or purpose. Databases have traditionally been held in filing cabinets or special card index systems, such as an index of books in a library. In the case of a library, each book was recorded on two or three cards in two or three index systems. One card was stored in the book title index, one in the book author index and sometimes one in the book publisher index. This meant that the data was duplicated or triplicated and therefore the system was difficult to maintain.

Computer databases perform all the functions of manual systems but are much more efficient. Duplication is eliminated and accuracy is much greater. It is much quicker and easier to locate information when it is stored on computer. Computer databases are used to store large amounts of data, usually on magnetic disk. Each collection of data is stored in a file, the size of which depends on the amount of data contained in it.

The popularity of the Internet in recent years has led to an explosion in the number of databases stored on computer. Numerous companies ask you to fill in a form when you visit their site. This information is automatically stored in a database on their computer. The use of this information is controlled in Ireland but many countries have no control over the use to which this information is put or to whom it is sold.

The list of examples of databases is endless but the following are just a few to start you off.

Company accounts	Payroll records
Employee personal details	Bank accounts
Insurance company records	Books in a library
Product information	Telephone directories

DATABASE MANAGEMENT SYSTEMS (DBMS)

When talking about databases many people confuse the actual database, as described above, with the computer program that allows them to work with a database. A database management system (DBMS) provides an interface between the user and the data stored in the database. A DBMS is a collection of computer programs that are used to create a database, manage a database, retrieve information from a database and present it in the desired manner.

Most large companies have their own DBMS specially written for their company. This is a very expensive approach to managing databases but it does allow the company to store and manage their data in whatever way they like as well as update and modify their system to meet their needs over time.

The alternative to producing your own DBMS is to purchase an off-the-shelf system. There are many of these systems available and it is this type of system that we will be covering in this section. There are many different DBMSs in use today, but all DBMSs operate similarly and therefore the things you learn in this section will apply to all DBMSs, even those specifically written for individual companies.

BASIC CONCEPTS

Before we begin our work with databases we must first understand some basic database concepts. These terms are standard to all databases and it is essential to have some knowledge of them in order to understand the work we will be performing in the following tasks. You should understand some of these terms now while others will become clearer as we deal with them specifically later.

Database   A collection of data that's related to a particular topic or purpose, as described above.

DBMS   A collection of computer programs used to manage a database, as described above.

Field   Each separate piece of data stored in a database is referred to as a field. A field could contain a person's name, a book title, an author, an account balance, an employee's date of birth, etc. A field may contain no data, in which case it is referred to as a blank field.

Record   This is a collection of data about one person, thing or event. It contains all the fields that make up the data for a single entry in the database or a particular topic.

Table   This is a collection of records about a particular subject. It is presented in table format so that it is easy to read and understand. Each column constitutes a particular field. Each row constitutes one particular record.

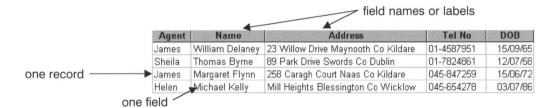

Figure 5.1

Query   This is a question you ask about the data stored in a database. A query usually results in a selection of data being presented to the user. It should be noted, even at this stage, that when a query is saved it is only the question which is saved and not the answer or result.

Report   This is a custom-designed presentation of data from a database. This is used to present data for viewing by other people who require additional information in order to understand the data being displayed. Reports are generally printed for viewing by managers and other relevant personnel.

Form   Instead of working with data in tabular format it may be presented one record at a time. This is done using a form that you design so that the fields are displayed in whatever layout you like (see Figure 5.2). The DBMS will then display one record at a time in this format. It is possible to enter, change and view records using the form view or table view.

Car Rental - Customer Booking

Agent's Name: [   ]

Customer Name: [   ]
Customer Address: [   ]

Contact Tel No: [   ]   Customer DOB: [   ]

Figure 5.2

Primary Key This is the field that identifies each record as unique, i.e. different from any other record. Typically it would be an identity number such as employee number, part number, book number, account number, etc. Two of the major uses of a primary key are to prevent the input of duplicate records and to create an index.

DATABASE PROGRAMS (DBMSs)

There is great diversity in the appearance of different database programs (DBMSs), but they all have the same components. We will be using one program as an example of how to perform the tasks in this section. If you are using a different program then you may adjust the notes to reflect your particular program.

LOADING THE DATABASE PROGRAM

The database program may be loaded from the desktop, if there is an icon on the desktop, as follows:

➤➤   ▮▸ Database icon .

If the program is not available from the desktop then it may be loaded from the Start menu, as follows:

➤➤   ▮▸ Start .

➤➤   ▮▸ All Programs.

continued

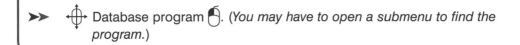

➤➤ ⊕ Database program 🖱. (*You may have to open a submenu to find the program.*)

Task 5.1.1

Create a new database and save it with the filename **Tennis Club**.

CREATING A NEW DATABASE

One point worth noting at this stage is that most database programs require the file that will contain the database to be created and saved before any data can be entered into the database. This means that the process of creating a new database involves saving it and giving it a filename. This is at variance to most other programs, where the file may be worked on and saved afterward.

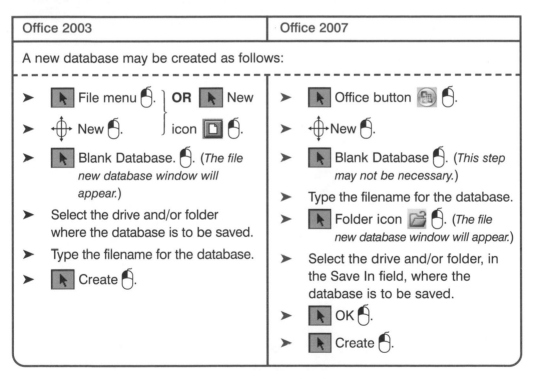

Office 2003	Office 2007
A new database may be created as follows:	
➤ 🔲 File menu 🖱. ⎤ **OR** 🔲 New ➤ ⊕ New 🖱. ⎦ icon 🔲 🖱. ➤ 🔲 Blank Database. 🖱. (*The file new database window will appear.*) ➤ Select the drive and/or folder where the database is to be saved. ➤ Type the filename for the database. ➤ 🔲 Create 🖱.	➤ 🔲 Office button 🖱. ➤ ⊕ New 🖱. ➤ 🔲 Blank Database 🖱. (*This step may not be necessary.*) ➤ Type the filename for the database. ➤ 🔲 Folder icon 📂 🖱. (*The file new database window will appear.*) ➤ Select the drive and/or folder, in the Save In field, where the database is to be saved. ➤ 🔲 OK 🖱. ➤ 🔲 Create 🖱.

The database will be created and saved. The database main screen will be presented. The Access **2007** main screen is shown in Figure 5.3.

Note: It may be a good idea to maximise the screen size at this stage if the program does not automatically do so.

Once the program has been loaded the screen may look something like the following.

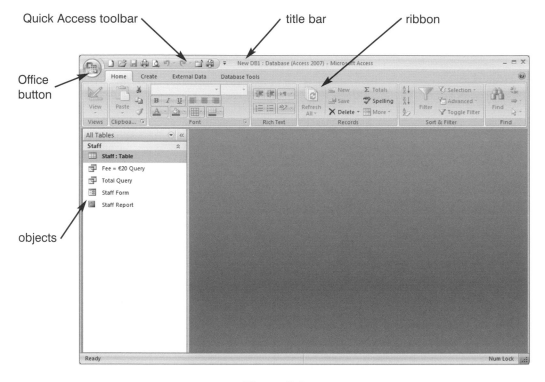

Figure 5.3

In Access **2003** the various objects are selected by simply pointing to the object type (Table, Form, etc.) and clicking the left mouse button. The individual objects will then appear as a list on the right. All the objects appear to be very similar, so care should be taken to ensure that you have selected the object you require.

In Access **2007** the individual objects all appear on the left-hand side. The icon in front of each object indicates what type of object it is. When using the program it is a good idea to form the habit of adding the object type as part of the object name, e.g. Staff Table, Male Staff Query, Application Form, Staff Details Report, etc.

Task 5.1.2

(a) Create a new table with the field names, field types, size or format shown in Figure 5.4. (You may add a short description for each field, if your program allows it.)
(b) Nominate the Memb No field as the primary key field.
(c) Ensure that all dates entered must be after 01/01/1972 (the date the club started).
(d) Save the table as **Members Table**.

Field Name	Field Type	Size or Format
Memb No	Number	Integer
FullName	Text	20
Address	Text	50
Date	Date/Time	Short Date
Fee	Currency	Currency
Full	Logical (Yes/No)	Yes/No

Figure 5.4

CREATING A NEW TABLE

When new data is to be entered into a database it requires a table to be created to accommodate the data.

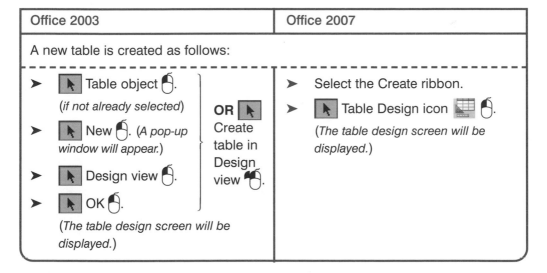

Creating Fields

The table design screen is used to specify the fields that will make up the new table.

> Each field is created as follows:
>
> ➤➤ Enter the field name in the first blank Field Name cell.
>
> ➤➤ Press the tab key to move to the Data Type cell.
>
> ➤➤ ⬛ Down arrow icon 🖱.
>
> ➤➤ Select the required data type.

continued

➤➤ Press the tab key to move to the description cell.

➤➤ Enter a description of the field, if required. (*Whatever is typed here will appear on the bottom of the screen when entering records.*)

➤➤ Type or select additional field properties, such as the field size and/or format, in the bottom half of the screen.

➤➤ Repeat the steps for each field.

Nominate a Primary Key

A primary key field is nominated as follows:

➤➤ Place the cursor anywhere in the row of the field to be nominated 🖰.

➤➤ 🖰 Primary key icon 🔑 🖰.

(*A small key will appear on the left-hand side of the row.*)

Save the Table

Office 2003	Office 2007
The table is saved as follows:	
➤ 🖰 File menu 🖰.	➤ 🖰 Office button 🖰.

➤➤ 🖰 Save as 🖰. (*The save as window will appear.*)

➤➤ Type the table name.

➤➤ 🖰 OK 🖰.

Note: It is a good idea to add the word 'Table' after the name – Access **2007** automatically adds the word 'Table' to all new tables.

It must be remembered that when you save a table it is not saved as a separate file, but rather it is saved as a table in the database that has been created.

Close the Table

The table design window can be closed as follows:

>> Window close icon ☒ 🖱.

(The program will ask you if you wish to save the table, or changes to the table, if you have not already done so.)

Note: If you wish to go directly to the datasheet view of the table you may point to the view icon ▦ and click the left mouse button. (On the home ribbon in **2007**.)

Data Types

There are a number of common data types available in most databases. The types include text, memo, number, date/time, currency, counter, yes/no.

The main data types are:

Text   Any string of letters or digits up to 255 characters.

Number   Any integer or real number.

Date/Time Dates and/or times in a range of formats.

Currency Monetary values.

Logical   A logical field which can only contain one of two values, usually yes/no or a box which is ticked for yes or blank for no.

Field Properties

Most data types require the specification of field properties. The fields that require additional field properties specified are:

Text:	Field	Number of characters. (You may change the size at a later time but remember that if you shorten the field you may lose some of the data in the field.)
Number:	Field Size	Integer or single (in most cases).
	Format	General number, e.g. 345.789.
	Currency	e.g. 45.50.
	Fixed	Number of decimal places.
	Standard	Two decimal places.
	Per cent	
	Scientific	
	Decimal Places	0 to 15 (used with fixed numbers).
Date/Time:	Format	Specify format from list of options.

Validation rule may be used to ensure that data meets a particular requirement. Some simple validation rules are:

>01/01/1972   Must be a date after 01/01/1972.

<>NULL   Must have a value in this field (cannot be null).

Like "P??"   Must be three characters, beginning with P.

Task 5.1.3

(a) Open the Members Table in datasheet view.
(b) Enter the following records into the **Members Table**.
(c) Print the table.

Memb No	FullName	Address	Date	Fee	Full
2001	Goff Harry	78 Mill Lane Naas Co Kildare	25/06/1998	€650.00	☑
2002	Furlong Kevin	Canal View Naas Co Kildare	15/11/1988	€650.00	☑
2003	Collins Helen	23 Canal Banks Naas Co Kildare	14/07/1972	€485.00	☐
2004	Griffin Liam	Beech Grove Clane Co Kildare	12/09/1989	€275.00	☐
2005	Fennell Sarah	64 Millbrook Kilcullen Co Kildare	25/09/1972	€650.00	☑
2006	Doyle Jeffery	Main Street Naas Co Kildare	05/02/1981	€650.00	☑
2007	Fleming Linda	54 Ashgrove Naas Co Kildare	06/12/1992	€485.00	☐
2008	Collins Brian	Gate Lodge Clane Co Kildare	22/07/1997	€485.00	☐
2009	Collins Keith	248 Willowside Clane Co Kildare	27/09/1972	€650.00	☑
2010	Burke Joan	56 Broadbank Naas Co Kildare	03/08/1999	€650.00	☑

Figure 5.5

OPENING A TABLE

A table may be opened in either datasheet view or design view. Datasheet view will display all the records in the table. Design view will display the design screen for the table. Alterations may be made to the design of the table in design view.

A table is opened as follows:

Datasheet View

Office 2003	Office 2007
➤ 🖱 Tables object 👆. ➤ 🖱 Table name 👆. ⎤ OR 🖱 ➤ 🖱 Open 👆. ⎦ Table name 👆👆.	➤ 🖱 Table name 👆👆.

Design View

Office 2003	Office 2007
➤ 🔲 Tables object 🖱. ➤ 🔲 Table name 🖱. ➤ 🔲 Design 🖱.	➤ 🔲 Table name 🖱. ➤ 🔲 Design View icon 📝 🖱.

ENTERING RECORDS INTO A TABLE

Once the table structure has been created it is then possible to enter the records into the table. New records may be entered into a table at any time, not just after it has been created.

Records may be added to a table in either datasheet view or form view. The records will be added to the table regardless of what view it is in.

Datasheet View

Records are entered in datasheet view as follows:

➤➤ Open the table in datasheet view. (*as described above*)

➤➤ 🔲 New record icon ▶✱ 🖱 (*If the table already has records entered.*)

➤➤ Type the entries in each field. (*Use the tab key* ↹ *to move from field to field.*)

➤➤ Close the table when finished.

When the first record has been entered, it may be a good idea to adjust the column widths so that all the data in each field appears on-screen. Column widths are adjusted as follows:

Method 1

➤➤ 🔲 Line between column labels 🖱.

(*The cursor changes to a black, double-headed arrow* ↔.)

➤➤ Drag the line to the required width 🖱.

Method 2

➤➤ 🔲 Line between columns 🖱🖱.

Even if the column width appears too big or too small, it will still hold the data as specified in the table structure. For example, if a field was specified as twenty characters, then even if the width of that field (column) in the table is bigger or smaller it will still accept a maximum of twenty characters, even if the field appears much bigger.

Form View

In order to enter records in form view, a form must first be created. We will be creating forms later so we will leave entering records in form view until then.

PRINTING A TABLE

A table may be printed at any time. A printout may be produced while the table is either open or closed (some programs require the table to be open in order to print it). As with all printouts it is a good idea to preview the printout first.

Preview a Table

A table may be previewed as follows:

➤➤ 🖱 Table name 🖱.   **OR**   Open the table.

➤➤ 🖱 Preview icon 🔍 🖱.

Office 2007

Note: In Access **2007**, if the print preview icon is not on the Quick Access toolbar then the table is previewed as follows:

➤ 🖱 Table name 🖱.   **OR**   Open the table.

➤ 🖱 Office button 🖱.

➤ ✛ Print.

➤ ✛ Print Preview 🖱.

Printing a Table

A table may be printed as follows:

➤➤ 🖱 Table name 🖱.   **OR**   Open the table.

➤➤ 🖱 Print icon 🖱.

Office 2007

Note: In Access **2007**, if the print icon is not on the Quick Access toolbar then the table is printed as follows:

➤ 🔲 Table name 🖱. **OR** Open the table.

➤ 🔲 Office button 🔘 🖱.

➤ ✛ Print 🖱.

Task 5.1.4 (Additional)

(a) Close the Members Table (if it is open).
(b) Close the Tennis Club database.
(c) Exit the DBMS program.

CLOSING A DATABASE

Each database should be closed when you are finished working on it. It is a good idea to close any open objects before closing the database.

A database is closed as follows:

➤➤ 🔲 Window close icon ❌ 🖱.

EXITING THE DBMS PROGRAM

Each time you are finished with the DBMS program you must exit the program.

Office 2003	Office 2007
A program is exited as follows:	
➤ 🔲 File menu 🖱.	➤ 🔲 Office button 🔘 🖱.
➤ ✛ Exit 🖱.	➤ ✛ Close Database 🖱.

Task 5.1.5

(a) Load the DBMS program (if not already loaded).

(b) Open the **Tennis Club** database (if not already open).

OPENING A DATABASE

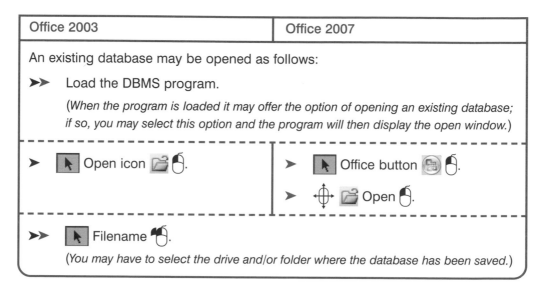

Office 2003	Office 2007
An existing database may be opened as follows:	
➤➤ Load the DBMS program.	
(When the program is loaded it may offer the option of opening an existing database; if so, you may select this option and the program will then display the open window.)	
➤ ▸ Open icon 🖿 🖱.	➤ ▸ Office button 🖳 🖱.
	➤ ✛ 🖿 Open 🖱.
➤➤ ▸ Filename 🖱.	
(You may have to select the drive and/or folder where the database has been saved.)	

The database will be opened and the database main screen will be presented.

Note: In Access **2003** it may be a good idea to maximise the screen size at this stage.

Task 5.1.6

Delete the **Full** field from the Members Table.

DELETING A FIELD FROM A TABLE

It may sometimes be necessary to remove a field from a table, but it must be remembered that when a field is removed all the data stored in that field will be permanently deleted from the database.

Office 2003	Office 2007
A field is deleted as follows:	
➤ ▸ Table object 🖱. *(if this is not already selected)*	➤ ▸ Table name 🖱.

continued

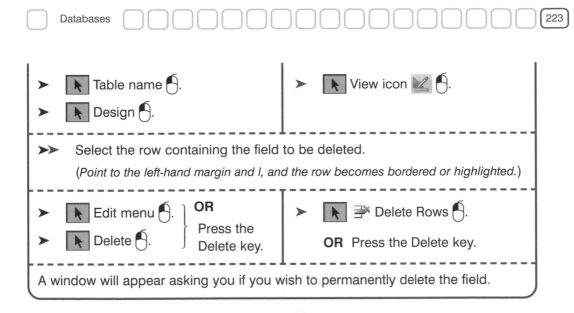

➤ ⬛ Table name 🖰.

➤ ⬛ Design 🖰.

➤ ⬛ View icon ✎ 🖰.

➤➤ Select the row containing the field to be deleted.

(*Point to the left-hand margin and I, and the row becomes bordered or highlighted.*)

➤ ⬛ Edit menu 🖰. ⎫ **OR**

➤ ⬛ Delete 🖰. ⎬ Press the Delete key.

➤ ⬛ ≕ Delete Rows 🖰.

OR Press the Delete key.

A window will appear asking you if you wish to permanently delete the field.

Task 5.1.7

(a) Recreate the **Full** field in the Members Table.

(b) Re-enter the data in the **Full** field.

Task 5.1.8

Enter the following two records to the Members Table.

Memb No	FullName	Address	Date	Fee	Full
2011	Fleming Liam	54 Ashgrove Naas Co Kildare	12/08/1996	€650.00	☑
2012	Keating Mark	Westgate Newbridge Co Kildare	13/09/1999	€485.00	☐

Figure 5.6

Task 5.1.9 (Additional)

Enter the additional records shown in the Members.doc file in the Database folder on the CD into the Members Table.

Task 5.1.10

Delete the following records from the Members Table.

Memb No	FullName	Address	Date	Fee	Full
2001	Goff Harry	78 Mill Lane Naas Co Kildare	25/06/1998	€650.00	☑
2002	Furlong Kevin	Canal View Naas Co Kildare	15/11/1988	€650.00	☑

Figure 5.7

DELETING RECORDS FROM A TABLE

It is sometimes necessary to remove records that are no longer required from a table.

Records are removed from a table as follows:

➤➤ Open the table in datasheet view.

➤➤ Select the row containing the record.

(*Point to the left-hand margin and* 🖱. *The row appears bordered or highlighted.*)

➤➤ 🖱 Delete record icon ✖ / ✖ 🖱. **OR** 🖱 Press the Delete key.

(*A window will appear telling you that you are about to delete a record.*)

➤➤ 🖱 Yes 🖱. (*The record will be deleted.*)

Task 5.1.11

Re-enter the records that you deleted in **Task 5.1.10**.

Task 5.1.12

(a) Change Kevin Furlong's address to Canal View Prosperous Co Kildare.
(b) Change Liam Griffin's date to *12/09/1999*.
(c) Change Joan Burke's fee to *485.00*.

EDITING RECORDS IN A TABLE

It is often necessary to make changes to records in a table, which is accomplished by editing the record(s).

Records are edited as follows:

➤➤ Open the table in datasheet view.

➤➤ Select the position in the record. (*Place the cursor in the data to be edited* 🖱.)

continued

➤➤ Backspace to delete to the left. **OR** Press the Delete key to delete from the right.

➤➤ Type to enter data.

Task 5.1.13 (Additional)

Perform the operations specified in **Tasks 5A-1** on the CD.

QUERIES

The major purpose of producing a database is to be able to retrieve information from the database in a format that is useful to the operator. The main method of retrieving information from a database is by using a query. A query may be thought of as a question you ask – the DBMS will search the database table(s), assemble the information and present it, usually in table format.

It should be noted that when you save a query, you are saving the question and not the answer to the query. This means that each time you use the query the DBMS will search the table and retrieve the information, even if this is done immediately after closing the same query.

Task 5.2.1

(a) Open the database named **Tennis Club** (if not already open).
(b) Produce a query that will select all the records where the **fee** is 650 (€650.00) and display all the data about these members.
(c) Save this query with the filename **Fee 650 Query**.
(d) Print one copy of the query.
(e) Close the query.

DESIGNING A NEW QUERY

The simplest method of obtaining information from a database is to design a query. We will be using the design view to create queries.

Office 2003	Office 2007
A query is designed as follows:	
➤ ▸ Query object 🖱. (*if this is not already selected*)	➤ Select the Create ribbon. ➤ ▸ Query Design icon 📇 🖱.

continued

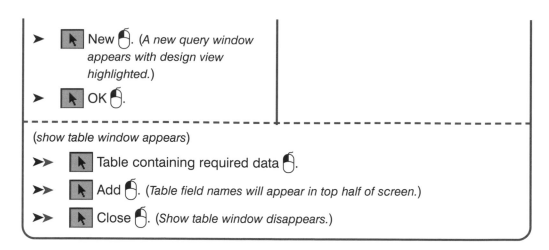

➤ ▣ New 🖱. (*A new query window appears with design view highlighted.*)

➤ ▣ OK 🖱.

- -

(*show table window appears*)

➤➤ ▣ Table containing required data 🖱.

➤➤ ▣ Add 🖱. (*Table field names will appear in top half of screen.*)

➤➤ ▣ Close 🖱. (*Show table window disappears.*)

With Access the screen should look like the following. This screen allows the query to be built up in a number of simple steps.

This screen has two distinct sections. The top half contains the table(s) that contains the data. The bottom half, which is called the QBE (query by example) grid, is where the output of the query is constructed.

Figure 5.8

Selecting Fields

The first step in building a query is to select the fields that you want included in the output. It is not always necessary to include all fields from the table. Fields are added to the query output by adding them to the QBE grid. The fields should be added in the order in which they are to be displayed in the output.

Fields are added to the QBE grid as follows:

➤➤ ▮ Required field in table .

➤➤ Repeat for all fields required in the query output.

(The fields will appear on the field row of the QBE grid.)

Viewing a Query

Once the fields have been added to the QBE grid, the query may be displayed on the screen.

The query is displayed as follows:

➤➤ ▮ Datasheet view icon ▦ .

The query will be displayed in table format on the screen.

You will notice that all the records appeared in the output, and in fact the output is exactly the same as the table. This is because we have not yet selected particular records to be included in the output and therefore the program automatically selects all the records.

Returning to Design

If you wish to make alterations after viewing your query, you may return to the design screen.

The design screen is displayed as follows:

➤➤ ▮ Design View icon ▨ 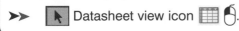.

Criteria

The criteria is the rule used to select the required records from the table. The criteria used to select the records is typed on the criteria row of the QBE grid. The required records are selected for inclusion in the query by checking each record with whatever is entered in the criteria section for that field. If the record matches the criteria then it is included, if it does not match then it is not included.

If you want all the members who pay a fee of €650.00, then you simply type **650** in the criteria row under the field name **Fee**. This will select all the records that have 650 in the **Fee** field. In this case the criteria must match the entry in the field exactly.

Note: The € symbol is not entered in the criteria as this is not part of the field contents. The € is displayed in the output because the field is defined as a currency field in the design of the table.

We will examine criteria in more detail later.

SAVING A QUERY

If you wish to retain the query for use again then it must be saved as a query.

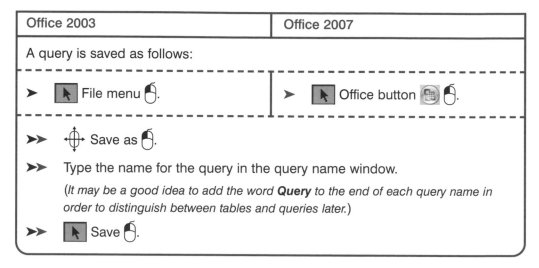

Office 2003	Office 2007
A query is saved as follows:	
➤ ▣ File menu 🖱.	➤ ▣ Office button 🖱.
➤➤ ⊕ Save as 🖱.	
➤➤ Type the name for the query in the query name window.	
*(It may be a good idea to add the word **Query** to the end of each query name in order to distinguish between tables and queries later.)*	
➤➤ ▣ Save 🖱.	

The query name will appear in the list of queries (**2003**) or the objects list (**2007**), in alphabetical order.

CLOSING A QUERY

When you are finished with a query you may return to the database main screen by closing the query. The query may be closed from either the design view or datasheet view.

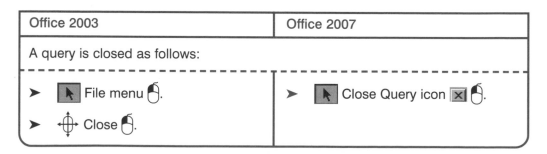

Office 2003	Office 2007
A query is closed as follows:	
➤ ▣ File menu 🖱.	➤ ▣ Close Query icon ☒ 🖱.
➤ ⊕ Close 🖱.	

If you have not saved the query then a window will appear asking if you wish to save this query.

PRINTING A QUERY

A query may be printed at any time. A printout may be produced while the query is either open or closed. Note that some programs require the query to be open in order to print it. As always, it is a good idea to preview the printout before printing.

Preview a Query

A query may be previewed as follows:

➤➤   Query name. **OR**   Open the query.

➤➤   Preview icon.

Office 2007

Note: In Access **2007**, if the print preview icon is not on the Quick Access toolbar then the query is previewed as follows:

➤   Query name. **OR**   Open the query.

➤   Office button.

➤   Print.

➤   Print Preview.

Printing a Query

A query may be printed as follows:

➤➤   Query name. **OR**   Open the query.

➤➤   Print icon.

Office 2007

Note: In Access **2007**, if the print icon is not on the Quick Access toolbar then the query is printed as follows:

➤   Query name. **OR**   Open the query.

➤   Office button.

➤   Print.

Task 5.2.2

(a) Open the **Tennis Club** database (if not already open).
(b) Open the **Fee 650 Query** in design view.
(c) Modify the design to perform the following:

- Have the output sorted on the **Date** field.
- Don't show the **Fee** field in the output.

(d) View the output and modify the design if the output is not correct.
(e) Save the query again with the same query name.
(f) Close the query.

OPENING A QUERY

A query may be opened in either datasheet view or design view. Datasheet view will display all the records from the table(s) as defined by the query. Design view will display the design screen for the query. Alterations may be made to the query in design view.

A query is opened as follows:

Datasheet View

Office 2003	Office 2007
➤ 🖱 Query name 🖱. ⎤ **OR** 🖱 ⎥ Query ⎥ name 🖱. 🖱 Open 🖱. ⎦	➤ 🖱 Query name 🖱.

Design View

Office 2003	Office 2007
➤ 🖱 Query name 🖱. ➤ 🖱 Design 🖱.	Open in Datasheet view. ➤ 🖱 View icon 📐 🖱.

Note: It is possible to switch between datasheet view and design view by simply pointing to the view icon and clicking the left mouse button.

SORTING QUERY OUTPUT

You may have the output sorted in ascending or descending order by any field in the QBE grid. If there is no stipulation on how the output is to be sorted then it automatically means in ascending order. **Sorting** is sometimes referred to as **organising**.

The output is sorted (organised) as follows:

➤➤ 🔲 Required sort field (in the QBE grid) 🖱.

➤➤ 🔲 Down arrow icon ▾ 🖱.

➤➤ 🔲 Ascending, descending or (not sorted) as required 🖱.

When sorting output, it is normally only sorted on one field. If you ask the program to sort the output on two fields it will usually sort on the first field, which has an entry on the sort row, and ignore anything else in that row.

In some cases there will be a number of records with the same entry in a sorted field, then the output may be sorted on a second field within the first field. The first field to be sorted is referred to as the **primary sort** and the second field to be sorted is referred to as the **secondary sort**, e.g. if we asked to have the output sorted on the **Fee** field and then on the **Date** field, then we would place the Fee field before the Date field in the QBE grid and sort both fields. All the records with the same **fee** will be grouped together (primary sort) and be displayed in order of the **Date** field (secondary sort).

SHOWING/HIDING FIELDS IN QUERY OUTPUT

It is sometimes necessary to include a field in the QBE grid that you do not want printed in the output. When a field is inserted in the QBE grid it is automatically registered to be shown in the output. The following procedure is used to prevent a field in the QBE grid from being displayed or printed.

A field is excluded from the output as follows:

➤➤ 🔲 Square in the show field 🖱. (*The tick will disappear from the square, which indicates that this field is not to be shown in the output.*)

Task 5.2.3

(a) Open the Tennis Club database (if not already open).

(b) Produce a new query that will perform the following:

- Select all records for the members who live in Naas (remember to use the * wild card).
- Display all fields in the output with the names in alphabetical order.

(c) Display the output on-screen and modify the design if not correct.

(d) Save this query with the filename **Naas Query**.

(e) Close the query.

QUERY SELECTION CRITERIA

We have already used the criteria section in the QBE grid to select specific records from the table(s). We will now examine some of the options that you may use in the criteria section when selecting records.

When entering criteria it is not always necessary to enter the complete contents of a field. Sometimes you may only know part of the field contents and you may wish to see all the records that have this part in that field. For example, if you were looking for someone's address and you only knew part of it, then you would want all the records that contain that part in the Address field.

There are two wild card operators that may be included in the criteria when making out a query. The two operators are the ? and the * symbols. The ? can be used to take the place of a single character and the * can be used to take the place of a number of characters.

When making out criteria the following rules apply:

56 Main Street Naas   This will select all records with the words '56 Main Street Naas' in this field.

?? Main Street Naas   This will select all records with any two-digit number in front of 'Main Street Naas' in this field.

Main*   This will select all records beginning with the word 'Main' in this field.

***Naas**   This will select all records ending with the word 'Naas' in this field.

Street   This will select all records with the word 'Street' anywhere in this field.

tree   This will select all records with the word 'tree' anywhere in this field. (This will include street.)

We may also use some logical operators in the criteria. The following are the most common logical operators:

< 2005   All records with a value less than 2005 in this field.

<= 2005   All records with a value less than or equal to 2005 in this field.

> 2005   All records with a value greater than 2005 in this field.

>= 2005   All records greater than or equal to 2005 in this field.

<>2005   All records with a value not equal to 2005.

Between 2003 and 2007   All records with a value between **2003** and **2007** in this field, including both values. (Not all programs recognise this operator but it may be constructed as follows: **>=2003 AND <=2007**.)

DBMSs allow the use of the logical operators **AND** and **OR**. Some programs provide an **OR** row for the criteria, but generally it is more satisfactory not to use the **OR** row. The **AND** operator allows you to select records which meet two criteria. The **OR** operator allows you to select records with one value **OR** another value in a field.

Example

>450 **AND** <500	All records with a value greater than 450 and less than 500.
2005 **OR** 2008	All records with 2005 or 2008 in this field.
millbrook **OR** millhouse	All records with millbrook or millhouse in this field.

Other useful operators are:

Null	All records that have nothing in this field.
Not...	All records except those matching whatever follows the **NOT** operator, e.g. **NOT Naas**.
Not Null	All records that do not have this field blank.

Any of the above criteria is simply typed on the criteria row. Most programs automatically add quote marks and # symbols as required. Some programs insist on you adding quote marks and # symbols manually.

It is possible to enter criteria in a number of fields in order to obtain the required records. For example, if you wanted all the members whose fee is €650.00 and who joined the club after 01/01/1998, then you would enter the criteria **650** into the Fee field and the criteria **>01/01/1998** in the date field.

Task 5.2.4

(a) Open the Tennis Club database (if not already open).
(b) Produce a new query that will perform the following:

- Select all the members whose fee is less than 500.
- Display all fields in the output with the records sorted with the highest fee first.

(c) Display the output on-screen and modify the design if not correct.
(d) Save this query with the filename **Fee under 500 Query**.
(e) Close the query.

Task 5.2.5

(a) Produce a new query that will perform the following:

- Select all records where the fee is 650 and the member joined after 01/01/1998.
- Display all fields in the output with the names in alphabetical order.

(b) Display the output on-screen and modify the design if not correct.
(c) Save this query with the filename **Fee 650 after 01/01/1998 Query**.
(d) Close the query.

Task 5.2.6

(a) Produce a new query that will perform the following:

- Select all records for all the members who live in Clane and who joined the club before 01/01/2000.
- Display all fields in the output with the dates in order, newest member first.

(b) Display the output on-screen and modify the design if not correct.
(c) Save this query with the filename **Clane before 01/01/2000 Query**.
(d) Close the query.

Task 5.2.7

(a) Produce a new query that will perform the following:

- Select all records for all the members who live in Clane or Naas.
- Display only the **Name** and **Address** fields.

(b) Display the output on-screen and modify the design if not correct.
(c) Save this query with the filename **Clane or Naas Query**.
(d) Close the query.

FILTERING

Most DBMSs have a filtering function that allows records to be filtered. If a table, query or form is displayed on-screen you may quickly want to see all the records that match the entry in one particular field, e.g. you might want to see all the members who paid a fee of €650.00. Applying a filter will display this information.

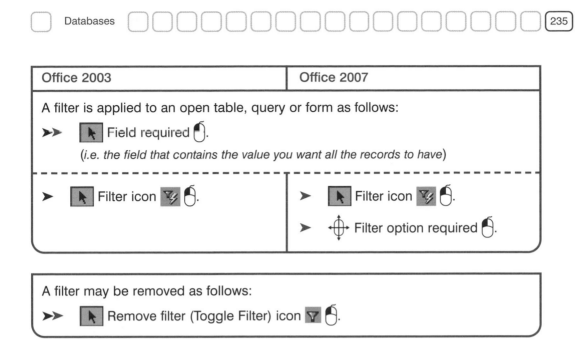

Office 2003	Office 2007
A filter is applied to an open table, query or form as follows:	
➤➤ ▣ Field required 🖱. *(i.e. the field that contains the value you want all the records to have)*	
➤ ▣ Filter icon 🔽 🖱.	➤ ▣ Filter icon 🔽 🖱. ➤ ✥ Filter option required 🖱.

A filter may be removed as follows:

➤➤ ▣ Remove filter (Toggle Filter) icon 🔽 🖱.

INDEXING

When databases become very large, they usually contain several linked tables. In such cases it may take a long time to find particular records – e.g. if you have a table containing a list of several thousand names along with a number of other fields in the table, and that table is linked to a number of other tables containing data relating to each person. If you regularly search the database for particular names then you would be using the Name field in the search criteria. Each time you search the table the DBMS must go through each field in the tables as it searches for the name.

If a separate table (index) were created that contained only the Name field, then the DBMS would be able to quickly search for a particular name in the index without having to go through other fields. This is what happens with indexing. The DBMS searches the index and then when it finds the record(s) it returns all the information requested from the various tables.

When a table is created and a primary key is set, this primary key becomes a unique field (no duplicates allowed) but it also becomes an index field. Thus, if we were searching a very large database using a criteria in the primary key field it would produce a solution much faster than a criteria in one of the other fields because this is an indexed field.

We can create an index for any field in the table when we are designing a table. This is one of the properties in the table design that you may set for any field, not just the primary key. When setting an index you may usually set it to one of the following:

- Indexed with no duplicate values allowed in the field (the same as a primary key).

- Indexed with duplicate values allowed.

Note: Indexing is only useful when dealing with large databases.

Task 5.2.8 (Additional)

Carry out the operations specified in **Task 5A-2** on the CD.

FORMS

As already mentioned, forms may be used to input and view records. However, in order to use a form it must be created and saved in the database. If the form is used to input or edit records, the data will automatically be added to or edited in the table.

Task 5.3.1

(a) Open the **Tennis Club** database (if not already open).
(b) Create a simple form containing all the fields in the Members Table.
(c) Save the form as **Members Form**.

CREATING A FORM

The simplest method of producing a form is to use the form wizard to create the initial form and then to modify the form to suit your requirements.

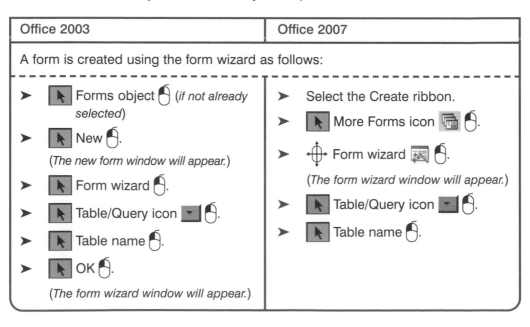

Office 2003	Office 2007
A form is created using the form wizard as follows:	
➤ Forms object (*if not already selected*)	➤ Select the Create ribbon.
➤ New.	➤ More Forms icon.
(*The new form window will appear.*)	➤ Form wizard.
➤ Form wizard.	(*The form wizard window will appear.*)
➤ Table/Query icon.	➤ Table/Query icon.
➤ Table name.	➤ Table name.
➤ OK.	
(*The form wizard window will appear.*)	

The form wizard will then guide you through the rest of the creation of the form. The necessary steps are shown in the following box.

1 Select the fields to be included in the form.

A list of fields, which you may select, will be displayed in the available fields box.

Fields are selected as follows:

➤➤ ⬛ First field to be included in the form ⬚. (*This field may already be highlighted.*)

➤➤ ⬛ Add icon ▷ ⬚.

(*The field will be transferred to the selected fields box.*)

➤➤ Repeat the procedure until all the required fields have been included.

Note: All the fields may be transferred as follows:

➤➤ ⬛ ⟫ ⬚.

When all the required fields have been included:

➤➤ ⬛ Next ⬚.

2 The next step is to select the layout of the form. This is the layout of the fields on the finished form. The most common type would be the single column. This may be modified later to produce a form with a number of fields on each row.

Select the layout required as follows:

➤➤ ⬛ Layout required ⬚. (*from the options offered*)

➤➤ ⬛ Next ⬚.

Note: In Access **2007**, if the form is to be modified later, it is advisable to select 'Justified' layout as this is the simplest layout to modify.

3 The next step is to select the style required. This is the background and the style of the labels and fields on the form.

Select the style required as follows:

➤➤ ⬛ Style required ⬚. (*from the options offered*)

➤➤ ⬛ Next ⬚.

4 Finally, enter a title for the form by typing it in the space provided. Remember that it is a good idea to add the word 'Form' to the name.

The form will usually require some modifications, so it is a good idea to modify the form at this stage by:

➤➤ ⬛ Modifying the form's design ⬚.

➤➤ ⬛ Finish ⬚.

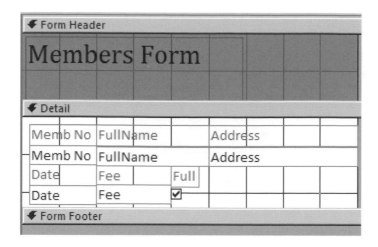

Figure 5.9

The form design will then appear on the screen in design view and should look something like Figure 5.9.

Design view allows you to make modifications to the form, such as layout and adding any additional headings, graphics, instructions, etc.

Each field consists of two parts. The first part is the field label and the second part is the field itself, where the data is entered and displayed. The two parts may be moved independently, allowing the layout to be modified as required.

It is possible to switch between form view and design view in the normal way.

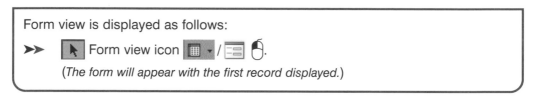

Form view is displayed as follows:

➤➤ ▶ Form view icon 📼 ▾ / 🗏 🖱.

(*The form will appear with the first record displayed.*)

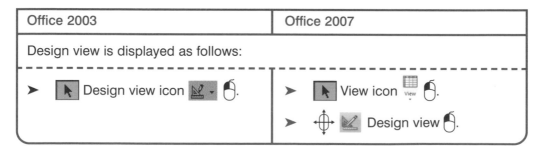

Office 2003	Office 2007
Design view is displayed as follows:	
➤ ▶ Design view icon 📝 ▾ 🖱.	➤ ▶ View icon ⊞ 🖱. ➤ ⊕ 📝 Design view 🖱.

Task 5.3.2

(a) Open the **Tennis Club** database (if not already open).

(b) Open the Members form in design view (if not already open).
(c) Widen the form so that it is the full width of the screen in form view. (You may have to switch between form view and design view a couple of times to achieve the correct width.)
(d) Lay out the fields as shown in Figure 5.10.
(e) Create a header space and insert the heading shown below.
(f) Create a footer space and insert the footer shown below.
(g) Insert a suitable Clip Art picture in the position shown below.
(h) Save the form again with the same form name.

Figure 5.10

CUSTOMISING A FORM

The width of a form may be altered by dragging the right margin to the required position. Position the cursor on the right-hand edge of the form (the cursor changes to a cross with two arrows ←╂→), hold down the left mouse button and drag the edge to the required width.

In order to work on a field or label, that field or label must be selected. A field or label is selected by simply pointing to the field or label and clicking the left mouse button. The field or label will appear with handles (small squares), as shown below.

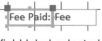

field label selected

Figure 5.11

field selected

Figure 5.12

You may move the fields and/or labels by selecting them and dragging them to the required position. The field and label are moved by selecting the field and then pointing to the edge of the field or label (a hand or four-headed arrow will appear), then holding down the mouse button and dragging the field and label to the required position. A field or label may be moved independently by pointing to the larger square (a hand with only one finger or a four-headed arrow will appear), holding down the left mouse button and dragging the field or label to the required position.

The size of each field or label may be adjusted by pointing to one of the side handles, holding down the mouse button and dragging the field or label to the required size. The field text may be edited by positioning the mouse in the label field and clicking the left mouse button. Text may then be added or deleted.

The form header may be lengthened or shorted by positioning the cursor on the top edge of the detail band (the cursor changes to a cross with two arrows ╪). Hold down the left mouse button and drag the detail section down to create/alter header space. The detail and form footer space is altered in the same way.

Additional data is added to the form by creating label frames and typing the text in each frame.

A label frame is produced as follows:

➤➤ ▣ Label tool **Aa** 🖰.

➤➤ Position the cursor on the form 🖰.

➤➤ Drag the mouse to the right and down to create a frame 🖰.

➤➤ Type text in the frame. (*If you don't type something in the frame, it will disappear.*)

While the form is being modified it is possible to switch between form view and design view, as described above.

INSERTING GRAPHICS IN A FORM

Office 2003	Office 2007
A graphic may be inserted on a form as follows: ➤➤ Open the form in design view.	
➤ ▣ Insert menu 🖰. ➤ ⊕ Picture 🖰. **OR** Object 🖰. (*Select Microsoft Clip Gallery for Clip Art 2003 only.*)	➤ ▣ Logo Icon 🖾 🖰.
➤➤ Select the picture or Clip Art. (*may need to locate the folder containing the graphic*)	

The graphic is positioned by simply pointing to the graphic, holding down the left mouse button and dragging the graphic to the required position on the form.

The graphic may be resized by selecting the graphic and then pointing to a handle (one of the small squares on the corners), holding down the left mouse button and dragging the graphic to the required size.

Note: It may be necessary to change the Size Mode property to 'Stretch' before resizing the graphic.

The properties are changed as follows:

➤➤ ▣ Clip/Picture 🖱. (*A pop-up menu will appear.*)

➤➤ ✛ Properties 🖱. (*The properties window will appear.*)

➤➤ ▣ All tab 🖱. (*if not already selected*)

➤➤ Change the Size Mode to 'Stretch'.

➤➤ Close the properties window.

CLOSING A FORM

Office 2003	Office 2007
The form is closed as follows:	
➤ ▣ File menu 🖱. ➤ ▣ Close 🖱.	➤ ▣ Close Form icon ☒ 🖱.

If you have not saved the form then a window will appear asking if you wish to save this form.

OPENING A FORM

Office 2003	Office 2007
The form is opened as follows:	
➤ ▣ Form object 🖱. ➤ ▣ Form name 🖱.	➤ ▣ Form name 🖱.

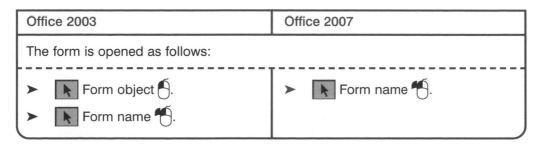

VIEWING RECORDS USING A FORM

Once the form has been created it will appear in the list of forms. This form may then be used to view each record.

Records may be viewed by first opening the form and then using the record selection icons at the bottom of the screen. These icons perform the functions listed below by simply pointing to the icon required and clicking the left mouse button.

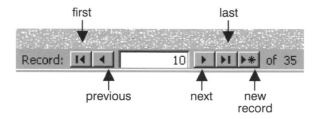

Figure 5.13

Task 5.3.3

(a) Open the **Tennis Club** database (if not already open).

(b) Enter the following records into the Members Table using the Members Form.

Memb No	FullName	Address	Date	Fee	Full
2031	O'Reilly Henry	56 Willow Grove Clane Co Kildare	15/08/2004	€650.00	☑
2032	Griffin Mary	The Banks Kilcullen Co Kildare	25/10/2004	€250.00	☐

Figure 5.14

ENTERING RECORDS IN FORM VIEW

Records are added in form view as follows:

➤➤ Open the form, in 'Form View'.

➤➤ ⬚ New record icon ▶* 🖱.

➤➤ Type the entries in each field. (*Use the tab key to move from field to field and use the mouse to tick any boxes.*)

Task 5.3.4 (Additional)

Carry out the operations specified in **Task 5A-3** on the CD.

REPORTS

Reports are used to assemble information and present it in a manner that is attractive and clear. Reports are generally produced for viewing by people who may not be familiar with the information or for inclusion in a publication.

Reports are also used to produce mailing labels. These may be actual labels which would be attached to envelopes for posting, or labels for a variety of other purposes such as attaching to files, belongings, samples, etc.

Task 5.4.1

(a) Open the **Tennis Club** database (if not already open).
(b) Create a simple report containing all the fields in the Members Table, sorted on the **Name** field.
(c) Save the report as **Members Report**.

CREATING A REPORT

The simplest method of producing a report is to use the report wizard to create the initial report and then to modify the report to suit your requirements.

Office 2003	Office 2007
A report is created using the report wizard as follows:	
➤ Reports object 🖱.	➤ Select the Create ribbon.
➤ New 🖱.	➤ Report wizard 🔍 🖱.
(The new report window will appear.)	*(The report wizard window will appear.)*
➤ Report wizard 🖱.	➤ Table/Query icon ▾ 🖱.
➤ Table/Query icon ▾ 🖱.	➤ Table or query name 🖱.
➤ Table or query name 🖱.	*(A report may be produced from a table or query.)*
(A report may be produced from a table or query.)	
➤ OK 🖱.	
(The report wizard window will appear.)	

The report wizard will then guide you through the creation of the report. The following selections will need to be made.

1 Select the fields to be included in the report. A list of fields you may select will be displayed in the available fields box.

Fields are included as follows:

➤➤ ▶ First field to be included in the report 🖱. (*This field may already be highlighted.*)

➤➤ ▶ Add icon ` > ` 🖱.

(*The field will be transferred to the selected fields box.*)

➤➤ ▶ Next field to be included in the report 🖱.

➤➤ ▶ Add icon ` > ` 🖱.

➤➤ ▶ Repeat the procedure until all the required fields have been included.

Note: It is a good idea to select the fields in the order in which you wish them displayed in the report.

All the fields may be transferred as follows:

➤➤ ▶ ` >> ` 🖱.

(*When all the required fields have been included.*)

➤➤ ▶ Next 🖱.

2 The next step is to decide if you want the report grouped in any way. For example, if you wanted members grouped by membership (full or not full) then you would select the Full field as the grouping field.

Fields are grouped as follows:

➤➤ ▶ Field to be grouped 🖱.

➤➤ ▶ Add icon ` > ` 🖱. (*The right-hand box will display the grouping.*)

➤➤ ▶ Next 🖱.

Most DBMSs provide a range of grouping options that may be selected.

3 The next step is to decide if you want the records sorted (organised) in any way. Most programs allow you to sort the records by up to four fields.

Records are sorted as follows:

➤➤ ▶ Selection icon for the first sort field ` ▾ ` 🖱.

(*The list of fields will be displayed.*)

➤➤ ▶ Field to be sorted 🖱.

continued

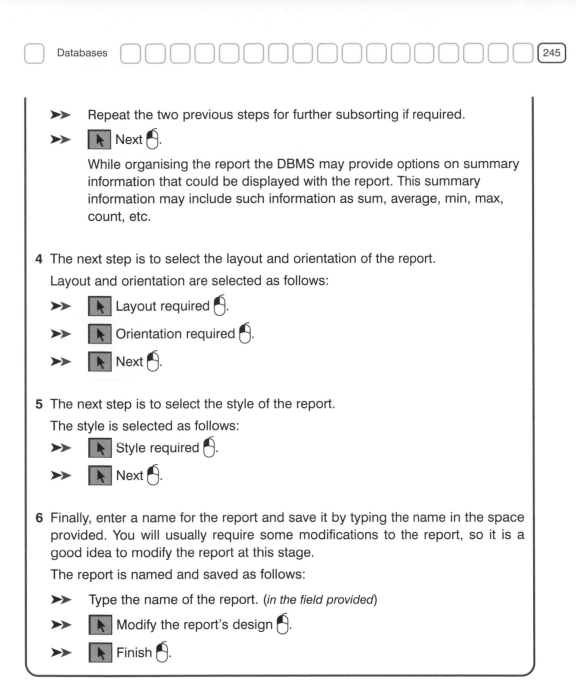

➤➤   Repeat the two previous steps for further subsorting if required.

➤➤   Next.

While organising the report the DBMS may provide options on summary information that could be displayed with the report. This summary information may include such information as sum, average, min, max, count, etc.

4   The next step is to select the layout and orientation of the report.

Layout and orientation are selected as follows:

➤➤   Layout required.

➤➤   Orientation required.

➤➤   Next.

5   The next step is to select the style of the report.

The style is selected as follows:

➤➤   Style required.

➤➤   Next.

6   Finally, enter a name for the report and save it by typing the name in the space provided. You will usually require some modifications to the report, so it is a good idea to modify the report at this stage.

The report is named and saved as follows:

➤➤   Type the name of the report. (*in the field provided*)

➤➤   Modify the report's design.

➤➤   Finish.

The report design will then appear on the screen in design view. This allows you to make modifications to the report, such as adding headings or additional information, before printing it. You may switch between print preview and design view in the same way as with the query and the form.

Preview a Report

Office 2003	Office 2007
A report may be previewed as follows: ➤➤ 🔺 Report name 🖱. **OR** Open the report. ➤➤ 🔺 Preview icon 🔍 🖱.	
Note: In Access **2007**, if the print preview icon is not on the Quick Access toolbar then the report is previewed as follows:	
	➤ 🔺 Report name 🖱. **OR** Open the report. ➤ 🔺 Office button 🖳 🖱. ➤ ✛ Print. ➤ ✛ Print Preview 🖱.

Printing a Report

Office 2003	Office 2007
A report may be printed as follows: ➤➤ 🔺 Report name 🖱. **OR** Open the report. ➤➤ 🔺 Print icon 🖱.	
Note: In Access **2007**, if the print icon is not on the Quick Access toolbar then the report is printed as follows:	
	➤ 🔺 Report name 🖱. **OR** Open the report. ➤ 🔺 Office button 🖳 🖱. ➤ ✛ Print 🖱.

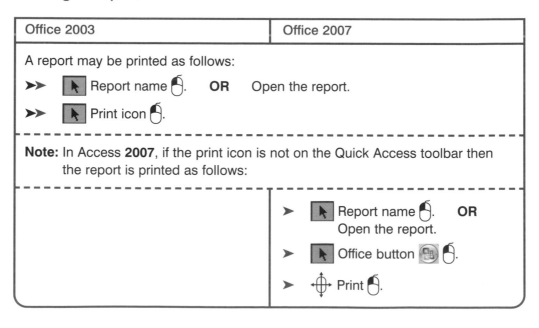

Task 5.4.2

(a) Open the **Tennis Club** database (if not already open).

(b) Open the **Members Report** in design view.

(c) Modify the report as follows:

- Create space in the **report header** and insert the headings shown in Figure 5.15.
- Lay out the **page header** so that the column headings appear as shown below.
- Lay out the **detail** so that the column contents appear as shown below.
- Insert the total and average fees in the **report footer** as shown below.
- Insert a suitable Clip Art picture in the position shown below.

(d) Save the report again with the same name.

Note: The page footer will be at the bottom of the page.

Members Report

Current Membership Report for Tennis Club

No	Name	Address	Date	Fee	Full
2010	Burke Joan	56 Broadbank Naas Co Kildare	3/08/1999	€485.00	☑
2008	Collins Brian	Gate Lodge Clane Co Kildare	2/07/1997	€485.00	☐
2003	Collins Helen	23 Canal Banks Naas Co Kildare	4/07/1972	€485.00	☐
2009	Collins Keith	248 Willowside Clane Co Kildare	7/09/1972	€650.00	☑
2006	Doyle Jeffery	Main Street Naas Co Kildare	5/02/1981	€650.00	☑
2005	Fennell Sarah	64 Millbrook Kilcullen Co Kildare	5/09/1972	€650.00	☑
2011	Fleming Liam	54 Ashgrove Naas Co Kildare	2/08/1996	€650.00	☑
2007	Fleming Linda	54 Ashgrove Naas Co Kildare	6/12/1992	€485.00	☐
2002	Furlong Kevin	Canal View Prosperous Co Kildare	5/11/1988	€650.00	☑
2001	Goff Harry	78 Mill Lane Naas Co Kildare	5/06/1998	€650.00	☑
2004	Griffin Liam	Beech Grove Clane Co Kildare	2/09/1999	€275.00	☐
2012	Keating Mark	Westgate Newbridge Co Kildare	3/09/1999	€485.00	☐

Total Fees €6,600.00

Average Fee €550.00

09 June 2003 *Page 1 of 1*

Figure 5.15

CUSTOMISING A REPORT

The report header may be lengthened or shortened by positioning the cursor on the top edge of the page header band (the cursor changes to a cross with two arrows ➕). Hold down the left mouse button and drag the page header section down to create/alter report header space.

The page header, detail and page footer space are altered in the same way as the report header. The report footer is created by dragging down the bottom of the report footer band.

Additional data is added to the report by creating label frames and typing the text in each frame.

A label frame is produced as follows:

➤➤ ▪ Label tool **Aa** 🖱.

➤➤ Position the cursor on the report 🖱.

➤➤ Drag the mouse to the right and down to create a frame 🖱.

➤➤ Type text in the frame. (*If you don't type something in the frame, it will disappear.*)

While the report is being modified it is possible to switch between print preview and design view, as described above.

In order to work on a field or label, that field or label must be selected. A field or label is selected by simply pointing to the field or label and clicking the left mouse button. The field or label will appear with handles (small squares), as shown below.

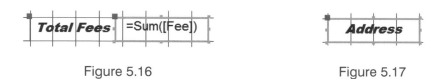

| Figure 5.16 | Figure 5.17 |

You may move the fields and/or labels by selecting them and dragging them to the required position. The field or label is moved by pointing to the edge of the field or label (a hand or four-headed arrow will appear), holding down the mouse button and dragging the field and label to the required position. Some fields will have a label and a field. A field or label may be moved independently by pointing to the larger square (a hand with only one finger or a four-headed arrow will appear), holding down the left mouse button and dragging the field or label to the required position.

The size of each field or label may be adjusted by pointing to one of the side handles and dragging the frame to the required size. The field text may be edited by positioning the mouse in the label field and clicking the left mouse button. Text may then be added or deleted in the normal way.

PERFORMING CALCULATIONS IN A REPORT

There are a number of calculations that may be performed in a report. In order to perform a calculation it is necessary to produce the report and then view it in design view. Calculations are normally placed in the report footer, but they may also be placed in the report header or details sections.

Calculations are performed as follows:

➤➤   Text box tool **ab** 🖱.

➤➤   Position the cursor on the report 🖱.

➤➤   Drag the mouse to the right and down to create a frame 🖱. (*The text box will appear something like Figure 5.18.*)

Figure 5.18

The text box has two fields. The left field is for a label and the right field (the bound field) is for the result of the calculation. The process is completed as follows:

Label

➤➤   Label field 🖱.

➤➤   Highlight the text in the field and type the new text, e.g. 'Total Fees'.

Calculation

➤➤   Bound field 🖱.

➤➤   Type the formula, starting with the = sign.

Some simple formulae are:

Summation   =**Sum([**field name**])**, e.g. =**Sum([**Fee**])**

Addition   =**Sum([**field one**])**+**Sum([**field two**])**+**Sum([**field three**])**

Average   =**Avg([**field name**])** (**Note:** Most programs use Avg for Average.)

Maximum   =**Max([**field name**])**

Count   =**Count([**field name**])**

FORMATTING A FIELD IN A REPORT

When a bound field is inserted into a report it may need to be formatted to display the contents in a particular way, e.g. with a currency symbol.

> Fields may be formatted as follows:
>
> ➤➤ ▮ Field 🖱. (*A menu will appear.*)
>
> ➤➤ ⬦ Properties 🖱.
>
> ➤➤ Format the field as required.

INSERTING GRAPHICS IN A REPORT

Office 2003	Office 2007
A graphic may be inserted on a report as follows: ➤➤ ▮ Open the report in design view.	
➤ ▮ Insert menu 🖱. ➤ ▮ Picture. **OR** Object 🖱. (*Select Microsoft Clip Gallery for Cip Art 2003 only.*)	➤ ▮ Logo Icon 🖼 🖱.
➤➤ Select the picture or Clip Art. (*May need to locate the folder containing the graphic.*)	

The picture is positioned by simply pointing to the graphic, holding down the left mouse button and dragging the graphic to the required position on the report.

The graphic may be resized by selecting the graphic and then pointing to a handle (one of the small squares on the corners), holding down the left mouse button and dragging the graphic to the required size.

Note: It may be necessary to change the Size Mode property to 'Stretch' before resizing the graphic.

> The properties are changed as follows:
>
> ➤➤ ▮ Clip/Picture 🖱. (*A pop-up menu will appear.*)

continued

➤➤ ⬦ Properties 🖰. *(The properties window will appear.)*

➤➤ ▣ All tab 🖰. *(if not already selected)*

➤➤ Change the Size Mode to 'Stretch'.

➤➤ Close the properties window.

CLOSING A REPORT

The report is closed as follows:

➤➤ ▣ Window close icon ☒ 🖰.

(If you have not already done so, the program will ask you if you wish to save the report or changes to the report.)

Task 5.4.3 (Additional)

Carry out the operations specified in **Task 5A-4** on the CD.

Task 5.5.1

(a) Open the **Tennis Club** database (if not already open).
(b) Create mailing labels for all the members. The layout of the labels should be as follows:

```
<Member's Name>
    <Blank Line>
<Member's Address>
    <Blank Line>
<Date> <Blank Space> <Fee>
```

(c) Save the report as **Members Labels**.

MAILING LABELS

Mailing labels is one of the reports that may be created from a database using a DBMS. Labels may be produced from a table or a query so it is necessary to select the correct table or query during the process.

Office 2003	Office 2007
Mailing labels are created as follows:	

Office 2003 (left column):

- ➤ ▶ Reports object 🖱.
- ➤ ▶ New 🖱.
  (*The new report window will appear.*)
- ➤ ▶ Label wizard 🖱.
- ➤ Select Table/Query name.
- ➤ ▶ OK 🖱.

Office 2007 (right column):

- ➤ Select or open the table or query containing the data.
- ➤ Select the Create ribbon.
- ➤ ▶ Labels icon 🔲 🖱.

(*The label wizard window will appear.*)

The label wizard will guide you through the creation of the labels. The following will need to be selected.

1 Select the size of label to be used. This will usually be one of the standard label stationery products.

Label sizes are selected as follows:

- ➤➤ ▶ Filter by manufacturer field arrow ▾ 🖱. (*A list will appear.*)
- ➤➤ ▶ Manufacturer 🖱. (*usually Avery*)
- ➤➤ ▶ Product number 🖱. (*usually L7160*)
- ➤➤ ▶ Next 🖱.

2 Select the font and colour required.

The font and colour are selected as follows:

- ➤➤ ▶ Select the font, font size and colour. (*from the options offered*)
- ➤➤ ▶ Next 🖱.

3 Select the fields to be included in the labels. A list of fields which may be selected will be displayed in the Available fields box.

Fields are included in the labels as follows:

- ➤➤ ▶ First field to be included in the label 🖱. (*Field may already be highlighted.*)

continued

➤➤ [cursor] Add icon [>] [mouse]. (*The field will be transferred to the prototype label box.*)

➤➤ Press the Enter key to move onto a new line, or the space bar to leave a space.

➤➤ [cursor] Next field to be included in the label [mouse].

➤➤ [cursor] Add icon [>] [mouse].

➤➤ Repeat the procedure until all the required fields have been included.

Note: It is a good idea to select the fields in the order in which you wish them displayed on the label. You may use spaces, commas and additional text to appear on all labels, as required.

When all the required fields have been included:

➤➤ [cursor] Next [mouse].

4 The next step is to decide if you want the labels sorted (organised) in any way.

Labels are sorted as follows:

➤➤ [cursor] Field to be sorted [mouse].

➤➤ [cursor] Add icon [>] [mouse]. (*The right-hand box will display the sorting.*)

➤➤ Repeat the two previous steps for further subsorting, if required.

➤➤ [cursor] Next [mouse].

5 Finally, enter a name for the labels and save them by typing the name in the space provided. You will usually require some modifications to the layout of the labels, so it is a good idea to modify them at this stage.

The labels are named and saved as follows:

➤➤ Type the name of the labels. (*in the field provided*)

➤➤ [cursor] Modify the label design [mouse].

➤➤ [cursor] Finish [mouse].

The label design will then appear on the screen in design view. This allows the labels to be modified before viewing them. It is possible to switch between print preview and design view in the same way as with any report.

Design view is where the layout of the labels is finalised and any additional information added. Fields may be widened or narrowed by selecting the field and resizing in the normal way. Fields may be moved by dragging them to the required position.

Office 2003	Office 2007
The labels are printed in the normal way as follows: ➤➤ ▣ Print icon 🖱.	
Note: In Access **2007**, if the print icon is not on the Quick Access toolbar then the report is printed as follows:	
	➤ ▣ Report name 🖱. **OR** Open the report. ➤ ▣ Office button 🔳 🖱. ➤ ✛ Print 🖱.

Note: The label stationery should be placed in the printer.

Task 5.5.2 (Additional)

Carry out the operations specified in **Task 5A-5** on the CD.

RELATIONAL TABLES

Sometimes, for security or confidentiality reasons, a large table with a large number of fields may be split into two tables – with a smaller number of fields in each. These tables may then be linked together in what is known as a **one-to-one** relational database. In this arrangement each record in one table will only have one matching record in the second table.

Another, more common type of relation is to have a **one-to-many** relationship, where one record in the first table will be linked to many records in the second table. Most modern DBMSs allow the creation and management of relational tables.

When relational tables are used it is necessary to ensure that modifications to one table are correspondingly updated in other related tables. The use of rules when creating relations ensures that modifications are correct in all tables.

Task 5.6.1

(a) Create a new database and save it with the filename **Stock**.
(b) Create two tables as specified in figures 5.19 and 5.20 and save them as **Product Table** and **Supplier Table**.
(c) Enter the records shown in the figures below into the respective tables.

(d) Link the tables where the Supp ID in the Supplier Table is linked to the Supp ID in the Product Table.

(e) Produce a query which will perform the following:

- Display the product ID, price, supplier ID and the name (supplier).
- Select all items where the price is less than €5.00.

(f) Save the query with the filename **Less than €5 Query**.

Field Name	Field Type	Size
Prod ID	Number	Integer
Description	Text	20
Price	Currency	Currency
Supp ID	Number	Integer

Figure 5.19

Field Name	Field Type	Size
Supp ID	Number	Integer
Name	Text	20
Address	Text	40

Figure 5.20

Prod ID	Description	Price	Supp ID
4001	M6 Steel Bolt	€1.25	22
4002	M8 Steel Bolt	€1.65	22
4003	M10 Steel Bolt	€1.85	22
5001	Single Switch	€2.10	15
5002	Double Switch	€2.55	15
5003	Three gang Switch	€3.50	15
5004	Single Switch Box	€0.85	15
6001	0.5l White Paint	€2.85	18
6002	1.0l White Paint	€5.50	18
6003	2.0l White Paint	€10.00	18
6004	2.5l White Paint	€14.50	18
6005	5.0l White Paint	€28.00	18

Product Table

Figure 5.21

Supp ID	Name	Address
15	Modern Paints Ltd	Bluebell Ind Ext, Dublin 12
18	Electrical Supplies	Park West, Dublin 12
22	Steel Fastenings	City West, Dublin 24

Supplier Table

Figure 5.22

DEFINING RELATIONSHIPS BETWEEN TABLES

In order to create a relationship between tables, the tables must be closed. In Access **2007** the relationship icon is on the Database Tools ribbon.

A relationship is created between tables as follows:

➤➤ 🖰 Relationship icon ⬛ 🖰.

(The relationships window will appear with the show table window.)

Note: If the show table window does not automatically appear then:

- 🖰 Show table icon ⬛ 🖰.

- 🖰 First table name 🖰.

  (The table appears in the relationships window.)

- 🖰 Second table name 🖰.

  (The second table appears.)

- Close the show table window.

➤➤ 🖰 Field in one table 🖰.

➤➤ Drag the field to the field to be linked in the second table 🖰.

(The edit relationships window will appear.)

➤➤ 🖰 Create 🖰.

Example

Drag the **Supp ID** field in the **Supplier Table** to the **Supp ID** field in the **Product Table** and select Create. A line will appear between the two tables linking the two fields.

DELETING A RELATIONSHIP BETWEEN TABLES

A relationship between two tables may be deleted as follows:

➤➤ 🖰 Relationship icon ⬛ 🖰. *(The related tables will appear.)*

➤➤ 🖰 Line joining the tables 🖰. *(The line appears thicker.)*

➤➤ Press the Delete key and confirm in order to delete the relationship.

DESIGNING A QUERY USING RELATED TABLES

Office 2003	Office 2007
A query is designed as follows:	
➤ 🔲 Query object 🖱. (*if this is not already selected*) ➤ 🔲 New 🖱. (*A new query window appears, with design view highlighted.*) ➤ 🔲 OK 🖱. (*Show table window appears.*)	➤ Select the Create ribbon. ➤ 🔲 Query Design icon 🔳🖱.

➤➤ 🔲 First table containing required data 🖱.

➤➤ 🔲 Add 🖱. (*The first table will appear in top half of screen.*)

➤➤ 🔲 Second table containing required data 🖱.

➤➤ 🔲 Add 🖱. (*The second table will appear in top half of screen.*)

➤➤ 🔲 Close 🖱. (*new table window disappears*)

➤➤ 🔲 Required fields from both tables 🖱.

➤➤ Insert criteria.

➤➤ View the query and save if required.

Task 5.6.2 (Additional)

Carry out the operations specified in **Task 5A-6** on the CD.

DATABASE DESIGN

When producing simple databases it is not normally necessary to go through the design process. However, when dealing with larger projects the design process becomes invaluable in the production of a working database. We will examine the individual steps of the design process and then apply the process to a simple example project.

STAGES

The production of a database may be divided into the following stages:

- Design.

- Production or implementation.

- Evaluation.

If these steps are followed diligently then the final outcome should be successful in meeting the needs for which the database was intended.

DESIGN

The design stage is the most important stage in the production of a database. It is, however, also the stage that is often neglected – or only given a half-hearted effort. The production of a database normally begins with a need. This need may originate from a system that is not meeting its current requirements or from a new situation that needs a database to store data and produce specific results.

The design stage may be divided into a number of specific steps, as follows:

- Overview and aims.

- Input data identified.

- Specification of data fields.

- Output queries or reports identified.

- Layout of form.

Overview and Aims

The design process will generally begin with a brief overview of the present situation and/or the needs to be addressed by the database. This helps to set the project in context and focus the attention on a specific situation.

The aims of the database should be clearly identified and stated. This will generally involve two specific steps.

1 A list of **specific** problems to be addressed by this database. These problems must be very specific and should be items a database and DBMS are capable of

addressing. Problems such as speed, presentation, accuracy, etc. would more correctly be identified in the overview and not in this section. Examples of problems that might be identified here are:

- Find the names of all the members who live in Naas.

- List the students who obtained a grant.

- Produce a list of all the books that cost more than €10.00, for viewing by the head librarian.

2 A list of solutions to the problems listed. This list will be expressed in general terms at this stage, as the fields and tables will not have been designed yet. Examples of solutions that might be identified here are:

- The list of names of the members who live in Naas may be obtained by producing a query that will select the members who live in Naas from a table containing the details of all the members.

- The list of students who obtained a grant may be obtained by producing a query that will select the students who obtained a grant from a table containing the details of all students.

- The list of books costing more than €10.00 may be obtained for the head librarian by producing a report based on a query that selects the required books from a table containing the details of all books.

Input Data Identified

This step involves the identification of each piece of data that will be input into the database. The input data is raw data and is divided into individual pieces that will be contained in separate fields. Examples of input data are:

- Member's name.
- Address.
- Cost of an item.

The method used to collect this data should be specified at this stage. The methods used to collect data vary greatly but some examples are:

- Taking data from an existing system.
- Using a survey form.
- Stock lists.
- Membership records.

In any event, a data capture form should be produced that will clearly identify the input data. The data capture form may be a form that is specially produced for the purpose of collecting the data, such as a survey form. Another type of data capture form would be the existing manual records that contain all the data that will be input into the database.

Specification of Data Fields

The specification of data fields would identify the field name, type, size, format and any other special attributes. Examples of data field specification might be:

Field Name	Field Type	Size or Format	Other
Name	Text	20	
Address	Text	50	
Date	Date/Time	Short Date	Only dates after 01/01/1985
Fee	Currency	Currency	Display the symbol

Figure 5.23

Output Queries and Reports

This step involves the identification of each query and report that will be produced in order to generate output from the database. The fields to be included in the queries and reports should be specified at this stage. Any additional information to be included in reports should be outlined.

Examples of output data are:

- Query listing all the members from Naas to include:
  Name.
  Address.
  Date of joining.
  Fee paid or not.

- Query listing all students who obtained a grant to include:
  Name.
  Address.
  Date of grant.
  Grant obtained.

- A report showing all the books that cost more than €10.00 to include the following:
  Book title.
  Book author.
  Book publisher.
  Cost.
  Suitable report header.
  Suitable report footer.
  Short note outlining comments on the report details.

FORM LAYOUT

It is not necessary to use a form with a database, but generally it is the method used to input data in a commercial database. The layout of the form should be efficient, i.e. related fields should be grouped together and there should be a natural flow from one field to the next. It is very difficult to enter records if the operator has to jump from one field at the top of the form to the next field at the bottom and then back to the top again for the next field.

The form should be pleasing to look at, have additional instructions built in if necessary, and have appropriate headings and labels.

PRODUCTION OR IMPLEMENTATION

Once the database has been designed it is then time to go to the computer and produce the database as designed. If the design stage has been performed adequately it should be possible to hand the design to someone else and they should be able to implement the database from the design specification.

The production stage will consist of the following:

- Creating the database.

- Creating a table(s).

- Creating a form(s).

- Inputting records.

- Creating queries.

- Creating reports.

EVALUATION

This is probably one of the most important aspects of the whole process. Once the database has been produced – and it has been carefully tested to ensure that all queries and reports are producing the correct results as specified in the design stage – it is time to examine the overall database and see if it could be improved. Items that could be re-examined would be listed and suggestions for modifications noted.

The actual implementation of modifications would involve going back to the design stage and redesigning the database. This alteration would be carried through the process to produce an updated database which would then be evaluated and if necessary redesigned again.

EXAMPLE

The following is a simple example of using the design process to produce a database. This is a very simple example intended to demonstrate the steps described above. In practice the database would be much larger and consequently the individual steps of the design would be correspondingly larger.

The presentation of the final project would be in a folder with the various sections clearly separated and labelled. This has not been done here due to space restrictions.

Overview and Aims

Kathleen Kenny runs a small, exclusive business dealing in rare jewellery. She collects items from a number of contacts in the business and then sells these to her customers.

Kathleen has approached me and asked if I could help her to keep track of her stock and allowing her to quickly find details of items which she has for sale. At present, all items are recorded in a ledger and then crossed out when they are sold. Since some items are in stock for long periods, even years, it is difficult to find items or even to know what is in stock at any particular time. I suggested that she use a database and she was very enthusiastic and asked if I could produce one for her.

We discussed the situation and identified the following requirements:

- Record details of all items in stock.

- Produce an easy method of adding items to stock as they are purchased.

- Remove items from stock as they are sold.

- Produce a list of items meeting the following criteria:
    - With a price less than €1,000.00.
    - In stock for more than a year.
    - All items stored in location C02.
    - All items in stock for more than six months and costing more than €1,500.00.

- Produce an attractive list of items for display or handing out to customers.

- Produce a list of items complete with a total value for all items in stock.

In order to produce the requirements listed above the following will be required in the database:

- A table for recording all items.

- A form for adding and deleting items of stock as they are purchased and sold.

- Create queries that will produce lists showing the following:
    - Items with a price less than €1,000.00.
    - Items in stock for more than a year, sorted by date of purchase.
    - All items stored in location C02.
    - All items in stock for more than six months and costing more than €1,500.00.

- An attractively produced report listing items for sale, sorted by price.

- A report listing all items and including a calculation to display the total value of stock, sorted by date.

Input Data

In order to collect the data for each item from Kathleen, a data capture form was required. The following form records the details of all items in stock.

Kathleen's Exclusive Jewellery	
Item No	
Description	
Location	
Date Purchased	
Selling Price	

Figure 5.24

The following data was obtained from the data capture forms that were completed from Kathleen's ledger. This is the data that will be input into the database.

Item	Description	Location	Date Purchased	Selling Price
2501	Cordoba Gold Bracelet	C06-T12	12/06/2003	€875.00
2502	Maltise Wrap Necklace	C08-T15	25/04/2002	€2,450.00
2503	Edwardian Gold Ring Cluster	C02-T11	13/11/2001	€1,285.00
2504	Ruby Pearl Earrings	C12-T05	11/02/2003	€985.00
2505	Victorian Bar Brooch	C02-T14	02/05/2001	€1,575.00
2506	Victorian Pearl Bangle	C06-T03	01/09/2002	€2,150.00
2507	Edwardian Gold Garnet Brooch	C07-T21	16/07/2003	€1,985.00
2508	Victorian Gold Chain Set	C04-T10	24/08/2003	€955.00
2509	Gold and Diamond Ring	C02-T14	12/11/2002	€2,155.00
2510	Blue Topaz Bar Brooch	C06-T04	15/04/2002	€1,565.00

Figure 5.25

Specification of Data Fields

The following table shows the specification for each data field.

Field Name	Field Type	Size or Format	Other
Item No	Number	Integer	Must be four digits exactly
Description	Text	50	
Location	Text	10	
Date	Date/Time	Short Date	Only dates after 01/01/1985
Price	Currency	Currency	With € symbol

Figure 5.26

Output Queries and Reports

The following queries will be required from the database:

- Items with a price less than €1,000.00.

- Items in stock for more than a year, sorted by date of purchase.

- All items stored in location C02.

- All items in stock for more than six months and costing more than €1,500.00.

The following reports will be required.

- Attractively presented report listing all items, to include:
  - Item no.
  - Description.
  - Location.
  - Price.

- The following additional information:
  - Heading 'Items for Sale'.
  - Company name and address.
  - Picture in the report header.
  - Report footer stating that all items may be viewed at the premises and that items may be acquired to order.
  - Items sorted by price, with highest first.

- A report listing all items, to include:
  - All fields, sorted by date.
  - Total value of stock, sorted by date.

Form Layout

The following is the layout of the database form as it will appear on-screen.

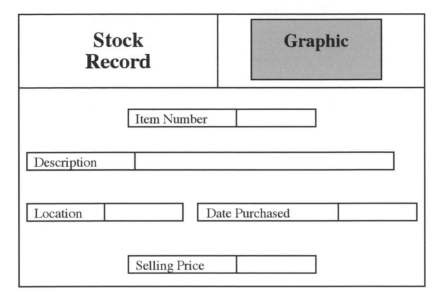

Figure 5.27

Production

The process of producing the database was relatively simple and the following shows the unique items table, the form and the output from the queries and reports.

Item No	Description	Location	Date	Price
2501	Cordoba Gold Bracelet	C06-T12	12/06/2003	€875.00
2502	Maltise Wrap Necklace	C08-T15	25/04/2002	€2,450.00
2503	Edwardian Gold Ring Cluster	C02-T11	13/11/2001	€1,285.00
2504	Ruby Pearl Earrings	C12-T05	11/02/2003	€985.00
2505	Victorian Bar Brooch	C02-T14	02/05/2001	€1,575.00
2506	Victorian Pearl Bangle	C06-T03	01/09/2002	€2,150.00
2507	Edwardian Gold Garnet Brooch	C07-T21	16/07/2003	€1,985.00
2508	Victorian Gold Chain Set	C04-T10	24/08/2003	€955.00
2509	Gold and Diamond Ring	C02-T14	12/11/2002	€2,155.00
2510	Blue Topaz Bar Brooch	C06-T04	15/04/2002	€1,565.00

Figure 5.28   Unique Items Table

Stock Record

Item Number:	0

Description:	

Location:		Date Purchased:	

Selling Price in €:	0.00

Figure 5.29   Unique Items Form

Item No	Description	Location	Date	Price
2501	Cordoba Gold Bracelet	C06-T12	12/06/2003	€875.00
2504	Ruby Pearl Earrings	C12-T05	11/02/2003	€985.00
2508	Victorian Gold Chain Set	C04-T10	24/08/2003	€955.00

Figure 5.30   Items Less Than €1,000 Query

Item No	Description	Location	Date	Price
2505	Victorian Bar Brooch	C02-T14	02/05/2001	€1,575.00
2503	Edwardian Gold Ring Cluster	C02-T11	13/11/2001	€1,285.00
2510	Blue Topaz Bar Brooch	C06-T04	15/04/2002	€1,565.00
2502	Maltise Wrap Necklace	C08-T15	25/04/2002	€2,450.00
2506	Victorian Pearl Bangle	C06-T03	01/09/2002	€2,150.00
2509	Gold and Diamond Ring	C02-T14	12/11/2002	€2,155.00

Figure 5.31   Over a Year Query

Item No	Description	Location	Date	Price
2503	Edwardian Gold Ring Cluster	C02-T11	13/11/2001	€1,285.00
2505	Victorian Bar Brooch	C02-T14	02/05/2001	€1,575.00
2509	Gold and Diamond Ring	C02-T14	12/11/2002	€2,155.00

Figure 5.32   Location CO2 Query

Item No	Description	Location	Date	Price
2502	Maltise Wrap Necklace	C08-T15	25/04/2002	€2,450.00
2505	Victorian Bar Brooch	C02-T14	02/05/2001	€1,575.00
2506	Victorian Pearl Bangle	C06-T03	01/09/2002	€2,150.00
2509	Gold and Diamond Ring	C02-T14	12/11/2002	€2,155.00
2510	Blue Topaz Bar Brooch	C06-T04	15/04/2002	€1,565.00

Figure 5.33   Over Six months and Greater Than €1,500 Query

Items for Sale

Kathleen Flanagan
Rare and Antique Jewellery
Main Street
Naas
Co Kildare
Phone 045-866427
E-Mail: Kate@rarejewellery.com

Item No	Description	Location	Price
2502	Maltise Wrap Necklace	C08-T15	€2,450.00
2509	Gold and Diamond Ring	C02-T14	€2,155.00
2506	Victorian Pearl Bangle	C06-T03	€2,150.00
2507	Edwardian Gold Garnet Brooch	C07-T21	€1,985.00
2505	Victorian Bar Brooch	C02-T14	€1,575.00
2510	Blue Topaz Bar Brooch	C06-T04	€1,565.00
2503	Edwardian Gold Ring Cluster	C02-T11	€1,285.00
2504	Ruby Pearl Earrings	C12-T05	€985.00
2508	Victorian Gold Chain Set	C04-T10	€955.00
2501	Cordoba Gold Bracelet	C06-T12	€875.00

All items may be viewed at the above address

If you let us know what type of item you are interested in, we may be able to source it for you

15 April 2003   Page 1 of 1

Figure 5.34   Product Listing

Stock Valuation Report

Item No	Description	Location	Date	Price
2505	Victorian Bar Brooch	C02-T14	02/05/2001	€1,575.00
2503	Edwardian Gold Ring Cluster	C02-T11	13/11/2001	€1,285.00
2510	Blue Topaz Bar Brooch	C06-T04	15/04/2002	€1,565.00
2502	Maltise Wrap Necklace	C08-T15	25/04/2002	€2,450.00
2506	Victorian Pearl Bangle	C06-T03	01/09/2002	€2,150.00
2509	Gold and Diamond Ring	C02-T14	12/11/2002	€2,155.00
2504	Ruby Pearl Earrings	C12-T05	11/02/2003	€985.00
2501	Cordoba Gold Bracelet	C06-T12	12/06/2003	€875.00
2507	Edwardian Gold Garnet Brooch	C07-T21	16/07/2003	€1,985.00
2508	Victorian Gold Chain Set	C04-T10	24/08/2003	€955.00

Total Value of Stock €15,980.00

14 April *Page 1 of 1*

Figure 5.35

Evaluation

When the database was completed I presented it to Kathleen. We discussed the use of the database and she quickly learned how to record new items and produce the various queries and reports.

After using the database for a short time Kathleen made the following suggestions:

- She found that she had not recorded the cost price of the items and therefore had to search through her purchase records when she needed to find out how much a particular item cost. If this could be included in the database it would help her greatly.

- Some customers come into the shop and want a particular item, such as a ring, necklace, bracelet, etc. Kathleen would like to be able to print out a list of items of a particular type.

- The location on the product report was confusing for customers. Some people thought that they had to go to another premises to find the items. Kathleen would like this removed from the report.

I examined the three problems listed above and made the following suggestions:

- The cost could easily be included by adding an extra field in the table.
  The list of particular items could be produced by adding a field in the table for the item type and then producing a query that would select items of a particular type.
  The product report could be modified to omit the location and then restyled.

6 Presentation and Graphics

SYMBOLS USED IN THIS CHAPTER

The symbols used in this chapter, and their meanings, are as follows:

Click the left mouse button.

Double-click the left mouse button.

Hold down the left mouse button.

Move the mouse to point to an item without clicking or holding any button.

Release the mouse button.

Point to an item on the screen.

Hold down the Shift key.

Hold down the Shift key and hold down the left mouse button.

INTRODUCTION

With the growth in the use of technology the use of computers and data projectors has increased greatly. This has also led to a growth in the use of presentation software such as Microsoft PowerPoint, Lotus Freelance Graphics and many others. These programs allow the user to produce slides combining text, graphics, sound, video, etc. The slides may then be embellished with transitions and animations to enhance a presentation.

Teachers and conference presenters often use these programs when presenting lecture material. However, there are many other applications for these programs, particularly in relation to graphics and animation.

This section will concentrate on the presentation aspect of these programs, which will include some simple graphics. The final part of the chapter will concentrate on more extensive graphics work.

With presentation programs, items are entered onto a slide. A presentation may have only one slide or any number of slides. Slides are normally the shape and proportion of a normal monitor but this may be changed as required. Each slide may be thought of as a white board onto which various items may be placed, such as text frames, picture frames, sound items, video items, etc. The slide itself does not allow text to be typed onto it directly – everything must be in a frame. Once frames have been created they may be edited, copied, deleted and moved around the slide and from slide to slide as required.

LOADING THE PRESENTATION PROGRAM

The presentation program is loaded from the desktop as follows:

➤➤ Presentation program shortcut icon 🖱.

If the program is not available from the desktop then it may be loaded from the Start menu as follows:

➤➤ Start 🖱.

➤➤ Programs.

➤➤ Presentation program 🖱. (*It may be necessary to open a submenu to find the program.*)

The program will be loaded and most programs will require the selection of a layout for the first slide. Slide selection will be discussed later so, for now, simply select a blank slide.

THE PRESENTATION SCREEN

When the presentation program is loaded the screen should look something like Figure 6.1.

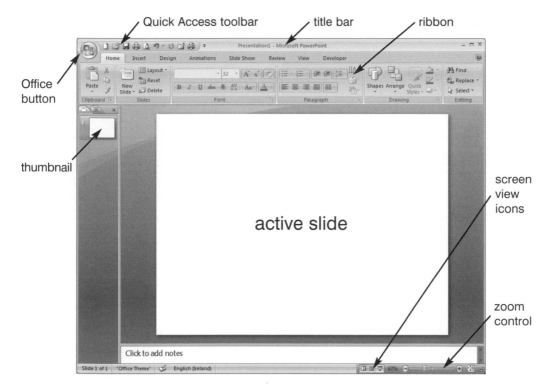

Figure 6.1

Task 6.1.1

(a) Load the presentation program (if not already loaded).

(b) Choose a blank slide from the layout options (if not already selected).

(c) Create a text frame that is the width of the slide, with a small margin between the frame and the left and right of the slide.

(d) Type the following in the frame:
My Lecture

(e) Select the text and format it as follows:

- Centre the text in the frame.
- Increase the size to approximately 80 pt.
- Bold the text.
- Change the font colour to blue.
- Apply a shadow.

(f) Save the presentation with the filename **My Lecture 1**.

(g) Close the presentation.

CHOOSING A SLIDE LAYOUT

When the presentation program is loaded a slide will be displayed. This slide may be a title slide or the slide layout window may also be displayed. If the slide layout window does not automatically appear (or if it is needed at any time) then it may displayed.

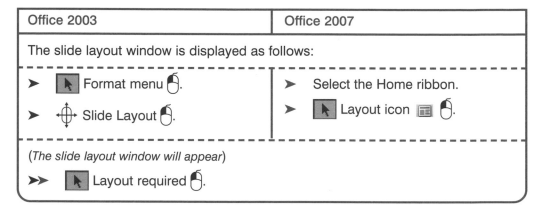

Office 2003	Office 2007
The slide layout window is displayed as follows:	
➤ Format menu. ➤ Slide Layout.	➤ Select the Home ribbon. ➤ Layout icon.
(*The slide layout window will appear*) ➤➤ Layout required.	

This window allows the particular layout for the slide to be selected. These layouts provide an easy method of arranging items on a slide. A blank slide may be used where one of the layouts is not suitable. The most common slide layouts are:

- Title slide.
- Bulleted list.
- Chart.
- Organisation chart.
- Text and chart.
- Text and graphic.

SCREEN VIEWS

Most programs will automatically display the screen in what is termed **normal view**, as shown above in Figure 6.1. However, the **screen view** icons, at the bottom of the screen, allow the screen to be viewed in other ways. It is a good idea to experiment with these to get to know what each one looks like. The screen view icons will contain the following: normal, slide sorter and slide show.

TEXT FRAMES

Office 2003	Office 2007
A text frame is created as follows:	
➤ ▣ Text tool icon 📧 🖱.	➤ Select the Insert ribbon. ➤ ▣ Text tool icon 📧 🖱.
➤➤ Any position on the slide 🖱.	
➤➤ Drag the mouse to the right and a rectangle will appear on the slide. Drag the mouse until the width of the rectangle is the width of the frame required 🖱.	

A small text frame will be displayed with a flashing cursor in it. Text may be inserted into the frame by simply typing the text. The frame will expand vertically as each line of text is typed or each time the Enter key is pressed.

Text Alignment

Text may be aligned using the alignment icons ▤▥▦ left, centre and right.

Text Enhancement

Text may be enhanced using the icons **B** *I* U bold, italics and underline.

Line Spacing

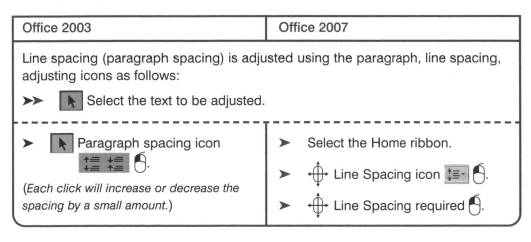

Office 2003	Office 2007
Line spacing (paragraph spacing) is adjusted using the paragraph, line spacing, adjusting icons as follows:	
➤➤ ▣ Select the text to be adjusted.	
➤ ▣ Paragraph spacing icon ▤▥ 🖱. *(Each click will increase or decrease the spacing by a small amount.)*	➤ Select the Home ribbon. ➤ ⊕ Line Spacing icon ▤ 🖱. ➤ ⊕ Line Spacing required 🖱.

DELETING A FRAME

A frame may be deleted as follows:

➤➤ Ensure the frame is active.

➤➤ Press the Delete key.

Note: If more than one frame is active then all the active frames will be deleted.

TEXT FONTS

The text in a frame may be changed either before or after the text is typed.

Changing the Text Font

The text font may be changed as follows:

➤➤ Select the text to be changed. (*if already typed*)

➤➤ ▶ Font arrow Times New Roma ▾ 🖱.

➤➤ ▶ Font required 🖱.

Changing the Font Size

Text in a frame may be increased or decreased using the increase font size or decrease font size icons as follows:

➤➤ Select the text to be changed.

➤➤ ▶ Increase **A** icon 🖱. **OR** ▶ Decrease **A** icon 🖱.

Each click of the mouse button will increase or decrease the font size by one step.

Alternatively:

➤➤ Select the text to be changed.

➤➤ Font size arrow 18 ▾ 🖱.

(*A list of font sizes will be displayed.*)

➤➤ Size required 🖱.

Both methods allow the user to change individual letters or words.

Changing the Font Colour

The font colour may be changed as follows:

➤➤ Select the text to be changed.

➤➤ ⬚ Font colour icon arrow **A** ▾ 🖱.

(*A range of font colours will appear.*)

➤➤ ⬚ Colour required 🖱.

If the font colour displayed by the font colour icon is correct, then it is only necessary to click on the icon to apply that colour.

Text Shadows

Selected text may have a shadow applied to it as follows:

➤➤ ⬚ Text shadow icon **S** 🖱.

SAVING A PRESENTATION

A presentation may be saved at any time as follows.

Saving for the First Time

Office 2003	Office 2007
➤ ⬚ File menu 🖱.	➤ ⬚ Office button 🖱.

➤➤ ⊕ Save as 🖱. (*The save as window will appear.*)

➤➤ Select the folder into which the file is to be saved (if necessary) in the 'Save in' field.

➤➤ Type a name for this file in the 'File name' field.

➤➤ ⬚ Save 🖱.

Saving after Giving the Presentation a Filename

➤➤ ▣ Save icon 🖫 🖱.

Saving as Other File Type

Every time the presentation program saves a file it will automatically save the file as a presentation file. Modern presentation programs allow individual slides in a file to saved as other types, e.g. .htm /.html (for publishing on a website), .pot/.potm (template), or .jpg (a picture).

A presentation or slide may be saved as another file type by selecting the type in the 'Save as type' field while saving, as described above.

Task 6.1.2

(a) Open the presentation named **My Lecture 1**.
(b) Create a text frame underneath the first frame that is the same width.
(c) Type the following in the frame:
     Presented by
     <*your name*>
(d) Select the text and format it as follows:

- Centre the text in the frame.
- Increase the size to approximately 48 pt.
- Bold the text.
- Change the font colour to purple.

(e) Position the frames on the slide so that they occupy the centre portion of the slide.
(f) Save the presentation with the same filename.

OPENING A PRESENTATION

Office 2003	Office 2007
A presentation is opened as follows:	
➤ ▣ Open icon 📂 🖱.	➤ ▣ Office button 🔘 🖱. ➤ ⬦ Open icon 📂 🖱.

continued

(The open window will appear, which is practically the same as the save as window.)

➤➤ Select the correct folder and a list of files will appear.

➤➤ [↖] Required file ⬋. } **OR** [↖] Required file ⬋.

[↖] Open button ⬋.

It may be necessary to select the drive and folder (in a similar way to that used when saving a file).

MAKING A FRAME ACTIVE

In order to perform any operation on a frame, the frame in question must be **active**. A frame is made the active frame by simply placing the mouse anywhere on a solid frame and clicking the left mouse button. In the case of objects that are not solid, i.e. lines or open shapes, they are made active by pointing to the edge of the object and clicking the left mouse button. When the frame is active it will be displayed with the frame handles (the small circles/squares) visible, as shown below.

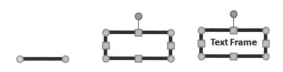

Figure 6.2

MOVING A FRAME

A frame may be moved to any location on the slide. First make it the active frame and then:

➤➤ [↖] Anywhere on a solid frame or on the edge of a nonsolid frame ⬋.

(The cursor changes to a four-headed black arrow ✛.)

➤➤ Drag the frame to its new position ⬋.

continued

Task 6.1.3

(a) Open the presentation named **My Lecture 1** (if not already open).
(b) Insert a short line between the two text frames.
(c) Change the line thickness to 6 pt and the colour to brown.
(d) Insert a rectangle, a square, a circle and an oval and position them on the slide as shown.

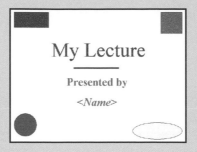

Figure 6.3

(e) Colour the four objects blue, red, green and yellow.
(f) Save the presentation again with the same filename.

INSERTING OBJECTS

Most of the objects which will be dealt with in the following pages are obtained from the Drawing toolbar in PowerPoint **2003**, which is usually displayed at the bottom of the screen. In the case of PowerPoint **2007**, the objects are found in the Shapes icon on the Home ribbon or on the Insert ribbon.

DRAWING LINES

A line may be produced as follows:

➤➤   Line tool.

➤➤   Select a starting point on the slide.

➤➤   Drag the mouse to form a line.

A straight line is drawn by simply holding down the Shift key before holding the mouse button and releasing the mouse button before releasing the Shift key.

Line Colour

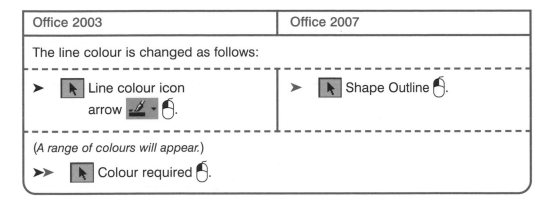

Office 2003	Office 2007
The line colour is changed as follows:	
➤ 🔺 Line colour icon arrow ✏️ ▾ 🖱️.	➤ 🔺 Shape Outline 🖱️.
(A range of colours will appear.) ➤➤ 🔺 Colour required 🖱️.	

If the line colour displayed by the line colour/shape outline icon is correct, then it is only necessary to click on the icon to apply that colour.

Line Style

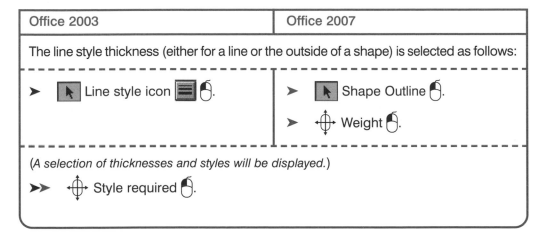

Office 2003	Office 2007
The line style thickness (either for a line or the outside of a shape) is selected as follows:	
➤ 🔺 Line style icon ▤ 🖱️.	➤ 🔺 Shape Outline 🖱️. ➤ ✛ Weight 🖱️.
(A selection of thicknesses and styles will be displayed.) ➤➤ ✛ Style required 🖱️.	

Most programs also provide an icon for applying dashed or arrowed styles on lines. There is an icon for dashed and arrowed lines on the drawing toolbar/shape outline selection.

DRAWING A RECTANGLE OR SQUARE

A rectangle or square may be produced as follows:

➤➤ 🔺 Rectangle tool ▣ 🖱️.

➤➤ Select a starting point on the slide 🖱️.

➤➤ Drag the mouse to form a rectangle 🖱️.

A square is drawn by simply holding down the Shift key before holding the mouse button and releasing the mouse button before releasing the Shift key.

Shape Colour

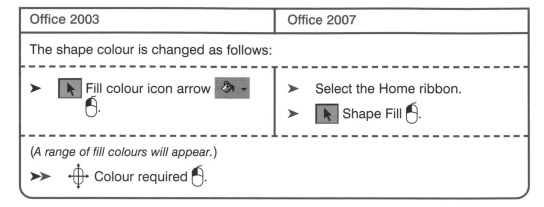

Office 2003	Office 2007
The shape colour is changed as follows:	
➤ Fill colour icon arrow 🎨 ▾.	➤ Select the Home ribbon.
	➤ Shape Fill.
(A range of fill colours will appear.)	
➤➤ ⊕ Colour required.	

The pallet will display a small number of colours but one of the other options displayed on the colour pallet may be selected:

No Fill   Produces a shape with no colour, effectively just a border.

More Fill Colours   Provides a range of colour options.

Fill Effects   Provides a range of texture and pattern options.

If the fill colour displayed by the fill colour icon is correct, then it is only necessary to click on the icon to apply that colour.

DRAWING AN OVAL OR CIRCLE

An oval (ellipse) or a circle may be produced as follows:

➤➤   Oval tool ⬭.

➤➤   Select a starting point on the slide.

➤➤   Drag the mouse to form an oval.

A circle is drawn by simply holding down the Shift key before holding the mouse button and releasing the mouse button before releasing the Shift key.

When drawing ovals and circles it is helpful to think in terms of drawing a rectangle or square that will fit around the oval or circle.

The oval/circle colour is changed in the same way as for a rectangle above.

RESIZING A FRAME

The size of a frame (or line) may be altered by first making the frame active and then:

➤➤　　One of the handles.

　　(*One of the resize arrows* ↔ ↕ ↗ ↘ *will appear on the handle.*)

➤➤　Drag the frame to the required size.

Note: When resizing a picture be sure to use a corner handle, not a side handle, to avoid distorting the picture.

Task 6.1.4

(a) Open the presentation named **My Lecture 1** (if not already open).
(b) Insert a new slide after the first slide. Select a bulleted list layout for this slide.
(c) Type the following in the heading box:
Introduction

(d) Change the font to Arial, 48 pt, bold, purple.
(e) Type the following two bullet points in the bulleted list box:

This lecture is intended to assist you in achieving top grades in your upcoming certificate examination.

I will also give you some helpful tips for studying for your examinations.

(f) Change the font to Arial, 36 pt, blue for these two bulleted points.
(g) Insert a suitable Clip Art picture in the bottom right-hand corner of the slide. The slide should look like the following.

> ### Introduction
>
> • This lecture is intended to assist you in achieving top grades in your upcoming certificate examination
> • I will also give you some helpful tips for studying for your examinations
>
>

Figure 6.4

(h) Save the presentation again with the same filename.

ADDING A SLIDE

A presentation would normally be made up of a number of slides.

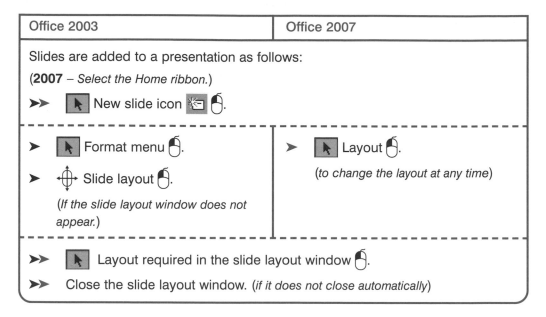

Office 2003	Office 2007
Slides are added to a presentation as follows: (**2007** – *Select the Home ribbon.*) ➤➤ 🖱️ New slide icon 🔲 🖱️.	
➤ 🖱️ Format menu 🖱️. ➤ ✛ Slide layout 🖱️. (*If the slide layout window does not appear.*)	➤ 🖱️ Layout 🖱️. (*to change the layout at any time*)
➤➤ 🖱️ Layout required in the slide layout window 🖱️. ➤➤ Close the slide layout window. (*if it does not close automatically*)	

A thumbnail for each slide is displayed on the left-hand side of the screen. Each slide may be selected by simply pointing to the particular thumbnail and clicking the left mouse button.

INSERTING CLIP ART

The insert Clip Art icon is on the Drawing toolbar in PowerPoint **2003** and on the Insert ribbon in PowerPoint **2007**. It may be necessary to be connected to the Internet in order to get Clip Art.

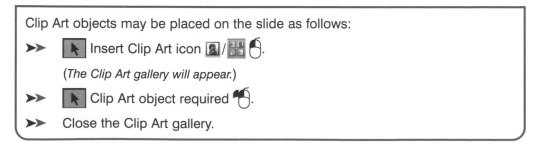

Clip Art objects may be placed on the slide as follows:
➤➤ 🖱️ Insert Clip Art icon 🖼️/🖼️ 🖱️.
   (*The Clip Art gallery will appear.*)
➤➤ 🖱️ Clip Art object required 🖱️.
➤➤ Close the Clip Art gallery.

Once the Clip Art is inserted it will usually have to be resized and positioned on the slide in the same way as any other object.

INSERTING PICTURES

The Insert Picture icon is on the Drawing toolbar in PowerPoint **2003** and on the Insert ribbon in PowerPoint **2007**.

A picture that has been saved may be placed on the slide as follows:

➤➤ 〔➤〕 Insert picture icon 〔🖼〕 👆. (*The insert picture window will appear.*)

➤➤ Locate folder where the picture is stored.

➤➤ 〔➤〕 Picture required 👆.

Once the picture is inserted it will usually have to be resized and positioned on the slide in the same way as any other object.

COPYING FRAMES

A single frame or a group of frames may be copied as follows:

➤➤ Make the frame(s) active.

(**2007** – *Select the Home ribbon.*)

➤➤ 〔➤〕 Copy icon 〔📋〕 👆.

➤➤ 〔➤〕 Paste icon 〔📋〕 👆.

Task 6.1.5

(a) Open the presentation named **My Lecture 1** (if not already open).
(b) Insert additional slides 3, 4, 5, 6 and 7 as shown below. Slides 3–6 should be on bulleted list slides. Slide 7 should be on a title slide. Use fonts as for slide 2.

Necessary Steps

- Attend classes
- Complete all homework
- Study every day
- Revise frequently
- Complete past papers

Figure 6.5

Study Procedure

- Make out a study timetable
- Don't study one subject for too long
- Take a break between each subject
- Take note of topics which are causing difficulty

Figure 6.6

Examination Tips

- Arrive early
- Read the paper thoroughly, at least twice
- Allocate time for each question
- Read each question again before attempting each part
- Stick to the time allocation for each question

Figure 6.7

Conclusion

- Remember there is more to life than examinations
- Do your best in preparation for each examination
- Answer every question to the best of your ability

Figure 6.8

Thank You

-----<Date>------

Figure 6.9

(c) Copy the Clip Art picture from slide 2 and insert it in the bottom right-hand corner of slides 3–6.

(d) Save the presentation again with the same filename.

(e) Print one copy of each slide.

PRINTING A SLIDE

Office 2003	Office 2007
A slide (or number of slides) may be printed in the normal way as follows: ➤➤ Print icon.	
Note: In PowerPoint **2007**, if the print icon is not on the Quick Access toolbar then the slide(s) may be printed as follows:	
	➤ Office button.
	➤ Print.

continued

> ⊕ Quick Print 🖰.

Note: (a) If there is more than one slide in the presentation then all the slides will be printed.

(b) Selected printing will be discussed later.

SELECTING A PRINTER

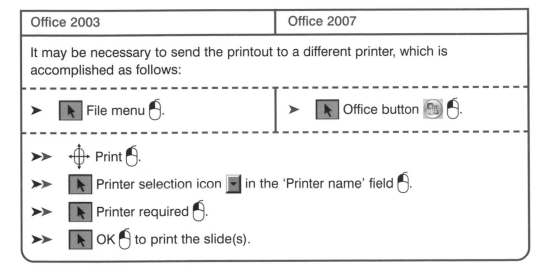

Office 2003	Office 2007
It may be necessary to send the printout to a different printer, which is accomplished as follows:	
➤ 🖰 File menu 🖰.	➤ 🖰 Office button 🖰.
➤➤ ⊕ Print 🖰.	
➤➤ 🖰 Printer selection icon ▾ in the 'Printer name' field 🖰.	
➤➤ 🖰 Printer required 🖰.	
➤➤ 🖰 OK 🖰 to print the slide(s).	

This printer will be the default printer until it is changed, the user logs off or the computer is shut down.

RUNNING (VIEWING) A PRESENTATION

Once two or more slides have been produced it is possible to view the presentation by running the slide show.

The presentation is viewed as follows:

➤➤   Select the first thumbnail.

➤➤   🖰 Slide show icon 🖳🖰.

➤➤   🖰 To move onto the next slide.

(The slides will appear on the screen one at a time.)

COPYING SLIDES

An efficient method is to copy an entire slide and then modify that to create a new slide. Slides are copied either in slide sorter view or in slide view, but slide sorter is usually easier.

Slides may be copied as follows:

➤➤   Select slide sorter view ⊞.

➤➤   ▣ Slide to be copied ⊖.

➤➤   ▣ Copy icon ▤ ⊖.

➤➤   Select the position for the copied slide. (*Position the cursor between two slides and ⊖. A vertical line will appear between the slides.*)

➤➤   ▣ Paste icon ▤ ⊖.

REARRANGING SLIDES

The most effective way of rearranging slides is to use the slide sorter view.

Slides are rearranged as follows:

➤➤   Select slide sorter view ⊞.

➤➤   ▣ Slide to be moved ⊖.

➤➤   ▣ Drag the slide to its new position ⊖.

Slides may also be rearranged in slide view by simply dragging the thumbnail to its new position in the left-hand panel. The only disadvantage in this case is that it may not be possible to see the slide detail.

ZOOMING

It is sometimes necessary to view a particular portion of the slide in more detail. The zoom control is used for this purpose.

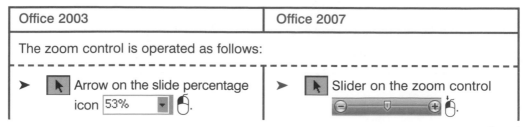

Office 2003	Office 2007
The zoom control is operated as follows:	
➤ ▣ Arrow on the slide percentage icon 53% ▾ ⊖.	➤ ▣ Slider on the zoom control ⊖ ▭ ⊕ ⊖.

continued

➤ ▮ Percentage required 🖱.

➤ Drag the slider to the required zoom 🖱.

Task 6.1.6 (Additional)

Produce the presentations specified in **Task 6A-1** on the CD.

Task 6.2.1

(a) Open the presentation named **My Lecture 1** (if not already open).
(b) Apply a template to the presentation.
(c) Apply a transition to slides 2–7.
(d) Animate the bullet points on slides 2–6.
(e) Run the slide show.
(f) Save the presentation with the filename **My Lecture 2**.

TEMPLATES

PowerPoint supplies a number of templates that may be used with a presentation. These templates produce a predefined layout and colour scheme that is applied to each slide. (It is also possible to create your own templates.)

Office 2003	Office 2007
A template may also be applied to an existing presentation as follows:	
➤ ▮ Slide Design icon 📧 🖱. *(The slide design window will appear.)* ➤ ▮ Slide design required 🖱. ➤ Close the slide design window.	Select the Design ribbon. ➤ ▮ Theme required 🖱.

After the slide design has been applied, some of the text colours will have changed. This is part of the slide design and the text colours usually match the background. The colour of the text may be changed again in the normal way.

APPLYING A TRANSITION TO A SLIDE

A transition is applied to each slide and this is the way the presentation moves from slide to slide when running a slide show.

Office 2003	Office 2007
A transition is applied to the selected slide as follows:	
➤ Slide Show menu. ➤ Slide transition icon. *(The Slide Transition window will appear.)*	➤ Select the Animation ribbon.
➤➤ Transition required.	
➤➤ Select a different speed for the transition *(if required)*.	
• Select an automatic time for the next transition. *(if not using the mouse to advance slides)*	
• Select a sound effect. *(if required)*	
• Select 'On Mouse Click' **OR** 'Automatically after'. *(as required)* *(insert time if using automatic)*	
➤➤ Apply to All slides. *(if the same transition is to apply to every slide)*	
➤ Close the Slide Transition window.	

ANIMATING SLIDES

Animation is the way in which the slide builds up, usually bullet point by bullet point. Graphics and charts may also be animated.

Office 2003	Office 2007
Animation is applied to an active slide as follows:	
➤ Slide Show menu. ➤ Custom animation.	➤ Select the Animation ribbon. ➤ Custom animation.
(The custom animation window will appear.)	
➤➤ Select the Thumbnail to be animated.	

continued

➤➤ Select the frame on the slide to be animated.

➤➤ 🖱 Add effects selection icon ⬭.

➤➤ Select the effect required.

➤➤ Select the animation Direction. (*if required*)

➤➤ Select the animation Speed. (*if required*)

➤➤ Repeat procedure for other animations.

➤➤ Close the Custom animation window.

Task 6.2.2 (Additional)

Produce the presentations specified in **Task 6A-2** on the CD.

Task 6.3.1

(a) Load the presentation program.
(b) Choose a title slide from the layout options.
(c) Apply a template to the presentation.
(d) Create the first slide as shown in Figure 6.10.
(e) Add a second slide with a bulleted list layout and create as shown in Figure 6.11.
(f) Add a third slide with an organisation chart layout and create as shown in Figure 6.12.
   Use 24 pt font size for the organisation chart heading.
(g) Add a fourth slide with a text and Clip Art layout and create as shown in Figure 6.13.
   Insert a suitable Clip Art picture.
(h) Add a fifth slide with a chart and text layout and create as shown in Figure 6.14.

	1st Qtr	2nd Qtr	3rd Qtr	4th Qtr
Houses	1.2	1.4	1.1	1.7
Aps.	2.8	3.5	2.6	1.9
Hotels	1.8	2.2	2.8	2.5
Comm.	0.78	1.05	0.89	0.68

Chart Information

(i) Add a sixth slide with a title layout and create as shown in Figure 6.15.
(j) Save the presentation with the filename **Jennings 1**.
   Adjust font sizes where necessary.

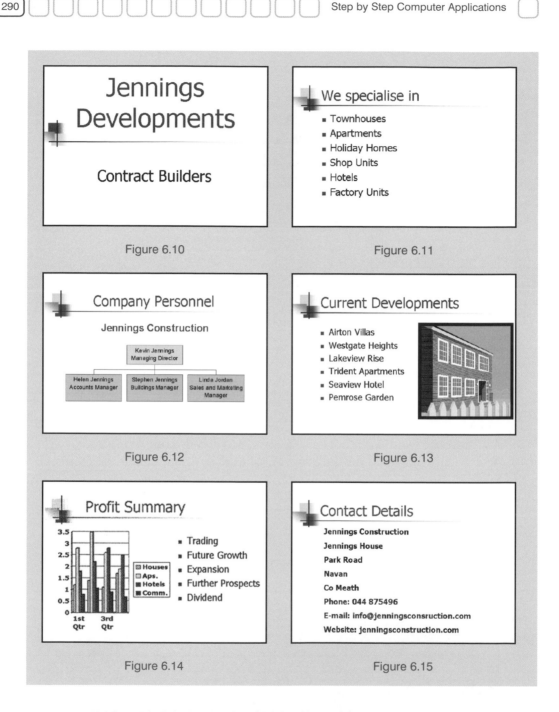

Figure 6.10

Figure 6.11

Figure 6.12

Figure 6.13

Figure 6.14

Figure 6.15

INSERTING AN ORGANISATION CHART

The simplest method of inserting an organisation chart is to select a slide from the slide layout that contains an insert object section. The slide will have a reserved area for a Table, Chart, Smart Art Graphic (this includes an organisation chart), Picture, Clip Art and Media Clip. Simply click on the required object and an appropriate window will be displayed.

Office 2003	Office 2007
An organisation chart is inserted, at any time, as follows:	
➤➤ Select the required layout. (*as described earlier*)	
➤ [icon] Insert Diagram or Organisation Chart icon [icon] 🖱. (*The diagram gallery window will appear.*) ➤ [icon] Organisation Chart 🖱.	➤ [icon] Smart Art icon [icon] 🖱. (*This is also on the Insert ribbon.*) (*The Smart Art Graphic window will appear.*) ➤ [icon] Hierarchy 🖱.
➤➤ [icon] Chart type required 🖱.	
➤➤ [icon] OK 🖱.	

Inserting Text

Text is inserted, in the chart, by simply selecting the relevant areas of the chart and typing the data in each section.

Changing Fonts

Font type and size are changed in the normal way.

Adding Extra Boxes

Office 2003	Office 2007
Additional boxes may be added to the chart as follows:	
➤ [icon] Box to which the new box is to be attached 🖱. ➤ [icon] Insert Shape selection icon 🖱. (*on the organisation chart toolbar*) ➤ ⊕ Type of box to be added 🖱.	➤ Select the Smart Art Tools Design ribbon. ➤ [icon] Add Shape selection icon Add Shape ▾ 🖱. ➤ ⊕ Shape of box to be added 🖱.

Changing Box Colour

The background colour for each box may be changed by selecting the Fill Colour icon in **2003** or Shape Fill icon in **2007**.

The background colour is changed as follows:

➤➤ � Select the box.

➤➤ Fill Colour/Shape Fill Selection icon 🖱.

   (*A colour pallet will be displayed.*)

➤➤ ▲ Colour required 🖱.

INSERTING CHARTS

The simplest method of inserting a chart is to select a slide from the slide layout that contains an **insert object** section. The slide will have a reserved area for a Table, Chart, Smart Art Graphic, Picture, Clip Art and Media Clip. Simply click on the required object and an appropriate window will be displayed.

Office 2003	Office 2007
A chart is inserted, at any time, as follows:	
➤ ▲ Chart icon 📊 🖱.	➤ Select the Insert ribbon.
	➤ ▲ Chart icon 📊 🖱.
	(*The insert chart window will appear.*)
	➤ ▲ Chart type required 🖱.
	➤ ▲ OK 🖱.

A chart will appear on the slide as well as a spreadsheet window that allows the input of data for the chart. Insert the required data in the table and the chart will be automatically updated. Where rows or columns are not required, the row or column should be deleted from the spreadsheet and not just the data in the cells.

   Close the spreadsheet data window when chart data and layout is complete.

Chart Colours

The colour of the bars of the chart may be changed as follows:

➤➤ ▲ Bar or pie segment 🖱. (*Handles will appear on selected item(s).*)

   (**2007** – *Select the Home ribbon.*)

continued

➤➤ ▶ Fill Colour/Shape Fill selection icon 🎨 ▾ 🖱.

➤➤ Select the colour required.

Note: It may be necessary to click a segment a number of times in order to select an individual segment.

Reopen a Chart

The chart window may be reopened at any time as follows:

➤➤ ▶ Chart on the slide 🖱.

If the data window does not open automatically then proceed as follows:

➤➤ ▶ View Datasheet/Edit Data icon ▦ / 🗇 🖱.

Changing the Chart Type

It is possible to change the chart type as follows:

➤➤ Reopen the chart window.

➤➤ ▶ Change Chart Type icon arrow 📊 ▾ / 📊 🖱.

➤➤ Select the chart type required.

Task 6.3.2

(a) Open the presentation named **Jennings 1** (if not already open).
(b) Apply a transition to slides 2–6.
(c) Animate the bullet points on slide 2.
(d) Animate the Clip Art and the bullet points on slide 4. (Use a chart effect such as Spiral for the Clip Art.)
(e) Animate the chart and the bullet points on slide 5. (Use a chart effect such as Dissolve for the chart.)
(f) Run the slide show and make corrections as necessary.
(g) Add a footer to each slide, with the exception of the first slide, as follows:
      Date   Name   Slide No
(h) Save the presentation with the filename **Jennings 2**.
(i) Print all the slides on one page.

INSERTING HEADERS AND FOOTERS

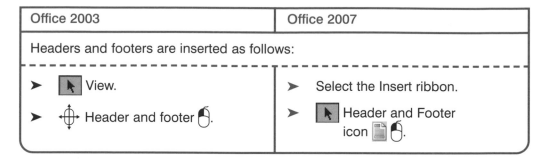

Office 2003	Office 2007
Headers and footers are inserted as follows:	
➤ ▶ View. ➤ ✛ Header and footer 🖱.	➤ Select the Insert ribbon. ➤ ▶ Header and Footer icon 📄🖱.

(*The header and footer window will be displayed.*)

This window is used to select the options to be placed on the slide and/or the handouts. The items that may be selected are:

- Date and time. (This can be set to a fixed date or to update automatically.)
- Slide number.
- Footer comment, e.g. name, title, etc.

PRINTING OPTIONS

When printing using the print icon, all slides will be printed on individual sheets. However, when printing an individual slide, a number of slides on one page, handouts or notes then it is necessary to display the print window.

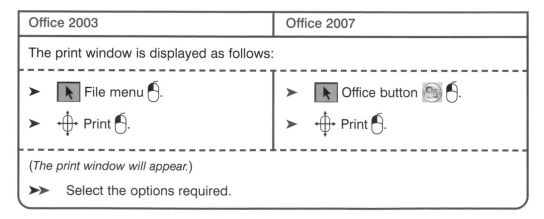

Office 2003	Office 2007
The print window is displayed as follows:	
➤ ▶ File menu 🖱. ➤ ✛ Print 🖱.	➤ ▶ Office button 🖱. ➤ ✛ Print 🖱.
(*The print window will appear.*) ➤➤ Select the options required.	

Print Range

- All slides.
- Current slide only – i.e. the slide in which the cursor is currently placed.

- The selected slides only.
- Particular slides – indicated by inserting the slide numbers.

Copies

- Select the number of copies to be printed.
- Collated – multiple copies collated or not collated.

Print What

- Slides, handouts, notes pages, outline view.

Handouts

- Select the number of slides on each page.
- Horizontal or vertical (the layout of the slides on the page).

Other Options

- Greyscale – shades of grey.
- Pure black and white – no grey.
- Scale to fit paper – used where odd-sized paper is used.
- Frame slides – used to place a frame around each slide.

Task 6.3.3

(a) Open the presentation named **Jennings 2** (if not already open).
(b) Change the background colour on every slide (select a colour of your choice).
(c) Change the organisation chart on slide 3 as follows:
Add a co-worker beside Linda Jordan with name 'Maeve Jennings', title 'Marketing Manager'.
(d) Change Linda Jordan's title to 'Sales Manager'.
(e) Add subordinates to each of the managers and insert the following names:
Liam Griffin, Kate Reilly, Larry Walsh and Noel Hughes.
(f) Change the bullet style for slides 4 and 5.
(g) Increase the spacing between the bullet points on slide 5.
(h) Hide slide 2.
(i) Run the slide show.
(j) Unhide slide 2.
(k) Save the presentation with the filename **Jennings 3**.

BACKGROUNDS

The background for individual slides or all slides may be changed, even when using a template.

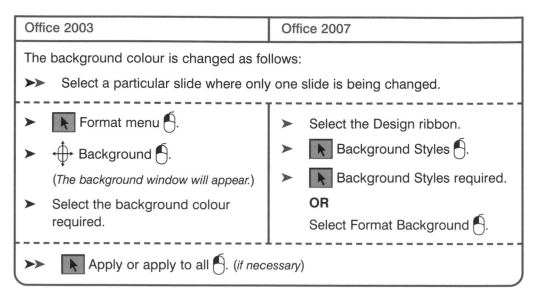

Office 2003	Office 2007
The background colour is changed as follows:	

➤➤   Select a particular slide where only one slide is being changed.

➤ Format menu.	➤ Select the Design ribbon.
➤ Background.	➤ Background Styles.
(*The background window will appear.*)	➤ Background Styles required.
➤ Select the background colour required.	**OR**
	Select Format Background.

➤➤   Apply or apply to all. (*if necessary*)

HIDING A SLIDE

Sometimes it may be advantageous to skip a slide during a presentation without deleting the slide. This can be accomplished by simply hiding the slide.

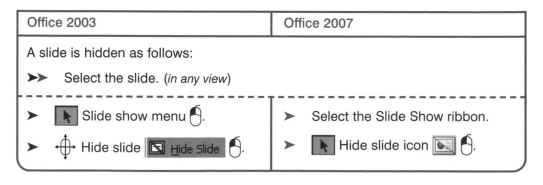

Office 2003	Office 2007
A slide is hidden as follows:	

➤➤   Select the slide. (*in any view*)

➤ Slide show menu.	➤ Select the Slide Show ribbon.
➤ Hide slide Hide Slide.	➤ Hide slide icon.

PAGE SETUP

The page setup is used to set the size and orientation for each slide. When producing slides for printing rather than show, it is useful to be able to select other page sizes.

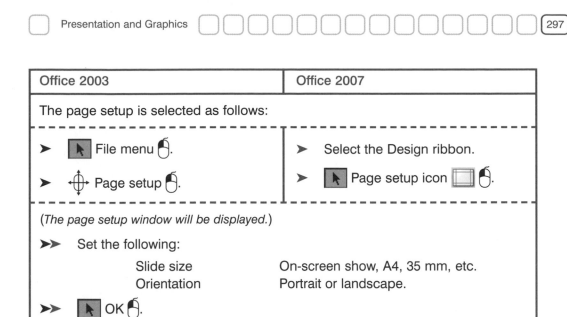

Office 2003	Office 2007
The page setup is selected as follows:	
➤ File menu.	➤ Select the Design ribbon.
➤ Page setup.	➤ Page setup icon.

(*The page setup window will be displayed.*)

➤➤ Set the following:

Slide size	On-screen show, A4, 35 mm, etc.
Orientation	Portrait or landscape.

➤➤ OK.

BULLETS AND NUMBERING

Office 2003	Office 2007
Bullets or numbering are applied to text either before or after entering the text.	

Applying

Bullets or numbering is applied as follows:

➤➤ Select the text. (*if already typed*)

➤➤ Bullet/numbering icon. (**2007** – *Select the Home ribbon.*)

Modifying

Bullet or numbering style may be changed as follows:

➤➤ Select the text.

➤ Format menu.	➤ Select the Home ribbon.
➤ Bullets and numbering....	➤ Bullets **OR** Numbering selection icon.

(*The bullet and numbering window will appear.*)

➤➤ Select the bullet or numbering style required.

continued

Spacing

The spacing between bullets or numbers may be changed as follows:

➤➤ Select the bulleted/numbered list.

➤ ▮ Format menu 🖰.

➤ ⊕ Line spacing 🖰.

(The line spacing window will appear.)

➤ Adjust the line spacing as required.

➤ Select the Home ribbon.

➤ ▮ Line spacing icon 🗘≡▾ 🖰.

➤ ⊕ Line Spacing required 🖰.

Task 6.3.4 (Additional)

Produce the presentations specified in **Task 6A-3** on the CD.

Task 6.4.1

(a) Load the presentation program (if not already loaded) and start a new presentation.
(b) Choose a title slide from the layout options.
(c) Apply a template to the presentation.
(d) Select the slide master and modify it as follows:

- Centre the text in the title and place a border on the frame (resize and reposition if necessary).
- Change the colour of the footer information.
- Insert a Clip Art picture in the top right-hand corner. (Resize so that it does not interfere with the titles.)

(e) Create the first (title) slide as shown in Figure 6.16. Insert the two rectangles on both sides and rotate them to the position shown.
(f) Add four slides, with layouts as shown, and create as shown below:

- Increase the spacing for the bullet points on slide 2.
- Change the style for the bullet points on slides 2 and 5.

- The data for slide 4 is as follows:

	Distinction	Merit	Pass	Fail
2003	38%	44%	14%	4%

- Apply a border and shadow to the Clip Art on slide 5.

(g) Add a sixth slide with a title layout (single frame) and delete the title text frame.

(h) Insert a Word Art frame and insert the text shown in Figure 6.21. Resize the Word Art frame if necessary so that the text occupies most of the slide.

(i) Add a footer to each slide, with the exception of the first slide, as follows:
    Date   Name   Slide No

(j) Save the presentation with the filename **New Age 1**.

Figure 6.16

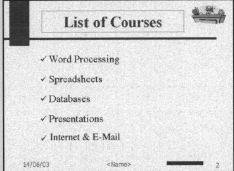

Figure 6.17

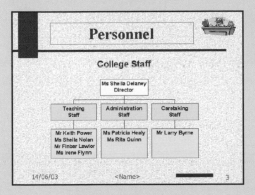

Figure 6.18

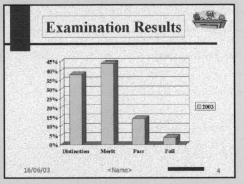

Figure 6.19

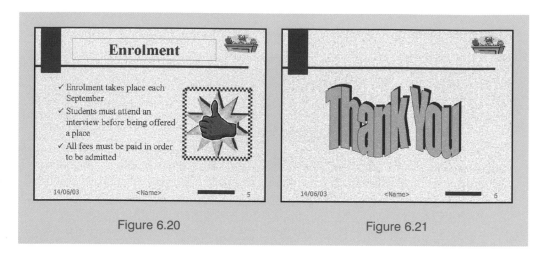

Figure 6.20　　　　　　　　　Figure 6.21

MASTER SLIDES

The font size, colour and position are controlled by the master slide. Any additional items that are to appear on all slides are placed on a master slide. Headers and footers also form part of the master slide.

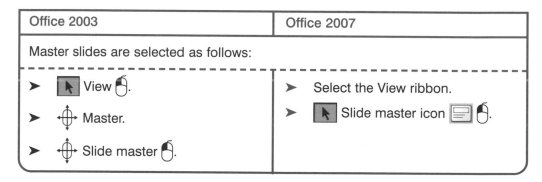

Office 2003	Office 2007
Master slides are selected as follows:	
➤ ▣ View 🖱.	➤ Select the View ribbon.
➤ ⬦ Master.	➤ ▣ Slide master icon 🖵 🖱.
➤ ⬦ Slide master 🖱.	

Anything added to the master slide, such as text, graphics, etc., will appear on all slides of the same type. However, it is possible to suppress the master page details on individual slides.

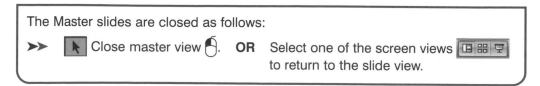

The Master slides are closed as follows:

➤➤ ▣ Close master view 🖱. **OR** Select one of the screen views ▣ ▦ ⬓ to return to the slide view.

Note: The title master, handout master and notes master may also be modified.

ROTATING AN OBJECT

It is possible to rotate some objects that are on a slide. If it is possible to rotate an object then the rotate icon will be active when the object is selected.

An object is rotated as follows:

➤➤ Select the object.

➤➤ 🖰 Green circle above the object 🖱.

(The rotate icon 🔄 *will appear.)*

➤➤ Move the mouse and the object will rotate.

➤➤ 🖱 When the object is in the required position.

BULLET/NUMBER STYLE

Office 2003	Office 2007
Bullet or numbering style may be changed as follows: ➤➤ Select the text 🖱.	
➤ 🖰 Format menu 🖱. ➤ 🖰 Bullets and numbering 🖱. *(The bullet and numbering window will appear.)*	➤ Select the Home ribbon. ➤ ✛ Bullets **OR** Numbering selection icon 🖱.
➤➤ Select the bullet or numbering style required.	

BORDERS AND SHADOWS

Borders

Office 2003	Office 2007
Any frame may have a border applied to it as follows: ➤➤ Select the frame.	
➤ 🖰 Line colour icon arrow 🖍▾ 🖱.	➤ Select the Home ribbon. ➤ 🖰 Shape outline 🖱.
(A range of colours will appear.) ➤➤ 🖰 Colour required 🖱.	

If the line colour displayed by the line colour/shape outline icon is correct, then it is only necessary to click on the icon to apply that colour.

Border Style

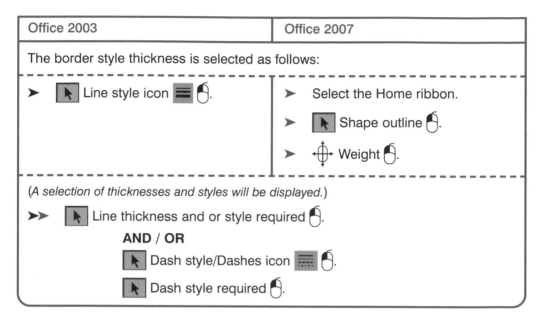

Office 2003	Office 2007
The border style thickness is selected as follows:	
➤ Line style icon	➤ Select the Home ribbon.
	➤ Shape outline.
	➤ Weight.
(*A selection of thicknesses and styles will be displayed.*)	
➤➤ Line thickness and or style required.	
AND / OR	
Dash style/Dashes icon.	
Dash style required.	

Note: If a thick dashed line is required then select a thick line and a dashed style.

Shadows

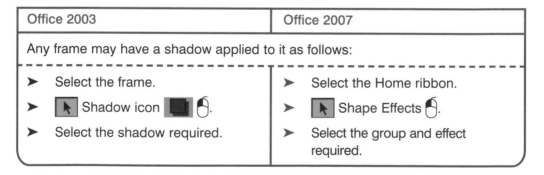

Office 2003	Office 2007
Any frame may have a shadow applied to it as follows:	
➤ Select the frame.	➤ Select the Home ribbon.
➤ Shadow icon.	➤ Shape Effects.
➤ Select the shadow required.	➤ Select the group and effect required.

Task 6.4.2

(a) Open the presentation named **New Age 1** (if not already open).
(b) Apply a transition to slides 2–6.
(c) Animate the bullet points on slide 2.
(d) Change the chart in slide 4 to a pie chart.
(e) Change the colour of each pie segment in the pie chart.

(f) Animate the segments of the pie chart (select 'By category' in the 'Introduce chart elements' in the 'Chart effects' tab).

(g) Animate the Clip Art and the bullet points on slide 5 (use a chart effect such as zoom in/out for the Clip Art).

(h) Spell check the presentation and make any corrections necessary.

(i) Run the slide show and make corrections as necessary.

Slide 1	Slide 2	Slide 3
New Age Training	**Courses**	**College Staff**
Specialist Computer Courses	The courses listed are the most popular ones at present.	All college staff are fully trained and very experienced.
Slide 4	Slide 5	Slide 6
Examination Results	**Enrolment**	**Thank You**
Our examination results are among the highest in the country.	Enrolment takes place each September, but students may enrol beforehand and in cases where classes are not full, enrolment may be up to the first night of the class.	

(j) Insert the following on the notes page for the slides indicated.

(k) Save the presentation again with the filename **New Age 2**.

(l) Print the notes pages for slides 2–5.

SPELL CHECKING

Presentation programs provide a facility for spell checking a presentation. However, it must be remembered that this facility simply checks every word on each slide to see if there is a matching word in one of the program's dictionaries.

The procedure for spell checking is as follows:

➤➤ Make the first slide active. (*not essential, but a good place to start*)

➤➤ 🖱 Spell check 🔤 🖱. (**2007** – *On the review ribbon.*)

(*The spell check window will appear.*)

The window will display the first word that is not in the dictionaries together with a list of possible correct words. One of a number of tasks may be performed:

(a) Select **ignore** to leave the word as it is.

continued

(b) Select the correct word from the list and select **change**.

(c) Type the word required and select **change**.

(d) Select **add** to add this new word to the dictionary.

ADDING NOTES TO SLIDES

Notes may be added to a presentation, either for the presenter or for the audience.

Notes are added as follows:

➤➤ Select normal view.

➤➤ Select notes pane. (*at bottom of screen*)

➤➤ Type the notes required.

OR

Office 2003	Office 2007
➤ ▶ View menu 🖰.	➤ Select the View ribbon.

➤➤ ▶ Notes page 🖰. (*The notes page for the selected slide will appear.*)

➤➤ Type the notes for selected page, in the position shown.

➤➤ ▶ Previous slide icon ▲. **OR** Next slide icon ▼ 🖰. (*underneath the right scroll bar*)

➤➤ Type notes on other pages.

Task 6.4.3 (Additional)

Produce the presentations specified in **Task 6A-4** on the CD.

GRAPHICS

Presentation programs are very powerful graphics programs. In addition to enabling the production of presentations they provide ways to produce and manipulate graphics. The following notes and tasks concentrate on the production of pictures using a presentation program.

Task 6.5.1

(a) Load the presentation program (if not already loaded).
(b) Start a new presentation and select a blank slide.
(c) Create a slide as shown.

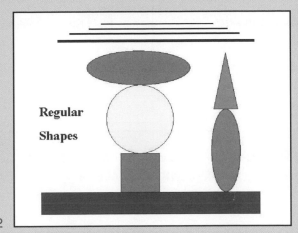

Figure 6.22

(d) Apply appropriate line thickness and colour to each object.
(e) Save the presentation with the filename **Regular Shapes**.
(f) Save the slide as a picture in .jpg format as **Regular Shapes**.
(g) Close the presentation.

INSERTING OBJECTS

Most of the objects which will be dealt with in the following pages are obtained from the Drawing toolbar in PowerPoint **2003**, which is usually displayed at the bottom of the screen. In the case of PowerPoint **2007**, the objects are found in the Shapes icon on the Home ribbon or on the Insert ribbon.

DRAWING LINES

A line may be produced as follows:

➤➤   ▶ Line tool ◳ 🖱.

➤➤   Select a starting point on the slide 🖱.

➤➤   Drag the mouse to form a line 🖱.

A straight line is drawn by simply holding down the Shift key before holding the mouse button and releasing the mouse button before releasing the Shift key.

Line Colour

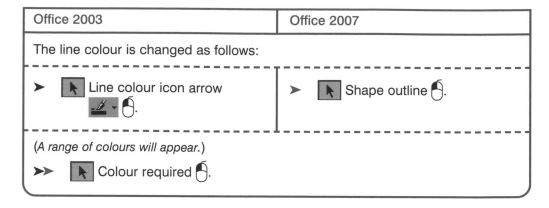

Office 2003	Office 2007
The line colour is changed as follows:	
➤ Line colour icon arrow.	➤ Shape outline.
(A range of colours will appear.) ➤➤ Colour required.	

If the line colour displayed by the line colour/shape outline icon is correct, then it is only necessary to click on the icon to apply that colour.

Line Style

Office 2003	Office 2007
The line style thickness (either for a line or the outside of a shape) is selected as follows:	
➤ Line style icon.	➤ Shape outline.
	➤ Weight.
(A selection of thicknesses and styles will be displayed.) ➤➤ Style required.	

Most programs also provide an icon for applying dashed or arrowed styles on lines. There is an icon for dashed and arrowed lines on the drawing toolbar/shape outline selection.

DRAWING A RECTANGLE OR SQUARE

A rectangle or square may be produced as follows:

➤➤ Rectangle tool.

➤➤ Select a starting point on the slide.

➤➤ Drag the mouse to form a rectangle.

A square is drawn by simply holding down the Shift key before holding the mouse button and releasing the mouse button before releasing the Shift key.

Shape Colour

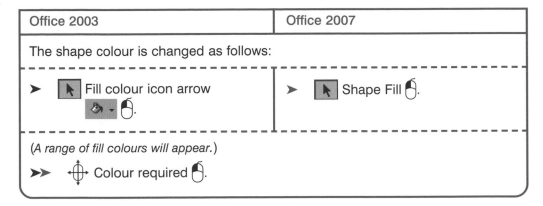

Office 2003	Office 2007
The shape colour is changed as follows:	
➤ ▮ Fill colour icon arrow ◈ ▾ 🖱.	➤ ▮ Shape Fill 🖱.
(A range of fill colours will appear.) ➤➤ ⊹ Colour required 🖱.	

The pallet will display a small number of colours but one of the other options displayed on the colour pallet may be selected:

No Fill   Produces a shape with no colour, effectively just a border.

More Fill Colours   Provides a range of colour options.

Fill Effects   Provides a range of texture and pattern options.

If the fill colour displayed by the fill colour icon is correct, then it is only necessary to click on the icon to apply that colour.

DRAWING AN OVAL OR CIRCLE

An oval (ellipse) or a circle may be produced as follows:

➤➤ ▮ Oval tool ▢ 🖱.

➤➤ Select a starting point on the slide 🖱.

➤➤ Drag the mouse to form an oval 🖱.

A circle is drawn by simply holding down the Shift key before holding the mouse button and releasing the mouse button before releasing the Shift key.

When drawing ovals and circles it is helpful to think in terms of drawing a rectangle or square that will fit around the oval or circle.

The oval/circle colour is changed in the same way as for a rectangle above.

DRAWING A TRIANGLE (AND OTHER REGULAR SHAPES)

If there **is** an icon for the shape required on the Drawing toolbar or the Home ribbon then the shape is produced in the same way as for the other shapes above.

Office 2003	Office 2007
If there **is not** an icon for the shape required then a triangle (and other regular shapes) may be produced as follows:	
➤ Auto shapes.	➤ Select the Insert ribbon.
➤ Basic shapes from the pop-up menu.	➤ Shapes icon.

➤➤   Triangle (or other basic shape) from the options offered.

➤➤   Select a starting point on the slide.

➤➤   Drag the mouse to form the shape.

RESIZING A FRAME

The size of a frame (or line) may be altered by first making the frame active and then:

➤➤   One of the handles.

(One of the resize arrows ↔ ↕ ↗ ↘ will appear on the handle.)

➤➤   Drag the frame to the required size.

Note: When resizing a picture be sure to use a corner handle, not a side handle, to avoid distorting the picture.

TEXT FRAMES

Office 2003	Office 2007
A text frame is created as follows:	
➤ Text tool icon.	➤ Select the Insert ribbon.
	➤ Text tool icon.

continued

➤➤   Any position on the slide 🖱.

➤➤   Drag the mouse to the right and a rectangle will appear on the slide. Drag the mouse until the width of the rectangle is the width of the frame required 🖱.

A small text frame will be displayed with a flashing cursor in it. Text may be inserted into the frame by simply typing the text. The frame will expand vertically as each line of text is typed or each time the Enter key is pressed.

Text Alignment

Text may be aligned using the alignment icons ▤▤▤ left, centre and right.

Text Enhancement

Text may be enhanced using the icons **B** *I* U bold, italics and underline.

SAVING IN PICTURE FORMAT

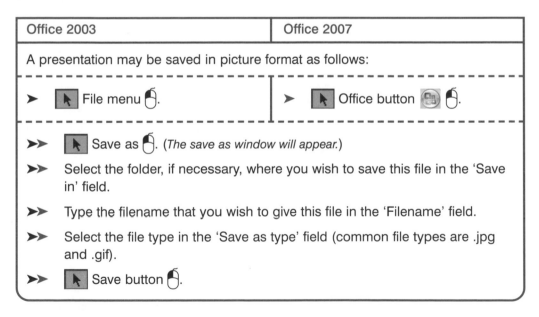

Office 2003	Office 2007
A presentation may be saved in picture format as follows:	
➤ File menu 🖱.	➤ Office button 🖱.

➤➤   Save as 🖱. (*The save as window will appear.*)

➤➤   Select the folder, if necessary, where you wish to save this file in the 'Save in' field.

➤➤   Type the filename that you wish to give this file in the 'Filename' field.

➤➤   Select the file type in the 'Save as type' field (common file types are .jpg and .gif).

➤➤   Save button 🖱.

The program may present a prompt, with a message asking 'Do you want to export every slide in the presentation or only the current slide?'. Select the option **Current Slide Only** to save a single picture.

It is always a good idea to save a picture first as a presentation, and then perform a second save as a picture. This allows the presentation to be opened again and modifications made.

Task 6.5.2

(a) Load the presentation program (if not already loaded).
(b) Start a new presentation and select a blank slide.
(c) Create a slide as shown in Figure 6.23 (apply a different colour to each shape).

Figure 6.23

(d) Move all the shapes to the centre of the slide so that they overlap (ensure that no shape is completely hidden).
(e) Perform the following operations on the shapes:

- Bring the rectangle to the front.
- Send the triangle to the back.
- Bring the oval forward one layer.
- Send the rectangle back three layers.

(f) Save the presentation with the filename **Shapes**.

STACKING FRAMES

When using presentation programs, the slide is built up in layers. Each object is produced on a separate layer and these layers are stacked on top of each other to produce the finished slide. The frames will cover each other in the order in which they were created. The first frame will be at the back and the last frame will be at the front.

Any frame may be moved closer or further from the top (front) by making the frame active and clicking one of the following icons:

Bring this frame to the front.

Send this frame to the back.

Bring this frame closer to the front.

Send this frame closer to the back.

Office 2003	Office 2007
If the icons are **not** on the toolbar, then proceed as follows:	
➤ ▦ Draw 🖱. (*on the drawing toolbar*) ➤ ⬥ Order 🖱.	➤ Select the Home ribbon. ➤ ▦ Arrange icon 🗗 🖱.
➤➤ ⬥ One of the options above.	

If any icon is not on the toolbar, then it may be a good idea to customise one of the toolbars to include the icon. In **2007**, the Quick Access Toolbar may have icons added to it.

Task 6.5.3

(a) Load the presentation program (if not already loaded).
(b) Start a new presentation and select a blank slide.
(c) Create a slide as shown.

Note: The clouds are free drawn and the front of the ship is a right-angled triangle, which may need to be rotated. The birds are from Clip Art.

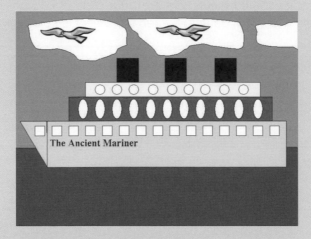

Figure 6.24

(d) Apply appropriate colours to each object.
(e) Save the presentation as **Ship**.
(f) Save the slide as a picture in .jpg format, with the filename **Ship**.
(g) Close the presentation.

FREEHAND DRAWING

Office 2003	Office 2007
Freehand drawing is produced using the scribble tool as follows:	
➤ ▮ AutoShapes 🔴. ➤ ▮ Lines 🔴.	➤ Select the Insert ribbon. ➤ ▮ Shapes icon 🔲 🔴.

➤➤ ▮ Scribble tool 🐍 🔴.

➤➤ Select a starting point on the slide 🔴. (*The cursor becomes a pencil.*)

➤➤ Draw the required shape 🔴.

This is a very useful tool but it must be remembered that unless the shape is **closed** (i.e. the end is joined to the start), it may not be possible to colour it correctly. If the shape is left **open**, then the shape will be closed with a straight line from the end point to the start point (if it is filled with a colour).

ROTATING AN OBJECT

It is possible to rotate some objects that are on a slide. If it is possible to rotate an object then the rotate icon will be active when the object is selected.

An object is rotated as follows:

➤➤ Select the object.

➤➤ ▮ Green circle above the object 🔴.

(*The rotate icon* 🔄 *will appear.*)

➤➤ Move the mouse and the object will rotate.

➤➤ 🔴 When the object is in the required position.

INSERTING CLIP ART

The Insert Clip Art icon is on the drawing toolbar in PowerPoint **2003** and on the Insert ribbon in PowerPoint **2007**. It may be necessary to be connected to the Internet in order to get Clip Art.

Clip Art objects may be placed on the slide as follows:

➤➤ ▮ Insert Clip Art icon ▦ / ▦ 🖱.

(The Clip Art gallery will appear.)

➤➤ Clip Art object required 🖱.

➤➤ Close the Clip Art Gallery.

Once the Clip Art is inserted it will usually have to be resized and positioned on the slide in the same way as any other object.

INSERTING PICTURES

The Insert Picture icon is on the drawing toolbar in PowerPoint **2003** and on the Insert ribbon in PowerPoint **2007**.

A picture that has been saved may be placed on the slide as follows:

➤➤ ▮ Insert Picture icon 🖼 🖱.

(The insert picture window will appear.)

➤➤ Locate the folder where the picture is stored.

➤➤ ▮ Picture required 🖱.

Once the picture is inserted it will usually have to be resized and positioned on the slide in the same way as any other object.

Task 6.5.4

(a) Load the presentation program (if not already loaded).
(b) Start a new presentation and select a blank slide.
(c) Create a slide as shown.

Figure 6.25

The picture consists of basic shapes (lines, rectangles/ squares), as described at the beginning of this section. The picture is produced as follows:

1 Rectangle for the sky.
2 Rectangle for the midsection.
3 Rectangle for the road.
4 Freeform for the clouds.
5 Rectangle for each building.
6 Rectangle for one window.
7 Copy and paste to form row of windows.
8 Group the windows and copy and paste for each row of windows.
9 Rectangle for doorways.
10 Line for the flagpole, triangle for the flag and rotate.
11 Dashed line for centre of roadway.
12 Insert Clip Art picture and resize if necessary.

(d) Apply appropriate colours to each object.
(e) Save the presentation as **Sky Scrapers**.
(f) Save the slide as a picture in .jpg format with the filename **Sky Scrapers**.
(g) Print one copy of the slide.
(h) Close the presentation.

GROUPING FRAMES

A number of frames may be grouped together to form a single group by firstly making the frames to be grouped active and then grouping them together.

Office 2003	Office 2007
Frames are grouped as follows:	
➤➤ ▶ A position outside the frames 🖰. (*It is sometimes necessary to start off the slide.*)	
➤➤ Drag the mouse to enclose the required frames 🖰.	
(*All the frames completely included will show with active handles.*)	
➤ ▶ Draw icon 🖰. (*on the drawing toolbar*)	➤ Select the Home ribbon.
	➤ ▶ Arrange icon 🖰.
➤ ✛ Group 🖰.	➤ ✛ Group 🖰.

The frames may be ungrouped by simply selecting 'Ungroup' instead of 'Group'.

A number of frames may be made active at the same time by selecting the first frame and then holding down the Shift key while selecting other frames.

The frames may be worked on (copied, moved, etc.) as if they were a single frame. Care must be taken to keep all the frames active by not clicking the mouse button while the objects are active.

Task 6.5.5

(a) Load the presentation program (if not already loaded).
(b) Start a new presentation and select a blank slide.
(c) Insert the picture **Sky Scrapers.jpg**, which you saved in the previous task.
(d) Resize the picture so that it is one-quarter the size of the slide and position it in the top left-hand corner of the slide.
(e) Copy the picture and paste it three times.
(f) Position the three pictures so that they occupy the other three quarters of the slide.
(g) Save the presentation as **Multi Picture**.
(h) Print one copy of the slide.

Task 6.5.6 (Additional)

Produce the presentations specified in **Task 6A-5** on the CD.

7 The Internet

SYMBOLS USED IN THIS CHAPTER

The symbols used in this chapter, and their meanings, are as follows:

Symbol	Meaning
🖱	Click the left mouse button.
🖱	Double-click the left mouse button.
🖱	Click the right mouse button.
⊕	Move the mouse to point to an item without clicking or holding any button.
▲	Point to an item on the screen.
⏎	Press the Enter key.

Note: The content of the World Wide Web (WWW) changes so frequently and websites appear and disappear at such a rapid rate that it is difficult to pick sites which will still be in use when you are reading this book. If a site address mentioned in this section does not give a response then simply use another address and continue the task.

INTRODUCTION

The use of the Internet and the WWW has revolutionised communications (the way in which information is acquired and business transacted). Most people now take the Internet and the WWW for granted and simply treat it as normal everyday life. It may be difficult to believe that all of this has happened in such a short period of time since its inception in 1989.

ORIGIN

The basic development of the Internet was done by the American military around 1970 with a system called ARPANET. The system they developed allowed various agencies to communicate with one another. The system also allowed the sharing of documents that contained only text, and the sending and receiving of electronic mail. This system later became an international system with agencies in London and Norway.

A breakthrough occurred in the early 1980s with the development of a common protocol called TCP/IP, which allowed the transfer of data between different types of computer systems. The number of servers connected to the Internet increased greatly to about 100,000 before 1990.

The concept of the WWW is accredited to Tim Berners-Lee and Robert Caillau, who wrote a proposal for an interface and **hypertext** to allow anyone to use the Internet. They further developed software for browsing the Internet, which was available free, and thus the original WWW was born. Marc Andreessen developed graphic capability for the browser and this ability led to a great explosion in the use of the WWW.

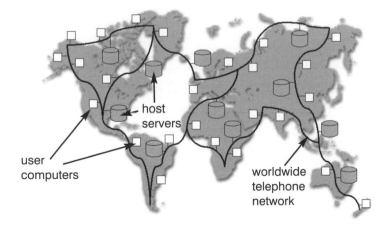

Figure 7.1

STRUCTURE OF THE INTERNET

The Internet uses the worldwide telephone network to permanently connect web server computers. These computers hold all the websites that are available for viewing on the WWW. WWW users connect to one of these servers, using the telephone line, or a wireless connection and then they have access to information stored on any server.

Modern developments have increased the access to the WWW by means of mobile phones and satellite communications. It is now possible to gain access to the WWW from almost anywhere in the world.

CONNECTING TO THE INTERNET

In order for an individual to connect to the Internet their computer must be equipped with a network connection, and a wireless facility or modem. In areas where broadband is not available it is possible to connect to the Internet over the telephone line using a modem. This is a device (card) which is fitted in the computer and allows it to connect to the telephone network. The download speeds using a modem are very slow – usually a maximum of 56 Kbps.

An account with an Internet service provider (ISP), such as Eircom, BT Ireland, etc. is also needed. Some of these accounts are free.

Any modern computer is capable of connecting to the Internet, but minimum requirements for an old computer would be:

CPU	Pentium I
CPU speed	300 MHz
RAM	128 MB
Hard disk	500 MB free space
Modem	56 K
Operating system	Windows 2000

The computer must also have a program (software) that will allow the user to interact with the WWW. This program is called a **web browser**, and the most common web browser programs in use are Microsoft Internet Explorer and Mozilla Firefox.

USES OF THE WWW

The uses of the WWW are vast and varied. New uses are being found every day and it is impossible to devise any sort of a list of uses, but the main uses can be broadly divided into the following areas.

Communication   The WWW has become an everyday communication tool. The great advantage is its speed and the ability to communicate graphic, sound and video information.

Training The amount of training information available on the WWW is vast. If you want to learn anything new, it is worth browsing the WWW to see what is available.

Research Any person involved in research, whether for a simple school project or a thesis for a PhD, uses the WWW to source information quickly.

Commerce The amount of business that is currently transacted via the WWW is enormous and growing every day. If you need anything, from a simple grocery item to an isolated mansion, it is possible to find it on the WWW.

Marketing Companies are finding that the WWW is a good place to market their goods and services. Consequently, a high proportion of websites devote large portions of their home page to advertising.

Other WWW Services

Along with searching the WWW for information the Internet provides a number of other services, such as:

E-mail Users send and receive text, graphics, audio, video, etc. directly to and from their computer.

Radio Users may receive live radio broadcasts from any station using the WWW to transmit their programs.

Audio Users may download audio files, e.g. songs, albums, for playing on their computer or other audio device.

Video Users may receive video and TV programs on their computer. These may be either live broadcasts from TV stations or video, e.g. films, from stored banks of video.

Video Phone and Chat This is a huge growth area, where users log on to a service provider such as Skype, Gismo, Yahoo Messenger etc. and they can see and talk to the person on another computer. Some of these services are also available on mobile phones with the necessary hardware and software. Most of these services also include a chat option where text may be typed on one computer and appears on the other person's computer.

Video and Picture Sharing There has been an explosion in this area. There are a number of video-sharing services available which contain vast volumes of shared pictures, video, audio files and data. Some of the most popular ones at present include YouTube, MySpace, Bebo, Google Video.

Online Games   There are numerous sites which allow the user to play games, either individually or with another person who is online at the same time.

Chat Rooms   Users enter into discussion groups online. Anyone in the group may contribute to the discussion by typing their comments on their own computer.

SAFETY ON THE WWW

Great care should be taken when using the WWW as it is being used in numerous ways to damage computers or steal user information. Personal information should only be divulged to legitimate companies and then only when necessary. There are a couple of areas in particular where care should be taken.

Viruses

Viruses are programs that infect a computer, destroy all the data on the computer, and render it unusable. The best method of protecting against such an occurrence is to install a good antivirus program and update it daily. Never accept e-mail from unknown sources and never open a file from an unknown source.

Pornography

The amount of pornographic material available on the WWW has grown phenomenally. This is all too easy to access and children often find themselves downloading pornographic images without specifically looking for them. There is no definitive solution to this problem other than direct user supervision. However, there are a number of filtering programs available (commonly called **Nanny** software) which prevent most of this material from being viewed on the computer.

Privacy

Cookies may be used to gather information about the user of a computer. However, it is very surprising how much information people are willing to reveal about themselves over the Internet. This can be done when filling in forms or when chatting in a chat room. Users should always be careful when revealing any information on the WWW.

OWNERSHIP OF THE INTERNET AND WWW

The Internet consists of many components – including the public telephone networks – so the Internet itself is not a single entity. Various people, companies and corporations own parts of the system and derive an income from that part. The telephone companies receive fees and charges for use of the lines.

The web servers charge for hosting websites, and the website owners derive income either directly from sales or from advertising on their website. A large number of companies just provide information via the WWW and do not receive income for doing so.

INTERNET AND WWW TERMS

Cookie
These are small text files that are delivered to a computer when a website is accessed. These were developed as harmless files to improve the communication between computers and websites. However, over the past few years they have been used to collect and return information about the computer user.

Digital Certificate
A digital certificate is like an electronic passport that is used to ensure that digital communications can be transmitted securely on the WWW. This identifies the user to the receiver and allows for secure transaction of commerce over the WWW.

Encryption
Encryption is the act of making a text unreadable by using an encryption algorithm. The text appears as a jumble of letters, digits and special characters, thus making the text secure. In order to decipher the text the receiver must use the same algorithm.

Firewall
This is a system used to prevent unauthorised access via the telephone system to a private network. This may be a special program (software), a piece of equipment (hardware) or a combination of both.

FTP
A standard, high-level protocol for transferring files from one computer to another. The most common protocol is TCP/IP.

HTML
Hypertext mark-up language (.htm or .html). A standard format used when saving a page for viewing on the WWW.

http
The hypertext transfer protocol is a set of rules for the transfer of data on the WWW.

The Internet
A worldwide collection of computers connected together using telephone lines.

ISP
An ISP (Internet service provider) provides a connection for individual computers or computer networks to connect to the Internet.

Link (Hyperlink)
This is a special portion of a web page that is specially configured to link to another page, a different position on the same page or even another website. A hyperlink may be a word(s), a graphic or even a position on the page or a graphic. A hyperlink will be recognised as the mouse pointer changes to a hand when it is positioned over the hyperlink.

Protected Website
A website that has restricted access. In order to gain access to these sites the user must register with the website and be given a username and password.

Search Engine	A database of information that is stored on the World Wide Web and is catalogued for easy access to information.
TCP/IP	The **T**ransmission **C**ontrol **P**rotocol/**I**nternet **P**rotocol is a standardised set of rules for connecting computers together and allowing the transfer of data.
URL	**U**niform **R**esource **L**ocation (http://www.————). This is the unique address of an individual page on a computer anywhere in the world.
Web Browser	Program used to browse the WWW, e.g. Internet Explorer.
Web Page	One page of information that is stored for displaying in a web browser. A single web page can be any length and width.
Web Server	A computer that is dedicated to storing websites and is permanently connected to the WWW.
Website	A collection of web pages.
WWW	The **W**orld **W**ide **W**eb (commonly referred to as the Web) is a global collection of websites containing information that can be accessed using the Internet.

THE INTERNET

The term **Internet** is short for internetworking. The Internet is a collection of worldwide computers and computer networks connected together using telephone lines. The information on all these computers may be shared by anyone connected to this worldwide network.

In order for an individual to connect to the Internet their computer must be equipped with a **modem**. This is a device (card) which is fitted in the computer and allows it to connect to the telephone network. (External modems are also available, or alternatively the computer may be part of a local area network which is connected to the Internet.) An account with an Internet service provider (ISP), such as Eircom, Smart, O2, BT, etc., is also needed. Some of these accounts are free.

WORLD WIDE WEB (WWW)

The WWW is a global network of computers that uses the Internet to connect and transfer data, pictures, sound and video worldwide. In order to allow this to happen there has to be a standard protocol for connecting computers together and transferring information. The development and adoption of **http** (hypertext transfer protocol) facilitated the development of the WWW.

In order to connect to the WWW a computer must also have a program (software) that will allow the user to interact with the WWW. This program is called a **web browser**, and the most common web browser programs in use are Microsoft Internet Explorer and Mozilla Firefox.

INTERNET SERVICE PROVIDER (ISP)

ISPs are the key to the operation of the WWW, as they provide a connection between individual computers and the Internet. There are a large number of these providers and great care should be exercised before signing up with one of them. A number of them provide free access but you will find that the online cost is high. Paying a subscription may reduce the cost and also provide some support if difficulties arise.

The method of connection may vary from dial-up to permanently online, but this should be balanced against the cost and need.

The cost of hosting your own website varies greatly between ISPs. However, the cost is not the only factor which should influence the choice of host. The following factors should also be considered:

- Space available.

- Speed of ISP connection to the Internet.

- User-to-line ratio.

- How many e-mail addresses are provided.

- Technical support provision.

The access speed is a major problem for Internet users and is influenced by the following:

- The computer's modem speed.

- The ISP connection speed.

- The number of users using the ISP.

- The number of people accessing a particular website.

- The type of telephone line linking the computer and the ISP.

URL

Each page on the WWW has a unique URL address. Each site will generally have a fairly short address so that people will remember it easily. Each site will have a home page that will automatically be displayed when the address of the site is entered. Each address has the same format, similar to the following.

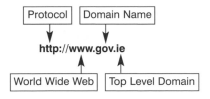

Figure 7.2

Most large websites will create a structure of folders and subfolders for storing their pages on the web server. As a website is browsed the URL may become longer with new parts being added, each one separated by a forward slash (/). This simply indicates that the page being viewed is stored in that particular folder. If the last part of the URL finishes with a filename extension then it is the name of the actual page.

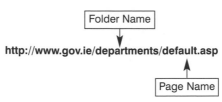

Figure 7.3

If an individual page from a site is required and the address for that page is known, then it is possible to go directly to that actual page. Actual pages usually end with the filename extension **.htm**, **.html** or **.asp**. However, with the growth in technology, the way in which websites are developed is changing rapidly and the display of the URL may be quite different.

When typing the URL address it is not necessary to type the **http://** portion of the address.

USEFUL URLs

www.irlgov.ie	Irish Government
www.education.ie	Department of Education and Science
www.fetac.ie	Further Education and Training Awards Council
www.ecdl.ie	European Computer Driving Licence
www.scoilnet.ie	Scoilnet
www.ncte.ie	National Centre for Technology in Education
www.ucd.ie	University College Dublin
www.dcu.ie	Dublin City University
www.tcd.ie	The University of Dublin, Trinity College
www.ucc.ie	University College, Cork
www.nui.ie	National University of Ireland (NUI)
www.nuig.ie	NUI Galway
www.nuim.ie	NUI Maynooth
www.ul.ie	University of Limerick

www.european-agency.org	The European Agency for Development in Special Needs Education
www.ireland.com	Information about Ireland
www.Irishtimes.ie	The *Irish Times* website
www.sunday-times.co.uk	The *London Sunday Times* website
www.gaa.ie	GAA
www.rte.ie	RTÉ
www.kildare.ie	County Kildare Community Network

WEBSITE

A website is a collection of web pages that are made available to anyone using the WWW. A website is produced and maintained by a company or organisation that wishes to communicate with the rest of the world using the WWW. Each site would have its own unique URL address. The size of these websites varies greatly depending on the amount of information the owner wishes to display. A site will consist of a number of pages that are linked together. The user may move from page to page by simply clicking the mouse button while pointing to a link on a page.

Most companies have their own domain name. These domain names must be registered with appropriate domain registries. URLs ending with **.ie** are all domains registered in Ireland.

LINKS (HYPERLINKS)

Most web pages will have a link, called a **hyperlink**, to another page or even to another website. This is a special portion of a page that is specially configured to link to another page. A hyperlink can be recognised because the mouse pointer changes to a hand as it is positioned over the hyperlink. Text hyperlinks will normally be in blue with the text underlined.

Hyperlinks are activated by simply pointing to the hyperlink and clicking the left mouse button. The program will then search the WWW for that page, download it to your computer and display it on-screen.

WEB BROWSERS

In order to view the pages stored on the WWW it is necessary to use a program capable of displaying the pages. These programs are referred to as **web browsers**.

Task 7.1.1

(a) Load the web browser program.
(b) Display the website, www.gov.ie
(c) Activate the link to the Government Departments.
(d) Activate the link to Attorney General.
(e) Use the Back button to return one page.
(f) Activate the link to the Agriculture and Food Department.
(g) Activate the link to Food Safety.
(h) Use the Back button three times to return to the government home page.
(i) Use the Forward button once to go to the Government Departments.
(j) Close the web browser.

Note: If this site has changed, use any website to perform the same operations.

LOADING THE WEB BROWSER

The web browser is loaded from the desktop as follows:

- 🔲 Web browser shortcut icon 🖱.

If the program is not available from the desktop then it may be loaded from the Start menu as follows:

- 🔲 Start 🖱.

- ⊕ All Programs.

- ⊕ Web browser 🖱.

The web browser will be loaded and the default site home page will be displayed on-screen. This is usually the home page of the ISP, or the site home page if connecting via a network.

title bar —   address bar   toolbar

menu bar —

web page title —

web page —

status bar —

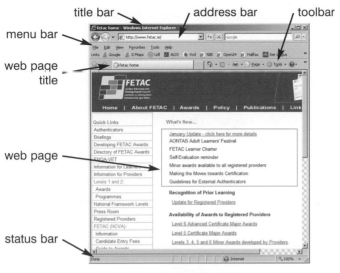

Internet Explorer

Figure 7.4

title bar —   toolbar   address bar

menu bar —

web page —

status bar —

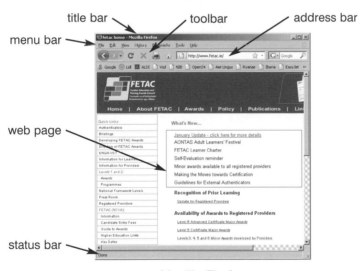

Mozilla Firefox

Figure 7.5

BROWSER TOOLBAR

The main icons on the web browser toolbar are as follows:

Explorer	Firefox	Function
		This icon is used to start the search of the WWW for the URL specified in the address field. The Enter key may be pressed instead of clicking this icon.

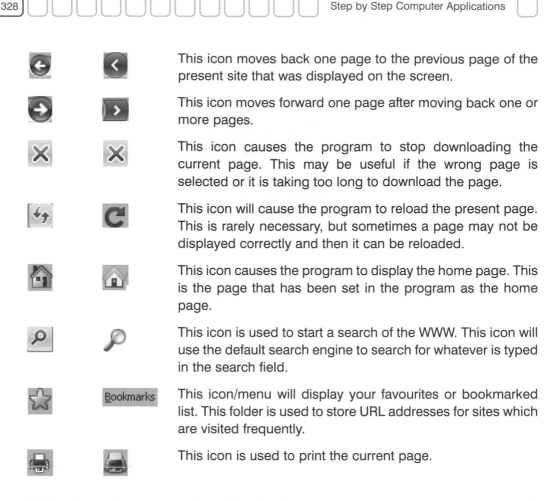

This icon moves back one page to the previous page of the present site that was displayed on the screen.

This icon moves forward one page after moving back one or more pages.

This icon causes the program to stop downloading the current page. This may be useful if the wrong page is selected or it is taking too long to download the page.

This icon will cause the program to reload the present page. This is rarely necessary, but sometimes a page may not be displayed correctly and then it can be reloaded.

This icon causes the program to display the home page. This is the page that has been set in the program as the home page.

This icon is used to start a search of the WWW. This icon will use the default search engine to search for whatever is typed in the search field.

This icon/menu will display your favourites or bookmarked list. This folder is used to store URL addresses for sites which are visited frequently.

This icon is used to print the current page.

All the above icons are activated by simply pointing to the icon and clicking the left mouse button ◀.

DISPLAYING A WEBSITE

Any website may be accessed by simply typing the URL address on the address line as follows:

- ▸ Address field 👆. (*The address will become highlighted.*)
- Type the URL address ⌨.

The program will search the WWW for that website and display the home page for the site.

When typing the URL address it is not necessary to type the **http://** portion of the address.

Task 7.1.2

(a) Load the web browser program.
(b) Display the website, www.education.ie.
(c) Activate the link to Education Personnel.
(d) Save the Education Personnel page.
(e) Preview the Education Personnel page.
(f) Change the page margins to 1 cm all round.
(g) Print one copy of the page.
(h) Use the Back button to return to the education home page.
(i) Save one of the graphic images in a folder of your choice and give it the filename **Education Picture**.
(j) Close the web browser.

SAVING A WEB PAGE

When a page is displayed on-screen it may be saved as follows:

- 🖱 File ⬦.

- 🖱 Save as ⬦. (*The save as window will appear.*)

- Select the drive and folder where the page is to be saved.

- Type the filename for this page.

- Select the type of file to be saved. (*web page complete, web page HTML, text file*)

- 🖱 Save ⬦.

Web Page Complete

When the web page is saved as this type, there will be a file with the same name that the page was saved under. There will also be a new subfolder with a similar name to the saved file, containing various elements of the saved page. In order to view the page later this subfolder and contents must be retained in its current folder. This page may be viewed offline in the web browser.

Web Page HTML

When the web page is saved as this type there will be a single page saved. This page may be displayed in the web browser as a single page image. The graphic images will not be displayed but the place holdings will.

Text File

Saving a page as this type means that only the text on the page will be saved. Any graphic images, place holders, etc. will not be saved. This page can then be viewed in any text-editing program, e.g. Notepad, WordPad.

SAVING GRAPHICS

Most graphic images on websites are generally quite small. They are usually either **.jpg** or **.gif** format.

Graphic images may be saved on disk as follows:

- ▣ Graphic image ✋. (*A menu will appear.*)

- ⊕ Save picture/image as ✋. (*A save window will appear.*)

- Select the drive and folder where the image is to be saved.

- Type the filename for this graphic.

  (*It may be necessary to include the filename extension.*)

- ▣ Save ✋.

PRINT PREVIEW

It is a good idea to preview a page before printing. This is especially true in the case of web pages, as they have no definite size. The print preview displays how the web page will appear on an A4 page.

A page is previewed as follows:

- ▣ File menu ✋.

- ⊕ Print Preview ✋.

If the web page does not fit on the A4 page then the orientation of the page may need to be changed.

Note: Some browsers may not have a preview option.

PRINTING

The page displayed on-screen may be printed as follows:

- ▶ Print icon 🖱.

The page will be printed, but because it is a web page it may be of any length or width, and therefore it may be printed on more than one page. If the web page is wider than an A4 page then the right side of the page may be missing and it will be necessary to print the page in landscape.

Print Options

The print window allows a number of options to be selected. The most common options available are:

- Number of copies to be printed.
- Print selected frames.
- Print selected pages.

The print window is accessed as follows:

- ▶ File menu 🖱.
- ⊕ Print 🖱.

PAGE SETUP

The page setup is used to alter page header and/or footer, page margins and page orientation.

The page setup window is accessed as follows:

- ▶ File menu 🖱.
- ⊕ Page setup 🖱.

Note: Some websites override page margins when printing a web page.

Task 7.1.3 (Additional)

Perform the operations specified in **Task 7A-1** on the CD.

Task 7.2.1

(a) Load the web browser program.

(b) Display a search engine of your choice.

(c) Type the following in the search field: **House to let in Costa del Sol**.

(d) Select one of the search results and view the contents.

(e) Use the Back button to return to the search results page.

(f) Select a different one of the search results and view the contents.

(g) Save this page as a HTML file.

(h) Print one copy of the page in landscape orientation.

(i) Close the web browser.

SEARCH ENGINES

Search engines are databases that continuously browse the web and collect, store and catalogue data from the WWW. This data is stored in large databases that are accessible by users of the search engine. This means that it is only necessary to interrogate the search engine database when looking for data on the WWW. Without these search engines it would be necessary to have the address of the particular site which the user wished to visit.

The data stored in each search engine's database is different and some search engines specialise in particular areas. If the information required is not found on one search engine then it is a good idea to try another one.

Most search engines provide facilities that allow the web to be searched in a number of ways, as follows:

The WWW   This is the normal search option and will search through the search engine's database for matches to the search request.

Images   Search for images that match the criteria.

Groups   Allows the user to restrict the search to a particular group type, e.g. business, arts, science.

The web browser programs generally provide a search engine for performing searches of the WWW. There are a large number of commercial search engines available. These engines come and go from time to time, but the following is a list of some of the current popular search engines:

www.google.com	www.yahoo.com	www.msn.com
www.ask.com	www.alltheweb.com	www.lycos.com
www.altavista.com	www.go.com	www.dogpile.com
www.excite.com	www.lygo.com	www.mamma.com

SEARCHING THE WWW

Each search engine provides a field where the word (or words) being looked for are typed. Then there is a button which is usually labelled 'Search' , 'Go', 'Look' or a similar word. Clicking this button will usually result in the program displaying pages of sites. It is generally a good idea to type a few words in quote marks and see what happens first.

When typing search words it is generally a good idea to use all lower case letters unless it is certain that a word is in capital letters or begins with a capital letter. There are also a few conventions which may be useful and generally work with most search engines:

horse	Searches for word 'horse'.
horse racing	Searches for word 'horse' or the word 'racing'.
+horse+racing	Searches for words 'horse' and 'racing' not necessarily near one another (may type **and** or **+**).
horse NEAR racing	Searches for word 'horse' near the word 'racing'.
'horse racing'	Searches for words 'horse racing', words must be adjacent.
key*	Searches for words starting with 'key'. This would include key, keying, keyhole, etc.
sink**	Searches for all forms of the word 'sink'. This would include sink, sinking, sank, sunk.
(horse NOT racing)	Searches for word 'horse' but not the word 'racing'.
horse-racing	The – sign or the **NOT** may be used more than once in the search field.

The search engine will display the results of the search. The number of websites found will be displayed and a brief summary of the first ten or twenty will be displayed. Any of the websites displayed may then be visited by simply pointing to a link for that website and clicking the left mouse button. Further matching websites may be accessed by selecting any of the numbers at the bottom of the page. This will display another ten or twenty matching websites. This process may be continued until all matching sites have been exhausted.

Task 7.2.2

(a) Load the web browser program.
(b) Display a search engine of your choice.
(c) Carry out a search of the WWW for the word **cycling**.
(d) Display any web page which gives information about cycling from the search results.
(e) Use the Back button to return to the search engine results page.

(f) Refine your search to include cycling in **Ireland**.

(g) Display any web page that gives information about cycling in Ireland from the search engine results.

(h) Use the address field to select and display one of the sites previously visited.

(i) View the history of websites visited today.

(j) Delete all history.

(k) Close the web browser.

REVISITING WEBSITES

When sites are visited their address remains stored in the address field.

The user may quickly return to a recently visited website as follows:

- Address field selection icon .
- Address required .

When typing an address a number of addresses may appear under the address field as the address is typed. These are previously visited websites and if the correct one is displayed then it may be selected by simply pointing to it and clicking the left mouse button.

HISTORY

The website addresses visited over the past number of days will be stored in a folder called **History**. This History folder may be used to access a website or simply to view the websites visited.

The history is displayed as follows:

Explorer

- Favourites icon .
- History button History .

Firefox

- History menu .

Task 7.2.3

(a) Load the web browser program.
(b) Display the website, www.kildare.ie
(c) Search the kildare.ie website for the word 'equine'.
(d) Display any web page that gives information about equines on the kildare.ie website.
(e) Use the Back button to return to the kildare.ie search facility.
(f) Search the kildare.ie website for the word 'migration'.
(g) Display any web page that gives information about migration on the kildare.ie website.
(h) Close the web browser.

SEARCHING WITHIN A WEBSITE

Websites very often provide a search facility within the website itself. This function is recognised by a search field on a page in the site.

This search facility is operated in the same way as the search facility in one of the search engines, but it will only search the particular site for the information requested. The use of quote marks and additional features may of limited benefit on some sites.

Task 7.2.4 (Additional)

Perform the operations specified in **Task 7A-2** on the CD.

Task 7.3.1

(a) Load the web browser program.
(b) Display a search engine of your choice.
(c) Save this website address in a folder named Search Engines in the favourites/bookmarks – you will need to create the folder as you save it.
(d) Display another search engine.
(e) Save this website address in the Search Engine's folder in the favourites/bookmarks.
(f) Display a third search engine.
(g) Save this website address in the Search Engine's folder in the favourites/bookmarks.
(h) Use the favourites/bookmarks to display the first search engine.
(i) Close the web browser.

FAVOURITES OR BOOKMARKS

Web browsers provide a simple method of storing website addresses which may be used frequently. This facility is called **favourites** by Internet Explorer and **bookmarks** by Mozilla Firefox. Once the website address is stored, it is a simple matter to select favourites or bookmarks and click the website required from the list saved. (It may be necessary to open a folder to find the website.)

To provide an easy means of connecting to that site in the future.

Explorer

A website is stored in favourites as follows:

- Locate the website and display it on-screen.
- ▣ Add to Favourites icon ⬕ 🖱.
- ⊕ Add to Favourites 🖱. (*The add a favourite window will appear.*)
- Type a name for this website.
- Select a folder into which you wish to save this website.
- ▣ Add 🖱.

Firefox

A website is stored in bookmarks as follows:

- Locate the website and display it on-screen.
- ▣ Bookmark icon ☆ 🖱. (*The edit this bookmark window will appear.*)
- Type a name for this website.
- Select a folder into which you wish to save this website.
- ▣ Done 🖱.

Note: When saving the website in favourites or bookmarks it is possible to create a new folder into which the web page (and subsequent web pages) can be saved.

Deleting a Favourite/Bookmark

Any stored website may be deleted as follows:

- ▣ Favourites/bookmarks menu 🖱.
- ▣ Website 🖱.
- ⊕ Delete 🖱.

CHANGING THE HOME PAGE

It is possible to change the page that is displayed each time the user loads the web browser. This page may be different for each user who logs into the same computer. The page which is displayed is called the home page.

The home page is set as follows:

-  Tools menu 🖱.

- ✛ Internet options/Options 🖱.
  (The internet options/options window will be displayed.)

- Use current/Use Current Pages 🖱.

- Apply 🖱. (Explorer)

- OK 🖱.

Task 7.3.2

(a) Load the web browser program.
(b) Display a search engine of your choice.
(c) Make this the home page.
(d) View the page in full screen.
(e) Restore the view to the previous view.

CHANGING THE VIEW DISPLAY

When a large site is being displayed on a small screen it is possible to have the page take up the full size of the screen.

The full screen is displayed as follows:

- View 🖱.

- ✛ Full screen 🖱.

The screen is restored to its original size as follows:

- Hold the mouse at the top of the screen until the toolbars appear.

- Restore icon 🖱. *(in the top right-hand corner of the screen)*

Task 7.3.3

(a) Load the web browser program.
(b) Change the web browser configuration so that it does not download images.
(c) Display any web page.
(d) Change the web browser configuration so that it does download images.
(e) Refresh the web page.
(f) Close the web browser.

IMAGE BLOCKING

It is possible to stop the downloading of graphic images from a website and therefore obtain a faster download of the text.

Image blocking is accomplished as follows:

Explorer

- Tools menu.

- Internet options.

  (*The internet options window will be displayed.*)

- Advanced tab.

- Scroll down the list until the multimedia options are displayed.

- Remove the tick from the Show Pictures box.

- OK.

Firefox

- Tools menu.

- Options.

  (*The options window will be displayed.*)

- Content tab.

- Remove the tick from Load Images Automatically.

- OK.

Task 7.3.4 (Additional)

Perform the operations specified in **Task 7A-3** on the CD.

Task 7.4.1

(a) Load the web browser program.
(b) Display any web page that requires you to complete a form, e.g. free e-mail account, car hire enquiry, hotel reservation, airline reservation.
(c) Complete the form – you do not need to send it.
(d) Close the web browser.

COMPLETING FORMS

There are a large number of websites that ask the user to complete a form in order to register with them or to receive information. When purchasing something over the WWW it is usually necessary to complete a form and give credit card details. Before entering personal details (particularly credit card details) the user should be sure that it is necessary and that the website is not just collecting data.

Forms on the WWW are similar to any other form, in the respect that there are fields that require data to be entered into them. Forms have a number of different types of fields.

General Field   Requests the input of data that is displayed as it is typed.

Required Field   Similar to a general field but it must have data entered into it, otherwise the form will not be accepted.

Selection Field   Requires the selection of one of the options offered. This type of field will be recognised by the selection icon ▾ on the right of the field.

Password Field   This type of field will generally not display what is being typed. Instead an asterisk (*) will appear in the field each time a character is entered.

Note: Great care should be taken when sending credit card details over the WWW. Ensure that the website is a secure one before entering credit card details. A secure site is indicated in the URL by the letter s after the **http** – so the URL starts **https://**.

Task 7.4.2

(a) Load the web browser program.
(b) Display any web page that contains text and graphic images.
(c) Load a word processing program.
(d) Copy a small portion of text into the word processing program.
(e) Copy any graphic image into the word processing program (resize if necessary).
(f) Close the web browser program.
(g) Print one copy of the word processing document.

COPYING INTO DOCUMENTS

It is possible to copy most information displayed on websites into a document.

Text is copied as follows:

- Select the text to be copied.
- Edit menu.
- Copy.
- Open the document into which the text is to be copied.
- Paste icon.

A graphic image is copied as follows:

- Graphic image. (*A menu will appear.*)
- Copy.
- Open the document into which the image is to be copied.
- Paste icon.

The image may be a link to another web page and it is a good idea to break any links associated with an image.

Links are broken or removed as follows:

- Graphic image in the document. (*A menu will appear.*)
- Remove hyperlinks.

Task 7.4.3

(a) Load the web browser program.
(b) Display the website, www.adobe.com
(c) Locate any download file – pick a small one.
(d) Download the file to a folder of your choice – the file may be deleted later.
(e) Close the web browser.

DOWNLOADING FILES

One great advantage of the WWW is the ability to transfer files to your computer. These files may be data files, programs or drivers for equipment such as printers, graphic cards, etc.

Files are downloaded as follows:

- Locate the file on the website. (*The file will have a link to download.*)

- ⬛ Download 🖱. (*The file download window will appear.*)

- Select save this program to disk. (*The save as window will appear.*)

- Select a folder of your choice to save the file into.

- ⬛ Save 🖱.

The file will start to download and a progress window will be displayed.

If the file downloaded is a program (or driver) then it is necessary to install that program (or driver) in the same way as if it were on a CD.

Note: Great care should be taken with data that is downloaded from the Internet to ensure that it does not contain a virus. Files that are downloaded should be checked for viruses before opening them.

Task 7.4.4 (Additional)

Perform the operations specified in **Task 7A-4** on the CD.

Task 7.5.1

(a) Load the web publishing program.

(b) Type the following text in 24 pt, bold, centred text on a blank page:

Web Page 1

This is my first web page

(c) Insert a Clip Art graphic in the centre of the page.

(d) Type the following text in 16 pt, bold, centred near the bottom of the page:

Link to Page 2

(e) Save the page in a folder of your choice in .htm format with the filename **Index.htm**.

(f) Start a new page (document/publication).

(g) Type the following text in 24 pt, bold, centred text on a blank page:

Web Page 2   Home

This is my second web page

(h) Insert a motion clip from Clip Art in the centre of the page.

(i) Type the following text in 16 pt, bold, centred near the bottom of the page:

Link to Page 1

(j) Save the page in the same folder in .htm format with the filename **Page2.htm**.

(k) Create a link from the words 'Link to page 2' to the file **Page2.htm**.

(l) Create a link from the words 'Link to page 1' to the file **Index.htm**.

(m) Create a link from the word 'Home' to the file **Index.htm**.

(n) Load the web browser.

(o) View the web pages and test the links – make modifications as required.

(p) Close the web browser.

CREATING A WEBSITE

There are many books dedicated to producing websites. In this task we are simply going to demonstrate the steps involved in producing very simple linked pages, which are the basic building blocks of a website.

The steps involved in creating a website are as follows:

1 Produce each page.

2 Save each page as a web page (.htm or .html).

3 Link pages using hyperlinks.

4 Test the website.

The following procedure relates to the production of web pages using Word.

Page Production

There are a number of very good programs available specifically for the production of web pages, e.g. Dreamweaver and FrontPage. However, word processing, presentation and desktop publishing programs will produce web pages and are very simple to use.

The process of producing a page is as follows:

- Type whatever text is required on the page.

- Insert whatever graphics are required.

- Insert a link word(s) or graphic (this will be used later) to create a link to another page.

Save Page

Each page is saved in the normal way, with the exception that it is saved as a web page. This is normally an option in the 'Save as type' field and will usually be .htm or .html.

Link the Pages

In order for the pages to operate as web pages they must be linked using hyperlinks. These links allow the web browser to call up another page when required.

Pages are linked as follows:

- Open the page.

- Select the link word(s) or graphic.

- [icon] Hyperlink icon [icons].
  (*The hyperlink window will appear.*)

- [icon] Browse for file [icon].
  (*The link to the file window will appear.*)

- Select the page to link to [icon].

- Repeat the process for other pages.

Viewing the Website

The website may be tested as follows:

- Load the web browser.

- Type the location of the first page (including the filename and extension) in the address field.

- Press the Enter key.

- Operate any links to ensure that they work properly.

Task 7.5.2 (Additional)

Perform the operations specified in **Task 7A-5** on the CD.

8 E-mail

SYMBOLS USED IN THIS CHAPTER

The symbols used in this chapter, and their meanings, are as follows:

Click the left mouse button.

Double-click the left mouse button.

Click the right mouse button.

Hold down the left mouse button.

Move the mouse to point to an item without clicking or holding any button.

Release the mouse button.

Point to an item on the screen.

Hold down the Ctrl button.

Hold down the Ctrl button and click the left mouse button.

Hold down the Shift key.

Hold down the Shift key and press the number eight.

Press the Enter key.

Note: The content of the WWW changes so frequently, and websites and e-mail addresses appear and disappear at such a rapid rate, that it is difficult to pick sites that will still be in use when you are reading this book. If a site address mentioned in this section does not give a response then simply use another address and continue the task.

INTRODUCTION

The term **e-mail** stands for electronic mail. The use of e-mail has revolutionised the way in which people communicate. E-mail can be thought of in the same way as a letter. The letter is written, any additional items (such as a photograph) are enclosed, the envelope is addressed to the receiver and posted. The letter will then travel to the recipient anywhere in the world. E-mail contains all the same features as a letter – along with some others – and with the additional advantage that it is sent and received almost instantly. Some of the advantages of e-mail are:

- Low cost.
- Speed.
- Send and receive worldwide.
- Send the same message to many recipients.
- Record of messages sent and received.

Everyone who has an account with an Internet service provider (ISP) usually has an e-mail address. Even if they do not have an account they may have an e-mail address in their place of work. Alternatively, anyone may sign up to a number of free e-mail services, such as Hotmail.com, Hotpop.com, Eircom.net, 123box.co.uk, etc.

Once a user has an e-mail account they may send and receive e-mail from anywhere in the world, provided they have access to a computer.

E-MAIL PROGRAMS

There are a large number of e-mail programs, many of which may be downloaded from the WWW. Outlook, Netscape Mail, Outlook Express, Eudora and IncrediMail are some popular e-mail programs that are used to send and receive e-mail.

E-MAIL ADDRESSES

The structure of an e-mail address is standard and everyone using e-mail will have a unique e-mail address. This is a worldwide address and can be used to send and receive e-mail anywhere in the world. The structure of an e-mail address is shown in Figure 8.1.

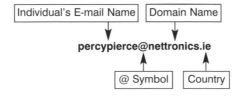

Figure 8.1

In some cases the country name will be replaced with **.com**, **.net**, **.org**, etc. Great care should be taken when typing e-mail addresses because if they are not typed exactly then the message will not be delivered or will be delivered to the wrong person.

E-MAIL SAFETY AND SECURITY

The use of e-mail is very convenient but there are a few areas where care should be taken. A major hazard with e-mail is the risk of receiving a virus, usually with an attachment. Viruses are programs that infect your computer and can destroy all the data on the computer and render it unusable. Another problem with using e-mail is the amount of unsolicited e-mail (called **junk mail** or **spam**) which may be received.

The following simple rules should help to avoid problems:

- Avoid opening attachments unless you know the origin.

- Avoid opening e-mail from unknown senders.

- Avoid opening e-mail with no subject.

- Avoid posting your e-mail address on the WWW.

- When completing forms look for the option to restrict the use of your e-mail address.

- Install an antivirus program.

The best method of protecting against viruses is to install a good antivirus program and update it weekly. Never accept e-mail from unknown sources and never open a file from an unknown source.

Where security is important then a digital signature can be obtained. This acts to prove that the sender of a document is who they claim to be. This is very important in commerce transactions, as anyone can put any name to an e-mail message.

Task 8.1.1

(a) Log on to a free e-mail provider, e.g. www.hotmail.com
(b) Register a new e-mail account – it is usually not necessary to complete all fields.
(c) Log out of the e-mail website.

FREE E-MAIL

It is not necessary to have an e-mail program, as there are a number of free e-mail providers and in these cases it is only necessary to log on to their website to send and receive e-mail, provided the user has signed up (registered) with them. Once this is done it is then possible to send and receive e-mail.

The method of acquiring a free e-mail account is similar with all providers, but they vary greatly in: the amount of space provided, the amount of information which must revealed, and the amount of advertising they display. So, it is a good idea to check out what is available before signing up with one. (A search of the WWW for 'free e-mail provider' should provide a selection.) In order to register a new account it is necessary to complete a form. Forms on the WWW are similar to any other form because there are fields that require data to be entered into them. Forms have a number of different types of fields.

General Field Requests the input of data, which is displayed as it is typed.

Required Field Similar to a general field but it must have data entered into it, otherwise the form will not be accepted.

Selection Field Requires the selection of one of the options offered. This type of field will be recognised by the selection icon ▼ on the right of the field.

Password Field This type of field will generally not display what is typed. Instead an asterisk (*) will appear in the field each time a character is entered.

When the form is complete it must be sent or submitted. If everything is correct on the form it will be accepted and after a short while it will be possible to log in and use the e-mail account.

Task 8.1.2

(a) Load the e-mail program – **OR** log on to free e-mail if not using a program.
(b) Select your Inbox folder – if not already selected.
(c) Read any messages in your Inbox.
(d) Select the other folders in turn to check their contents.
(e) Close the e-mail program – OR log out of the e-mail website.

LOADING AN E-MAIL PROGRAM

If a dedicated program is being used for sending and receiving e-mail then that program must be loaded from the desktop in the normal way, as follows:

- 🖱 E-mail shortcut icon 🖱.

If the program is not available from the desktop then it may be loaded from the Start menu in the normal way.

When the e-mail program is loaded the screen should look something like the one shown below, with the default **folder** displayed (usually the Inbox) but this may vary depending on the setup. A list of folders may be displayed on the left-hand side, from which the user may select the folder that is required. New folders may be created and customised.

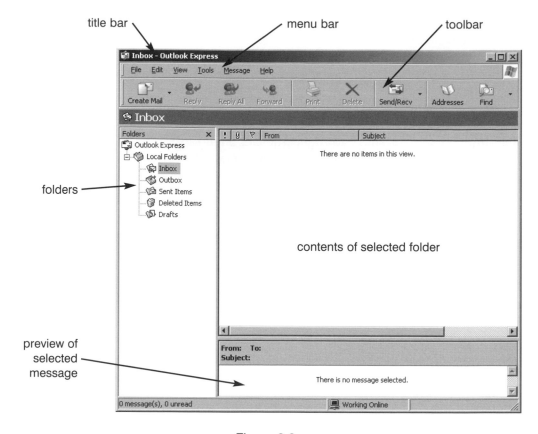

title bar

menu bar

toolbar

folders

preview of
selected
message

contents of selected folder

Figure 8.2

E-MAIL TOOLBAR

The main icons on the e-mail toolbar are shown below. The actual icon may vary from program to program but the function that it performs will be the same.

This icon is used to **compose or create** a new e-mail message.

This icon is used to **print** an e-mail message.

This icon is used to **delete** an e-mail message.

This icon is used to **reply** to an e-mail message.

This icon is used to **reply to all** recipients of an e-mail message.

This icon is used to **forward** an e-mail to another address.

This icon is used to **send and receive** any mail waiting to be sent and any mail waiting to be received from the remote mail server.

This icon is used to select your **address book**, provided an address book has been set up on your computer.

This icon is used to send an e-mail **to the Outbox** once it has been written. The mail may be automatically sent to the remote server or it may be necessary to click the **send/receive** icon, depending on the program setup.

This icon is used to **attach** a file to an e-mail. The file may be located anywhere on your computer.

This icon is used to set the message as **high priority**. When the message is received it will have the high priority indicator displayed.

To: This is where the address, to which the e-mail is **to be sent**, is typed.

Cc: This stands for **carbon copy** and is where the address to which a copy or copies of an e-mail is to be sent. Use a semicolon between e-mail addresses of multiple recipients.

Bcc: This stands for **blind carbon copy** and is where you type the address to which a copy or copies of an e-mail is to be sent, but the recipients entered here will not appear when the message is received.

Subject: It is normal practice to type a brief note of the **subject** of the e-mail. This is of great assistance to the recipient when viewing their e-mail. Many people will delete messages, with a blank Subject, without looking at them.

INBOX

The Inbox is where all mail received is displayed. Each message is displayed on a single line with the following information:

From This is the **sender** of the message.

Subject This is what the message is about. All e-mail messages should contain a **subject**.

Received This is the **date and time** that the e-mail was received by the remote server. This is not the date and time at which the e-mail is received by the recipient.

This indicates that this e-mail has been sent with a **high priority** rating.

✉ This indicates that this e-mail **has not been opened**.

✉ This indicates that this e-mail **has been opened**.

⚑ This indicates that this e-mail has been **flagged** for some reason.

📎 This indicates that this e-mail has at least one **attachment** with it.

OUTBOX

The Outbox is where all mail that is ready for delivery is displayed. Each message is displayed on a single line with the same information as in the Inbox.

SENT ITEMS

The Sent Items folder is where all the e-mail that have been sent are displayed. Each message is displayed on a single line with the same information as in the Inbox.

DELETED ITEMS

The Deleted Items folder is where all deleted e-mail are displayed. Each message is displayed on a single line with the same information as in the Inbox.

READING E-MAIL

Any e-mail that is displayed on the screen may be opened by simply double-clicking on the row containing the e-mail. The message will be displayed in a separate window together with any attachments. When finished reading the message the window should be closed in the normal way.

If the list of messages is long then the scroll bar may be used to scroll down the screen in the normal way.

Sorting Messages

Messages may be sorted by any of the column headings – just point to the heading and click the left mouse button. The list will be displayed in ascending order. Pointing to the same heading a second time and clicking the left mouse button will produce a list in descending order.

Attachments

The attachments may be read or run – depending on what sort of attachment it is – by simply pointing to the attachment and clicking the left mouse button. The program associated with the attachment will be loaded and the attachment displayed as a normal file. If the attachment is a program then it will perform whatever task it is meant to do.

Task 8.1.3

(a) Load the e-mail program – **OR** log on to free e-mail if not using a program.
(b) Select your Inbox folder – if not already selected.
(c) Select new mail message.
(d) Compose a simple message – either to yourself or to a friend if you have someone to work with.
(e) Spell check the message.
(f) Send the message.
(g) Select the Sent Items folder and check that the message is displayed.
(h) Select the Inbox folder.
(i) Check for new messages – select Send and Receive, if necessary.
(j) Read the message – either from yourself or a friend.
(k) Print the message.
(l) Close all open windows (messages).
(m) Close the e-mail program – **OR** log out of the free e-mail website.

COMPOSING AND SENDING E-MAIL

The procedure for composing and sending an e-mail is as follows:

- ▮↖ New mail icon 🖱. (*The new message window will appear.*)

- Type the recipient's e-mail address in the 'To...' field. If you wish to send the e-mail to more than one recipient, then simply separate each e-mail address with a semicolon and a space, or use the 'Cc...' field.

- Type the subject of the e-mail in the Subject field.

- Type the message in the main part of the window. The full range of text-editing facilities, such as cut, copy, paste and spell check, are available.

- ▮↖ The Send icon 🖱.

The e-mail will be sent to the Outbox for immediate delivery or delivery later, depending on the program settings.

If the program does not send outgoing mail immediately, then the e-mail is sent by pointing to the 'Send/Receive' button and clicking the left mouse button. All e-mail will be sent from the Outbox and any new messages will be received.

The following options are also available when sending e-mail:

- ▮↖ Priority icon 🖱. (*to indicate that the e-mail is high priority*)

continued

- Type the e-mail address of anyone who is to receive a copy of this e-mail in the 'Cc...' field. If a copy of this e-mail is to be sent to more than one recipient then simply separate each e-mail address with a semicolon and a space.

- Type the e-mail address of anyone who is to receive a blind copy of this e-mail in the 'Bcc...' field. If a copy of this e-mail is to be sent to more than one recipient then simply separate each e-mail address with a semicolon and a space.

SPELL CHECKING

It is a good idea to spell check a message before sending it.

Messages are spell checked as follows:

- Tools menu.

  OR Spelling icon. (*The spell check window will appear if there are any misspelled words.*)

- Spelling.

The window will display the first word that is not in the dictionaries, together with a list of possible correct words. The following tasks may then be performed:

(a) Select **ignore** to leave the word as it is.

(b) Select the correct word from the list and select **change**.

(c) Type the word required and select **change**.

(d) Select add to **add** this new word to the dictionary.

PRINT A MESSAGE

Any open message may be printed as follows:

- Open the message.
- Print icon.

More control over the printing process may be achieved as follows:

- Open the message.
- File menu.

continued

- ✛ Print 🖰. (*The print window will appear.*)
- Select the options required.
- ▣ OK 🖰.

Task 8.1.4

(a) Load the e-mail program.
(b) Select your Inbox folder – if not already selected.
(c) Select New Mail Message.
(d) Compose a simple message to yourself.
(e) Send a copy (Cc) to a friend.
(f) Mark the message as high priority.
(g) Send the message.
(h) Select the Inbox – if not already selected.
(i) Check for new messages – select Send and Receive, if necessary.
(j) Read the message (from yourself or a friend).
(k) Flag the message for follow-up before next Friday.
(l) Close all open windows (messages).
(m) Close the e-mail program – **OR** log out of the free e-mail website.

MARKING MESSAGES (PRIORITY, FLAGGING, READ, UNREAD)

Most e-mail programs provide a method of marking messages with a priority indicator and/or a flag.

Priority

A message can be marked as high priority anytime before sending as follows:

-  Priority icon 🖰.

When the message is received it will have a priority indicator in the Inbox list. When the message is opened the priority will be indicated on a line over the From name.

Flagging

A message can be flagged for follow-up anytime after receiving it.

A message is flagged as follows:

- 🖱 Flag column in front of the message in the folder list 🖱.

OR

- 🖱 Actions menu 🖱.

- ✛ Follow Up.

- ✛ Action required 🖱.

The message will be displayed with a flag indicator in the folder. The flag may be removed in the same way as it was applied.

Read/Unread

When a message is opened it will automatically register as read and the symbol will change from unread to read. However, a message may be marked as read or unread at any time.

A message is marked read/unread as follows:

- Open the folder containing the message.

- 🖱 Message 🖱.

- 🖱 Edit menu 🖱.

- ✛ Mark as read/unread 🖱.

Task 8.1.5 (Additional)

Carry out the operations specified in **Task 8A-1** on the CD.

Task 8.2.1

(a) Load the e-mail program – **OR** log on to free e-mail if not using a program).
(b) Select your Inbox folder – if not already selected.
(c) Select New Mail Message.

(d) Compose a simple message – either to yourself or to a friend if you have someone to work with.

(e) Attach any small file that you have saved on disk.

(f) Send the message.

(g) Select the Inbox – if not already selected.

(h) Check for new messages – select Send and Receive, if necessary.

(i) Read the message (either from yourself or a friend).

(j) Open the attachment.

(k) Close the attachment – and the program used to read it, if necessary.

(l) Close all open windows (messages).

(m) Close the e-mail program – **OR** log out of the free e-mail website.

SENDING ATTACHMENTS

An **attachment** is a file that is included with an e-mail and must be inserted in an e-mail before it is sent. Attachments sent with an e-mail should be as small as possible. The type of file attached will usually govern the size of the file. For best results the following file types should be used wherever possible:

Text .txt

Pictures .gif, .jpg

Sound .wav, .mp2, .mp3, .ai, .aif

Video .mp4, .asf, .mov

An attachment is sent with the e-mail as follows:

- The Attachment icon. (*The insert file window will appear.*)
- Locate the file. (*in the same way as opening or saving a file*)
- The Insert button.

If an attachment is **not** to be sent with an e-mail then it may be removed at any time before it is sent as follows:

- Attachment. (*A pop-up window will appear.*)
- Remove.

OPENING ATTACHMENTS

Attachments that are received with e-mail can be opened or viewed as follows:

- ⬚ Attachment in the received e-mail 🖰.

The program necessary to display the attachment will load automatically and the attachment will be displayed.

If the program required to open the attachment is not installed on your computer then it may be possible to open it using another program – a window will usually appear asking for the selection of the program to be used. Very often, it will not be possible to open the attachment if it does not open automatically.

Task 8.2.2

(a) Load the e-mail program – **OR** log on to free e-mail if not using a program.
(b) Select your Inbox folder – if not already selected.
(c) Select New Mail Message.
(d) Compose a simple message – either to yourself or to a friend if you have someone to work with.
(e) Attach any picture that you have saved on disk.
(f) Send the message.
(g) Select the Inbox – if not already selected.
(h) Check for new messages – select Send and Receive, if necessary.
(i) Read the message – either from yourself or a friend.
(j) Save the attachment in a folder of your choice.
(k) Flag the message to be replied to before next Friday.
(l) Close all open windows (messages).
(m) Close the e-mail program – **OR** log out of the free e-mail website.

SAVING ATTACHMENTS

Attachments that are received with an e-mail can be saved as follows:

- ⬚ Attachment in the received e-mail 🖰. (*A pop-up menu will appear.*)

- ⬦ Save as 🖰.

- Select the folder, if necessary, where you wish to save this file in the 'Save in' field.

- Type the filename that you wish to give this file in the Filename field.

- ⬚ Save button 🖰.

> ## Task 8.2.3
>
> (a) Load the e-mail program – **OR** log on to free e-mail if not using a program.
> (b) Select your Inbox folder – if not already selected.
> (c) Delete one message – either received from yourself or your friend.
> (d) Select the Deleted Items folder.
> (e) Delete any messages in the Deleted Items folder.
> (f) Compose a simple message – either to yourself or to a friend if you have someone to work with.
> (g) Send the message.
> (h) Close the e-mail program – **OR** log out of the free e-mail website.

DELETING E-MAIL AND ATTACHMENTS

E-mail and attachments may be deleted by simply highlighting them and pressing the Delete key. Once the e-mail is deleted it will automatically delete any attachments. Deleted e-mail will be sent to the Deleted Items folder.

If the e-mail setup does not automatically empty the Deleted Items folder then this will have to be done on a regular basis.

> ## Task 8.2.4 (Additional)
>
> Carry out the operations specified in **Task 8A-2** on the CD.

> ## Task 8.3.1
>
> (a) Load the e-mail program.
> (b) Select your Inbox folder – if not already selected.
> (c) Check for new messages – select Send and Receive, if necessary.
> (d) Read any message – either from yourself or a friend.
> (e) Reply to the message.
> (f) Send the reply.
> (g) Close the e-mail program.

REPLYING TO AN E-MAIL

When an e-mail is received it may be necessary to answer the message. This can be done by simply selecting the Reply option. When this option is selected the address and the subject will be completed automatically, thus saving time and avoiding error.

If the original message was sent to a number of recipients then the choice of simply replying to the sender (Reply) or replying to everyone who the original message was sent to (Reply to All) will be offered.

An e-mail is replied to as follows:

- Open the e-mail.
- ▶ Reply icon **OR** the reply to all icon 🖱.
- Type an additional message in the main part of the window.
- ▶ Send icon 🖱. (*The e-mail will be sent to the outbox for immediate delivery or delivery later, depending on the setup.*)
- ▶ Send/Receive icon 🖱. (*if necessary*)

Task 8.3.2

(a) Load the e-mail program.
(b) Select your Inbox folder – if not already selected.
(c) Check for new messages – select Send and Receive, if necessary.
(d) Read the reply message – either from yourself or a friend.
(e) Forward the message – either to yourself or a friend.
(f) Send the message.
(g) Close the e-mail program.

FORWARDING AN E-MAIL

An e-mail may be forwarded as follows:

- Open the e-mail.
- ▶ Forward icon 🖱.
- Type an additional message in the main part of the window.
- ▶ Send icon 🖱. (*The e-mail will be sent to the outbox for immediate delivery or delivery later, depending on the setup.*)
- ▶ Send/Receive icon 🖱. (*if necessary*)

INCLUDING MESSAGE WITH REPLY

When an e-mail is replied to or forwarded the original message may be included or excluded with the reply.

The original message may be included or excluded as follows:

- 🔲 Tools menu 🖱.
- 🔲 Options 🖱.
- 🔲 Preferences 🖱.
- 🔲 E-mail Options button 🖱.
- Tick **OR** remove the tick for 'Include original message text' in the appropriate field(s).

Task 8.3.3

(a) Load a text-editing program, e.g. Notepad, WordPad, Word.
(b) Type a simple message – either to yourself or to a friend if you have someone to work with.
(c) Select the text.
(d) Copy the text.
(e) Minimise the text-editing program.
(f) Load the e-mail program.
(g) Start a new message – complete the To and Subject fields only.
(h) Paste the text from the text-editing program into the e-mail message.
(i) Spell check the message.
(j) Send the message.
(k) Close all windows.

COPY AND PASTE

When composing long messages it is often more efficient to compose the message first (e.g. in Word) and then insert the message into the e-mail later. This may be done by inserting the text directly into the e-mail by copying and pasting the text (e.g. from Word) or by inserting the text as an attachment (e.g. a Word file) to the e-mail, as already described above.

Text is copied into an e-mail as follows:

- Type the text in a text-editing program, e.g. Notepad, WordPad, Word.
- Select the text.
- Copy the text. (*instructions on next line*)
  🔲 File menu 🖱, ⊕ Copy 🖱 **OR** 🔲 Copy icon 🖱.

continued

- Start a new message in the e-mail program.

- Paste the text into the e-mail. (*instructions on next line*)

  🔼 File menu 🖱, ⊕ Paste 🖱   **OR**   🔼 Paste icon 🖱.

It is also possible to copy and paste text between e-mail messages. The procedure is as follows:

- Open the e-mail message containing the text.

- Copy the text.

- Open the e-mail message into which the text is to go.

- Paste the text.

Task 8.3.4 (Additional)

Carry out the operations specified in **Task 8A-3** on the CD.

Task 8.4.1

(a) Load the e-mail program.
(b) Create a new folder and name it My Mail – include a shortcut to the folder.
(c) Move some messages from the Inbox to My Mail.
(d) Add the Preview icon to the toolbar.
(e) Close all windows.

CREATING A NEW FOLDER

A new folder may be created as follows:

- 🔼 File menu 🖱.

- ⊕ New.

- 🔼 Folder 🖱.

- Type the name for the new folder.

- 🔼 Folder in which the new folder is to be created 🖱.

- 🔼 OK 🖱.

MOVING MESSAGES

Messages may be moved from one folder to another as follows:

- Open the folder containing the message to be moved.
- Display the folder into which the message is to be moved on the left.
- 🖰 Message 🖰.
- Drag the message into the folder on the left 🖰.

CUSTOMISING TOOLBARS

Icons may be added or removed to/from the e-mail toolbar. The position of an icon on a toolbar can also be changed.

Icons are added as follows:

- 🖰 Tools menu 🖰.
- ⊕ Customise 🖰. (*A customise window will appear.*)
- 🖰 Commands tab 🖰.
- 🖰 Icon to be added 🖰.
- Drag the icon onto the toolbar 🖰.

Icons are repositioned as follows:

- 🖰 Tools menu 🖰.
- ⊕ Customise 🖰. (*A customise window will appear.*)
- 🖰 Icon to be repositioned 🖰.
- Drag the icon to its new position on the toolbar 🖰.

Icons are removed as follows:

- 🖰 Tools menu 🖰.
- ⊕ Customise 🖰. (*A customise window will appear.*)
- 🖰 Button in the list of current toolbar buttons 🖰.

continued

- ▮ Remove button 🖱.

Task 8.4.2

(a) Load the e-mail program.

(b) Add the details and e-mail addresses of at least four friends to your address book.

(c) Send an e-mail to one person who you added to the address book (pick the name from the address book for the To field).

(d) Close all windows.

STORING ADDRESSES

It is possible to store the e-mail addresses of people to whom e-mail is frequently sent. This avoids the necessity of trying to remember their e-mail addresses and the possibility of typing the address incorrectly when typing it in a new message.

New addresses (contacts) are added manually as follows:

- ▮ Addresses icon 📖 🖱.
- ▮ New icon ▾ 🖱. (*A drop-down menu will appear.*)
- ✥ New Contact 🖱. (*The contact window will appear.*)
- Enter the details in the fields required.
- ▮ Save and Close icon 💾 🖱.

The sender's e-mail address may be quickly added to the address book any time after the e-mail has been received.

Senders' e-mail addresses are quickly added as follows:

- Open the e-mail.
- ▮ Senders name 🖱.
- ▮ Add to Address book/contacts 🖱. (*The contact window will appear.*)
- Enter the details in the fields required.
- ▮ Save and Close icon 💾 🖱.

Addresses may be removed from the address book as follows:

- ▣ Addresses icon ▣ ⟰.
- ▣ Name ⟰. ⎫ ▣ Name ⟰.
- ⊕ Delete ⟰. ⎭ **OR** Press the Delete key.
- Confirm to permanently delete.

SENDING E-MAIL TO RECIPIENTS IN THE ADDRESS BOOK

When sending new e-mail to a recipient stored in the address book the procedure is as follows:

- ▣ New/Create mail icon ⟰. (*The new message window will appear.*)

- ▣ To: button (*on the left of the 'To:' field*) ⟰.
  (*The 'Select names: Contacts' window will appear.*)

- ▣ Recipient(s) required ⟰.

- ▣ To: button ⟰. (*the recipient is transferred to the 'To:' box*)
  (*It is possible to add recipients to the Cc and Bcc fields in the same way.*)

- ▣ OK ⟰.
- Proceed as normal with the rest of the message.

Task 8.4.3

(a) Load the e-mail program.
(b) Create a group with three addresses from your address book.
(c) Send an e-mail to the group – pick the group from the address book for the To field.
(d) Close all windows.

STORING GROUPS

When e-mail are frequently sent to the same group of people it is handy to be able to select these e-mail addresses quickly. This is accomplished by creating a group and adding the members to the group. E-mail can then be sent to everyone in the group by simply selecting the group for the To field. Groups may be created from members of the contacts list or directly entered into the group.

Groups are created from existing contacts as follows:

- ▣ Addresses icon 📖 🖱.
- ▣ New icon ▾ 🖱. (*A drop-down menu will appear.*)
- ✛ New Group/Distribution List 🖱. (*The Properties/contact window will appear.*)
- Enter a name for the group.
- ▣ Select members icon 🖱.
- ▣ Member to be included 🖱.
- ▣ Select/Members button 🖱.
- Repeat the two previous steps for each member to be included.
- ▣ OK 🖱.
- ▣ OK **OR** Save and Close icon 🖱.

Groups are created directly as follows:

- ▣ Addresses icon 📖 🖱.
- ▣ New icon ▾ 🖱. (*A drop-down menu will appear.*)
- ✛ New Group/Distribution List 🖱. (*The Properties/contact window will appear.*)
- Enter a name for the group.
- ▣ New Contact 🖱.
- Enter the member's details 🖱.
- ▣ OK 🖱.
- Repeat the three previous steps for each member to be included.
- ▣ OK **OR** Save and Close icon 💾 🖱.

SEARCHING FOR E-MAIL

It may be difficult to find a particular e-mail when the list of e-mail gets long. It is possible to use the find/search facility to find e-mail containing specific word(s).

The search facility is operated as follows:

- Select the folder in which you wish to search.
- ▲ Find 🖱 (*if necessary*).
- Enter the search word(s) in the search field.
- ▲ Find Now/Search icon 🔍🖱.

Any message containing the search word will be displayed.

The search results are cleared as follows:

- ▲ New Search/Clear Search icon ✕ 🖱.

Note: If instant search has been installed then the search facility allows more control over the search function. This function allows specific sections of the e-mail to be searched, such as From, To, Subject etc.

Task 8.4.4 (Additional)

Carry out the operations specified in **Task 8A-4** on the CD.

CUSTOMISING FOLDERS

Each folder (Inbox, Outbox, etc.) will be displayed with a number of columns. The actual columns displayed will vary from folder to folder. It is possible to add, remove and reposition columns in each folder.

Adding/Removing Columns

A column is added or removed to/from a folder as follows:

- ▲ View menu 🖱.

- ⊕ Current View.

- ⊕ Customise Current View 🖱. (*A customise view window will appear.*)

- ▲ Fields button 🖱. (*The show fields window will appear.*)

- Select the field in the Available Fields window.

- ▲ Add button 🖱.

- ▲ OK 🖱.

- ▲ OK 🖱.

OR

- ⊕ Columns 🖱.
- Tick the columns to be displayed.
- OK 🖱.

Repositioning Columns

A column is repositioned as follows:

- ▲ View menu 🖱.

- ⊕ Current View.

- ⊕ Customise Current View 🖱. (*A customise view window will appear.*)

- ▲ Fields button 🖱. (*The show fields window will appear.*)

- Select the field in the right-hand window.

- Select Move Up to move to the left, or Move Down to move to the right.

- ▲ OK 🖱.

- ▲ OK 🖱.

OR

- ⊕ Columns 🖱.
- Move columns Up/Down as required.
- OK 🖱.

E-MAIL ETIQUETTE

With the growth in the use of e-mail there is a certain etiquette, sometimes referred to as **netiquette**, which has developed at the same time. The following are some points worth noting:

- Always add a subject in the Subject field.

- Keep messages short, especially when replying. If you wish to send a long letter then send it as an attachment, or compose it offline and paste it into the message.

- Spell check messages – even though poor typing is tolerated.

- Add any netcronyms (see examples below) to your dictionary so that they don't show up as mistakes.

- When using newsgroups, keep it short and simple. It is easy to be misunderstood.

- Respect newsgroup protocol.

Emoticons

These are symbols that are used to portray emotions in messages. Some of the more popular ones are as follows:

>:-<	Angry
:-S	Confused
:'(	Crying
:-|	Disappointed
:(	Frowning
()	Hug
((()))	Lots of Hugs
:*	Kiss
:D	Laughing
:-(	Sad
:-@	Screaming
|-)	Sleepy
:-)	Smiling
:-O	Surprised
;-)	Wink

Netcronyms

These are acronyms that are used in e-mail. Some of the more popular ones are as follows:

ADN	Any Day Now
AFAIK	As Far As I Know
AFK	Away From The Keyboard
BAK	Back At The Keyboard
BCNU	Be Seeing You
BRB	Be Right Back
BTW	By The Way
FAQ	Frequently Asked Question
FWIW	For What It's Worth
FYI	For Your Information
GMTA	Great Minds Think Alike
HTH	Hope This Helps
IIRC	If I Remember Correctly
IMHO	In My Humble Opinion
IMO	In My Opinion
MOF	Matter Of Fact
NAGI	Not A Good Idea
OTOH	On The Other Hand
RSN	Real Soon Now
TAT	Turn Around Time
TIA	Thanks In Advance
TPTB	The Powers That Be
TTYL	Talk To You Later

A number of text shortcuts are also appearing in e-mail messages, such as the following:

2	To/Too	**B4**	Before	**No1**	No one
2da	Today	**B4N**	Bye for now	**R**	Are
2moro	Tomorrow	**G2G**	Got to go	**Sry**	Sorry
2nite	Tonight	**Gr8**	Great	**U**	You
3dom	Freedom	**H2**	How to	**U@**	Where are you
4	For	**IC**	I see	**UOK**	You okay
4get	Forget	**IK**	I know	**W8**	Wait
4N	Foreign	**L8r**	Later	**Y**	Why